4WD TRAILS
CENTRAL UTAH

Warning: While every effort has been made to make the 4WD trail descriptions in this book as accurate as possible, some discrepancies may exist between the text and the actual trail. Hazards may have changed since the research and publication of this edition. Swagman Publishing, Inc., and the authors accept no responsibility for the safety of users of this guide. Individuals are liable for all costs incurred if rescue is necessary.

Printed in the United States of America

Front cover photo: Swasey's Cabin Trail

4WD TRAILS

CENTRAL UTAH

PETER MASSEY
AND JEANNE WILSON

SWAGMAN
PUBLISHING

Acknowledgements
Many people and organizations have made major contributions to the research and production of this book. We owe them all special thanks for their assistance.

First, we would like to thank the following people who have played major roles in the production of this book and have been key to completing it in a timely fashion.

Senior Field Researchers: **Donald McGann, Maggie Pinder**
Senior Researcher: **Timothy Duggan**
Researcher: **Christopher Munden**
Graphic Design and Maps: **Deborah Rust**
Finance: **Douglas Adams**
Office Administration: **Peg Anderson**

We would also like to thank the many people at the Bureau of Land Management offices throughout Utah, who spent countless hours assisting us. In particular, we would like to thank Dennis Willis, outdoor recreational planner at the Price Field Office, and Blaine Miller, archaeologist at the Price Field Office.

Staff at many offices of the National Forest Service also provided us with valuable assistance, particularly the offices in Price, Ferron, Teasdale, and Richfield.

We received a great deal of assistance from many other people and organizations. We would like to thank the Utah State Historical Society, the Denver Public Library Western History Department, Kari Murphy at the Moab to Monument Valley Film Commission, and the Moab Historical Society. Mrs. Betty Smith of Green River, Utah, was most helpful in providing information about Smith's Cabin.

The book includes many photos, and we are most thankful to the Bushducks—Donald McGann and Maggie Pinder, and Alan Barnett and Tara Thompson at the Utah State Historical Society.

With a project of this size countless hours are spent researching and recording the trail information, and we would like to thank Carol and Gary Martin of the Virginian Motel in Moab for providing a base camp for our researchers and for their helpful trail suggestions.

We would also like to draw our readers' attention to the website (www.bushducks.com) of our senior researchers, the Bushducks—Donald McGann and Maggie Pinder. It provides information on current 4WD trail conditions and offers their valuable assistance to anyone who is planning a backcountry itinerary.

Publisher's Note: Every effort has been taken to ensure that the information in this book is accurate at press time. Please visit our website to advise us of any changes or corrections you find. We also welcome recommendations for new 4WD trails or other suggestions to improve the information in this book.

SWAGMAN
PUBLISHING

Swagman Publishing, Inc.
P.O. Box 519, Castle Rock, CO 80104
Phone: 303-660-3307
Toll-free: 800-660-5107
Fax: 303-688-4388
www.4wdbooks.com

Contents

Before You Go

Why a 4WD Does It Better

The design and engineering of 4WD vehicles provide them with many advantages over normal cars when you head off the paved road:

- improved distribution of power to all four wheels;
- a transmission transfer case, which provides low-range gear selection for greater pulling power and for crawling over difficult terrain;
- high ground clearance;
- less overhang of the vehicle's body past the wheels, which provides better front and rear clearance when crossing gullies and ridges;
- large-lug, wide-tread tires;
- rugged construction (including underbody skid plates on many models).

If you plan to do off-highway touring, all of these considerations are important, whether you are evaluating the capabilities of your current 4WD or are looking to buy one; each is considered in detail in this chapter.

In order to explore the most difficult trails described in this book, you will need a 4WD vehicle that is well rated in each of the above features. If you own a 2WD sport utility vehicle, a lighter car-type SUV, or a 2WD pickup truck, your ability to explore the more difficult trails will depend on conditions and your level of experience.

A word of caution: Whatever type of 4WD vehicle you drive, understand that it is not invincible or indestructible. Nor can it go everywhere. A 4WD has a much higher center of gravity and weighs more than a car, and so has its own consequent limitations.

Experience is the only way to learn what your vehicle can and cannot do. Therefore, if you are inexperienced, we strongly recommend that you start with trails that have lower difficulty ratings. As you develop an understanding of your vehicle and of your own taste for adventure, you can safely tackle the more challenging trails.

One way to beef up your knowledge quickly, while avoiding the costly and sometimes dangerous lessons learned from on-the-road mistakes, is to undertake a 4WD course taught by a professional. Look in the Yellow Pages for courses in your area.

Using This Book

Route Planning

The regional map on pages 24 to 25 provides a convenient overview of the trails in the central portion of the state. Each 4WD trail is shown, as are major highways and towns, helping you to plan various routes by connecting a series of 4WD trails and paved roads.

As you plan your overall route, you will probably want to utilize as many 4WD trails as possible. However, check the difficulty rating and time required for each trail before finalizing your plans. You don't want to be stuck 50 miles from the highway—at sunset and without camping gear, since your trip was supposed to be over hours ago—when you discover that your vehicle can't handle a certain difficult passage.

Difficulty Ratings

We utilize a point system to provide a guide rating the difficulty of each trail. Any such system is subjective, and your experience of the trails will vary depending on your skill and the road conditions at the time. Indeed, particularly in Utah, any amount of rain makes the trails much more difficult, if not completely impassable.

We have rated the 4WD trails on a scale of 1 to 10—1 being passable for a normal passenger vehicle in good conditions and 10 requiring a heavily modified vehicle and an experienced driver who expects to encounter vehicle damage. Because this book is designed for owners of unmodified 4WD vehicles—who we assume do not want to damage their vehicles—most of the trails are rated 5 or lower. A few trails are included that rate as high as 7, while those rated 8 to 10 are beyond the scope of this book.

This is not to say that the moderate-rated trails are easy. We strongly recommend that inexperienced drivers not tackle trails rated at 4 or higher until they have undertaken a number of the lower-rated ones, so that they can gauge their skill level and prepare for the difficulty of the higher-rated trails.

In assessing the trails, we have always assumed good road conditions (dry road surface, good visibility, and so on). The factors influencing our ratings are as follows:

- obstacles such as rocks, mud, ruts, sand, slickrock, and stream crossings;
- the stability of the road surface;
- the width of the road and the vehicle clearance between trees or rocks;
- the steepness of the road;
- the margin for driver error (for example, a very high, open shelf road would be rated more difficult even if it was not very steep and had a stable surface).

The following is a guide to the ratings.

Rating 1: The trail is graded dirt but suitable for a normal passenger vehicle. It usually has gentle grades, is fairly wide, and has very shallow water crossings (if any).

Rating 2: High-clearance vehicles are preferred but not necessary. These trails are dirt roads, but they may have rocks, grades, water crossings, or ruts that make clearance a concern in a normal passenger vehicle. The trails are fairly wide, so that passing is not a concern, and mud is not a concern under normal weather conditions.

Rating 3: High-clearance 4WDs are preferred, but any high-clearance vehicle is acceptable. Expect a rough road surface; mud and sand are possible but will be easily passable. You may encounter rocks up to 6 inches in diameter, a loose road surface, and shelf roads, though these will be wide enough for passing or will have adequate pull-offs.

Rating 4: High-clearance 4WDs are recommended, though most stock SUVs are acceptable. Expect a rough road surface with rocks larger than 6 inches, but there will be a reasonable driving line available. Patches of mud are possible but can be readily negotiated; sand may be deep and require lower tire pressures. There may be stream crossings up to 12 inches deep, substantial sections of single-lane shelf road, moderate grades, and sections of moderately loose road surface.

Rating 5: High-clearance 4WDs are required. These trails have a rough, rutted surface, rocks up to nine inches, mud and deep sand that may be impassable for inexperienced drivers, and stream crossings up to 18 inches deep. Certain sections may be steep enough to cause traction problems, and you may encounter very narrow shelf roads with steep drop-offs and tight clearance between rocks or trees.

Rating 6: These trails are for experienced four-wheel drivers only. They are potentially dangerous, with large rocks, ruts, or terraces that may need to be negotiated. They may also have stream crossings at least 18 inches deep, involve rapid currents, unstable stream bottoms, or difficult access; steep slopes, loose surfaces, and narrow clearances; and very narrow shelf roads with steep drop-offs and possibly challenging road surfaces.

Rating 7: Skilled, experienced four-wheel drivers only. These trails include very challenging sections with extremely steep grades, loose surfaces, large rocks, deep ruts, and/or tight clearances. Mud or sand may necessitate winching.

Rating 8 and above: Stock vehicles are likely to be damaged and may find the trail impassable. Highly-skilled, experienced four-wheel drivers only.

Scenic Ratings

If rating the degree of difficulty is subjective, rating scenic beauty is guaranteed to lead to arguments. Utah contains a spectacular variety of scenery—from its grand canyons and towering mountains and buttes to its seemingly endless desert country. We love the wide-open remoteness of many areas of Utah, but realize they are not to everyone's liking. Nonetheless, we have tried to provide some guide to the relative scenic quality of the various trails. The ratings are based on a scale of 1 to 10.

Remoteness Ratings

Many of the trails in Utah are in remote country; sometimes the trails are seldom traveled, and the likelihood is low that another vehicle will appear within a reasonable time to assist you if you get stuck or break down. We have included a ranking for remoteness of +0 through +2. Summer temperatures can make a breakdown in the more remote areas a life-threatening experience. Prepare carefully before tackling the higher-rated, more remote trails (see "Special Preparations for Remote Travel," page 11). For trails with a high remoteness rating, consider traveling with a second vehicle.

Estimated Driving Times

In calculating driving times, we have not allowed for stops. Your actual driving time may be considerably longer depending on the number and duration of the stops you make. Add more time if you prefer to drive more slowly than good conditions allow.

Current Road Information

All the 4WD trails described in this book may become impassable in poor weather conditions. Storms can alter roads, remove tracks, and create impassable washes. Most of the trails described, even easy 2WD trails, can quickly become impassable even to 4WD vehicles after only a small amount of rain. For each trail, we have provided a phone number for obtaining current information about conditions.

Abbreviations

The route directions for the 4WD trails use a series of abbreviations as follows:

SO	CONTINUE STRAIGHT ON
TL	TURN LEFT
TR	TURN RIGHT
BL	BEAR LEFT
BR	BEAR RIGHT
UT	U-TURN

Using Route Directions

For every trail, we describe and pinpoint (by odometer reading) nearly every significant feature along the route—such as intersections, streams, washes, gates, cattle guards, and so on—and provide directions from these landmarks. Odometer readings will vary from vehicle to vehicle, so you should allow for slight variations. Be aware that trails can quickly change in the desert. A new trail may be cut around a washout, a faint trail can be graded by the county, or a well-used trail may fall into disuse. All these factors will affect the accuracy of the given directions.

If you diverge from the route, zero your trip meter upon your return and continue along the route, making the necessary adjustment to the point-to-point odometer readings. In the directions, we regularly reset the odometer readings—at significant landmarks or popular lookouts and spur trails—so that you won't have to recalculate for too long.

Most of the trails can be started from either end, and the route directions include both directions of travel; reverse directions are printed in blue below the main directions. When traveling in reverse, read from the bottom of the table and work up.

Route directions include cross-references whenever two 4WD trails included in this book connect; this allows for an easy change of route or destination.

Each trail includes periodic latitude and longitude readings to facilitate using a global positioning system (GPS) receiver. These readings may also assist you in finding your location on the maps. The GPS coordinates were taken using the NAD 1927 datum and are in the format dd°mm.mm'. When loading coordinates into your GPS receiver, you may wish to include only one decimal place, since in Utah, the third decimal place equals only about 2 yards and the second less than 20 yards.

Map References

We recommend that you supplement the information in this book with more-detailed maps. For each trail, we list the sheet maps and road atlases that provide the best detail for the area. Typically, the following references are given:

- Bureau of Land Management Maps,
- U.S. Forest Service Maps,
- Utah Travel Council Maps, Department of Geography, University of Utah—regions 1 through 5,
- *Utah Atlas & Gazetteer,* 1st ed. (Freeport, Maine: DeLorme Mapping, 1993)—Scale 1:250,000,
- Maptech-Terrain Navigator Topo Maps —Scale 1:100,000 and 1:24,000,
- *Trails Illustrated* Topo Maps; National Geographic Maps—Various scales, but all contain good detail.

We recommend the *Trails Illustrated* series of maps as the best for navigating these trails. They are reliable, easy to read, and printed on nearly indestructible plastic paper. However, the series does not cover many of the 4WD trails described in this book.

The DeLorme atlas is useful and has the advantage of providing you with maps of the entire state at a reasonable price. While its 4WD trail information doesn't go beyond what we provide, it is useful if you wish to explore the hundreds of side roads.

U.S. Forest Service maps lack the topographic detail of the other sheet maps and, in our experience, are also out of date occasionally. They have the advantage of covering a broad area and are useful in identifying land use and travel restrictions. These maps are most useful for the longer trails.

Utah Travel Council maps cover Utah in five regions. They provide good overviews with a handful of 4WD trails, although with little specific detail. Four of Utah's five regions are currently available: Southwestern #4, Southeastern #5, Northern #1, and Northeastern #3. Central map #2 has been out of print for several years and it is yet undetermined when it will be available.

In our opinion, the best single option by far is the Terrain Navigator series of maps published on CD-ROM by Maptech. These CD-ROMs contain an amazing level of detail because they include the entire set of 1,524 U.S. Geological Survey topographical maps of Utah at the 1:24,000 scale and all 59 maps at the 1:100,000 scale. These maps offer many advantages over normal maps:

- GPS coordinates for any location can be found, which can then be loaded into your GPS receiver. Conversely, if you have your GPS coordinates, your location on the map can be pinpointed instantly.
- Towns, rivers, passes, mountains, and many other sites are indexed by name so that they can be located quickly.
- 4WD trails can be marked and profiled for elevation change and distance from point to point.
- Customized maps can be printed out.

Maptech uses seven CD-ROMs to cover the entire state of Utah, but the CD-ROMs can be purchased individually. The CD-ROMs can be used with a laptop computer and a GPS receiver in your vehicle to monitor your location on the map and navigate directly from the display.

Cheaper CD-ROM topographic maps are published, but none that we know of compare with the Maptech series. DeLorme publishes an alternative series entitled *TopoUSA* that is modestly priced, especially considering that it covers the entire country. However, the level of topographical detail available on-screen bears no comparison to the Maptech series—which comes as no surprise when you find there are only six CD-ROMs in the entire set.

All these maps should be available through good map stores. The Maptech CD-ROMs are available directly from the company (800-627-7236, or on the internet at www.maptech.com).

Backcountry Driving Rules and Permits

Four-wheel driving involves special driving techniques and road rules. This section is an introduction for 4WD beginners.

4WD Road Rules

To help ensure that these trails remain open and available for all four-wheel drivers to enjoy, it is important to minimize your impact on the environment and not be a safety risk to yourself or anyone else. Remember that the 4WD clubs in Utah fight a constant battle with the U.S. Forest Service (USFS) and the Bureau of Land Management (BLM) to retain the access that currently exists.

The fundamental rule when traversing the 4WD trails described in this book is to use common sense. In addition, special road rules for 4WD trails apply:

■ Vehicles traveling uphill have the right of way.

■ If you are moving more slowly than the vehicle behind you, pull over to let the other vehicle by.

■ Park out of the way in a safe place. Blocking a track may restrict access for emergency vehicles as well as for other recreationalists. Set the parking brake—don't rely on leaving the transmission in park. Manual transmissions should be left in the lowest gear.

Tread Lightly!

Remember the rules of the Tread Lightly!® program:

■ Be informed. Obtain maps, regulations, and other information from the forest service or from other public land agencies. Learn the rules and follow them.

■ Resist the urge to pioneer a new road or trail or to cut across a switchback. Stay on constructed tracks and avoid running over young trees, shrubs, and grasses, damaging or killing them. Don't drive across alpine tundra; this fragile environment can take years to recover.

■ Stay off soft, wet roads and 4WD trails readily torn up by vehicles. Repairing the damage is expensive, and quite often authorities find it easier to close the road rather than repair it.

■ Travel around meadows, steep hillsides, stream banks, and lake shores that are easily scarred by churning wheels.

■ Stay away from wild animals that are rearing young or suffering from a food shortage. Do not camp close to the water sources of domestic or wild animals.

■ Obey gate closures and regulatory signs.

■ Preserve America's heritage by not disturbing old mining camps, ghost towns, or other historical features. Leave historic sites, Native American rock art, ruins, and artifacts in place and untouched.

■ Carry out all your trash, and even that of others.

■ Stay out of designated wilderness areas. They are closed to all vehicles. It is your responsibility to know where the boundaries are.

■ Get permission to cross private land. Leave livestock alone. Respect landowners' rights.

Report violations of these rules to help keep these 4WD trails open and to ensure that others will have the opportunity to visit these backcountry sites. Many groups are actively seeking to close these public lands to vehicles, thereby denying access to those who are unable, or perhaps merely unwilling, to hike long distances. This magnificent countryside is owned by, and should be available to, all Americans.

Special Preparations for Remote Travel

Due to the remoteness of some areas in Utah and the very high summer temperatures, you should take some special precautions to ensure that you don't end up in a life-threatening situation:

■ When planning a trip into the desert, always inform someone as to where you are going, your route, and when you expect to return. Stick to your plan.

■ Carry and drink at least one gallon of water per person per day of your trip. (Plastic gallon jugs are handy and portable.)

■ Be sure your vehicle is in good condition with a sound battery, good hoses, spare tire, spare fan belts, necessary tools, and reserve gasoline and oil. Other spare parts and extra radiator water are also valuable. If traveling in pairs, share the common spares and carry a greater variety.

■ Keep an eye on the sky. Flash floods can occur in a wash any time you see "thunderheads"—even when it's not raining a drop where you are.

■ If you are caught in a dust storm while driving, get off the road and turn off your lights. Turn on the emergency flashers and back into the wind to reduce windshield pitting by sand particles.

■ Test trails on foot before driving through washes and sandy areas. One minute of walking may save hours of hard work getting your vehicle unstuck.

■ If your vehicle breaks down, stay near it. Your emergency supplies are there. Your car has many other items useful in an emergency. Raise your hood and trunk lid to denote "help needed." Remember, a vehicle can be seen for miles, but a person on foot is very difficult to spot from a distance.

■ When you're not moving, use available shade or erect shade from tarps, blankets, or seat covers—anything to reduce the direct rays of the sun.

■ Do not sit or lie directly on the ground. It may be 30 degrees hotter than the air.

■ Leave a disabled vehicle only if you are positive of the route and the distance to help. Leave a note for rescuers that gives the time you left and the direction you are taking.

■ If you must walk, rest for at least 10 minutes out of each hour. If you are not normally physically active, rest up to 30 minutes out of each hour. Find shade, sit down, and prop up your feet. Adjust your shoes and socks, but do not remove your shoes—you may not be able to get them back on swollen feet.

■ If you have water, drink it. Do not ration it.

■ If water is limited, keep your mouth closed. Do not talk, eat, smoke, drink alcohol, or take salt.

■ Keep your clothing on, despite the heat. It helps to keep the body temperature down and reduces your dehydration rate. Cover your head. If you don't have a hat, improvise a head covering.

■ If you are stalled or lost, set signal fires. Set smoky fires in the daytime and bright ones at night. Three fires in a triangle denote "help needed."

■ A roadway is a sign of civilization. If you find a road, stay on it.

■ If hiking in the desert, equip each person, especially children, with a police-type whistle. It makes a distinctive noise with little effort. Three blasts denote "help needed."

■ To avoid poisonous creatures, put your hands or feet only where your eyes can see.

Obtaining Permits

Backcountry permits, which usually cost a fee, are often required for certain activities on public lands in Utah, whether the area is a national park, state park, national monument, Indian reservation, or BLM land.

Restrictions may require a permit for all overnight stays, which can include backpacking and 4WD or bicycle camping. Permits may also be required for day use by vehicles, horses, hikers, or bikes in some areas.

When possible, we include information about fees and permit requirements and where permits may be obtained, but these regulations change constantly. If in doubt, check with the most likely governing agency.

Assessing Your Vehicle's Off-Road Ability

Many issues come into play when evaluating your 4WD vehicle, though most of the 4WDs on the market are suitable for even the roughest trails described in this book. Engine power will be adequate in even the least powerful modern vehicle. However, some vehicles are less suited to off-highway driving than others, and some of the newest, carlike sport utility vehicles (SUVs) simply are not designed for off-highway touring. The following information should allow you to identify the good, the bad, and the ugly.

Differing 4WD Systems

All 4WD systems have one thing in common: The engine provides power to all four wheels rather than to only two, as is typical in most standard cars. However, there are a number of differences in the way power is applied to the wheels.

The other feature that distinguishes nearly all 4WDs from normal passenger vehicles is that the gearboxes have high and low ratios that effectively double the number of gears. The high range is comparable to the range on a passenger car. The low range provides lower speed and more power, which is useful when towing heavy loads, driving up steep hills, or crawling over rocks. When driving downhill, the 4WD's low range increases engine braking.

Various makes and models of SUVs offer different drive systems, but these differences center on two issues: the way power is applied to the other wheels if one or more wheels slip, and the ability to select between 2WD and 4WD.

Normal driving requires that all four wheels be able to turn at different speeds; this allows the vehicle to turn without scrubbing its tires. In a 2WD vehicle, the front wheels (or rear wheels in a front-wheel-drive vehicle) are not powered by the engine and thus are free to turn individually at any speed. The rear wheels, powered by the engine, are only able to turn at different speeds because of the differential, which applies power to the faster-turning wheel.

This standard method of applying traction has certain weaknesses. First, when power is applied to only one set of wheels, the other set cannot help the vehicle gain traction. Second, when one powered wheel loses traction, it spins, but the other powered wheel doesn't turn. This happens because the differential applies all the engine power to the faster-turning wheel and no power to the other wheels, which still have traction. All 4WD systems are designed to overcome these two weaknesses. However, different 4WDs address this common objective in different ways.

Full-Time 4WD. For a vehicle to remain in 4WD all the time without scrubbing the tires, all the wheels must be able to rotate at different speeds. A full-time 4WD system allows this to happen by using three differentials. One is located between the rear wheels, as in a normal passenger car, to allow the rear wheels to rotate at different speeds. The second is located between the front wheels in exactly the same way. The third differential is located between the front and rear wheels to allow different rotational speeds between the front and rear sets of wheels. In nearly all vehicles with full-time 4WD, the center differential operates only in high range. In low range, it is completely locked. This is not a disadvantage because when using low range the additional traction is normally desired and the deterioration of steering response will be less noticeable due to the vehicle traveling at a slower speed.

Part-Time 4WD. A part-time 4WD system does not have the center differential located between the front and rear wheels. Consequently, the front and rear drive shafts are both driven at the same speed and with the same power at all times when in 4WD.

This system provides improved traction because when one or both of the front or rear wheels slips, the engine continues to provide power to the other set. However, because such a system doesn't allow a difference in speed between the front and rear sets of wheels, the tires scrub when turning, placing additional strain on the whole drive system. Therefore, such a system can be used only in slippery conditions; otherwise, the ability to steer the vehicle will deteriorate and the tires will quickly wear out.

Some vehicles, such as Jeeps with Selec-trac™ and Mitsubishi Monteros with Active Trac 4WD™, offer both full-time and part-time 4WD in high range.

Manual Systems to Switch Between 2WD and 4WD. There are three manual systems for switching between 2WD and 4WD. The most basic requires stopping and getting out of the vehicle to lock the front hubs manually before selecting 4WD. The second requires you to stop, but you change to 4WD by merely throwing a lever inside the vehicle (the hubs lock automatically). The third allows shifting between 2WD and 4WD high range while the vehicle is moving. Any 4WD that does not offer the option of driving in 2WD must have a full-time 4WD system.

Automated Switching Between 2WD and 4WD. Advances in technology are leading to greater automation in the selection of two- or four-wheel drive. When operating in high range, these high-tech systems use sensors to monitor the rotation of each wheel. When any slippage is detected, the vehicle switches the proportion of power from the wheel(s) that is slipping to the wheels that retain grip. The proportion of power supplied to each wheel is therefore infinitely variable as opposed to the original systems where the vehicle was either in two-wheel drive or four-wheel drive.

In recent years, this process has been spurred on by many of the manufacturers of luxury vehicles entering the SUV market—Mercedes, BMW, Cadillac, Lincoln, and Lexus have joined Range Rover in this segment.

Manufacturers of these higher-priced vehicles have led the way in introducing sophisticated computer-controlled 4WD systems. Although each of the manufacturers has its own approach to this issue, all the systems automatically vary the allocation of power between the wheels within milliseconds of the sensors' detecting wheel slippage.

Limiting Wheel Slippage

4WDs employ various systems to limit wheel slippage and transfer power to the wheels that still have traction. These systems may completely lock the differentials, or they may allow limited slippage before transferring power back to the wheels that retain traction.

Lockers completely eliminate the operation of one or more differentials. A locker on the center differential switches between full-time and part-time 4WD. Lockers on the front or rear differentials ensure that power remains equally applied to each set of wheels regardless of whether both have traction. Lockers may be controlled manually by a switch or lever in the vehicle, or they may be automatic.

The Toyota Land Cruiser offers the option of having manual lockers on all three differentials, while other brands such as the Mitsubishi Montero offer manual locks on the center and rear differential. Manual lockers are the most controllable and effective devices for ensuring that power is provided to the wheels with traction. However, because they allow absolutely no slippage, they must be used only on slippery surfaces.

An alternative method for getting power to the wheels that have traction is to allow limited wheel slippage. Systems that work this way may be called limited-slip differentials, posi-traction systems, or in the center differential, viscous couplings. The advantage of these systems is that the limited difference they allow in rotational speed between wheels enables such systems to be used when driving on a dry surface. All full-time 4WD systems allow limited slippage in the center differential.

For off-highway use, a manually locking differential is the best of the above systems, but it is the most expensive. Limited-slip differentials are the cheapest but also the least satisfactory, as they require one wheel to be slipping at two to three mph before power is transferred to the other wheel. For the center differential, the best system combines a locking differential and, to enable full-time use, a viscous coupling.

Tires

The tires that came with your 4WD vehicle may be satisfactory, but many 4WDs are fitted with passenger-car tires. These are unlikely to be the best choice because they are less rugged and more likely to puncture on rocky trails. They are particularly prone to sidewall damage. Passenger vehicle tires also have a less aggressive tread pattern than specialized 4WD tires, providing less traction in mud.

For information on purchasing tires better suited to off-highway conditions, see "Special 4WD Equipment" on page 20.

Clearance

Road clearances vary considerably among different 4WD vehicles—from less than 7 inches to more than 10 inches. Special vehicles may have far greater clearance. For instance, the Hummer has 16-inch ground clearance. High ground clearance is particularly advantageous on the rockier or more rutted 4WD trails in this book.

When evaluating the ground clearance of your vehicle, you need to take into account the clearance of the body work between the wheels on each side of the vehicle. This is particularly relevant for crawling over larger rocks. Vehicles with sidesteps have significantly lower clearance than those without.

Another factor affecting clearance is the approach and departure angles of your vehicle—that is, the maximum angle the ground can slope without the front of the vehicle hitting the ridge on approach or the rear of the vehicle hitting on departure. Mounting a winch or tow hitch to your vehicle is likely to reduce your approach or departure angle.

If you do a lot of driving on rocky trails, you will inevitably hit the bottom of the vehicle sooner or later. When this happens, you will be far less likely to damage vulnerable areas such as the oil pan and gas tank if your vehicle is fitted with skid plates. Most manufacturers offer skid plates as an option. They are worth every penny.

Maneuverability

When you tackle tight switchbacks, you will quickly appreciate that maneuverability is an important criterion when assessing 4WD vehicles. Where a full-size vehicle may be forced to go back and forth a number of times to get around a sharp turn, a small 4WD might go straight around. This is not only easier, it's safer.

If you have a full-size vehicle, all is not lost. We have traveled many of the trails in this book in a Suburban. That is not to say that some of these trails wouldn't have been easier to negotiate in a smaller vehicle! We have noted in the route descriptions if a trail is not suitable for larger vehicles.

In Summary

Using the criteria above, you can evaluate how well your 4WD will handle off-road touring, and if you haven't yet purchased your vehicle, you can use these criteria to help select one. Choosing the best 4WD system is, at least partly, subjective. It is also a matter of your budget. However, for the type of off-highway driving covered in this book, we make the following recommendations:

- Select a 4WD system that offers low range and, at a minimum, has some form of limited slip differential on the rear axle.
- Use light truck, all-terrain tires as the standard tires on your vehicle. For sand and slickrock, these will be the ideal choice. If conditions are likely to be muddy, or traction will be improved by a tread pattern that will give more bite, consider an additional set of mud tires.
- For maximum clearance, select a vehicle with 16-inch wheels, or at least choose the tallest tires that your vehicle can accommodate. Note that if you install tires with a diameter greater than standard, the odometer will undercalculate the distance you have traveled. Your engine braking and gear ratios will also be affected.
- If you are going to try the rockier 4WD trails, don't install a sidestep or low hanging front bar. If you have the option, have underbody skid plates mounted.
- Remember that many of the obstacles you encounter on backcountry trails are more difficult to navigate in a full-size vehicle than in a compact 4WD.

Four-Wheel Driving Techniques

Safe four-wheel driving requires that you observe certain golden rules:

- Size up the situation in advance.
- Be careful and take your time.
- Maintain smooth, steady power and momentum.
- Engage 4WD and low-range gears before you get into a tight situation.
- Steer toward high spots, trying to put the wheel over large rocks.
- Straddle ruts.
- Use gears and not just the brakes to hold the vehicle when driving downhill. On very steep slopes, chock the wheels if you park your vehicle.
- Watch for logging and mining trucks and smaller recreational vehicles, such as all-terrain vehicles (ATVs).
- Wear your seat belt and secure all lug-

gage, especially heavy items such as tool boxes or coolers. Heavy items should be secured by ratchet tie-down straps rather than elastic-type straps, which are not strong enough to hold heavy items if the vehicle rolls.

Utah's 4WD trails have a number of common obstacles, and the following section provides an introduction to the techniques required to surmount them.

Rocks. Tire selection is important in negotiating rocks. Select a multiple-ply, tough sidewall, light-truck tire with a large-lug tread.

As you approach a rocky stretch, get into 4WD low range to give you maximum slow-speed control. Speed is rarely necessary, since traction on a rocky surface is usually good. Plan ahead and select the line you wish to take. If a rock appears to be larger than the clearance of your vehicle, don't try to straddle it. Check to see that it is not higher than the frame of your vehicle once you get a wheel over it. Put a wheel up on the rock and slowly climb it, then gently drop over the other side using the brake to ensure a smooth landing. Bouncing the car over rocks increases the likelihood of damage, as the body's clearance is reduced by the suspension compressing. Running boards also significantly reduce your clearance in this respect.

It is often helpful to use a "spotter" outside the vehicle to assist you with the best wheel placement.

Slickrock. When you encounter slickrock, first assess the correct direction of the trail. It is easy to lose sight of the trail on slickrock, as there are seldom any developed edges. Often the way is marked with small rock cairns, which are simply rocks stacked high enough to make a landmark.

All-terrain tires with tighter tread are more suited to slickrock than the more open, luggier type tires. As with rocks, a multiple-ply sidewall is important. In dry conditions, slickrock offers pavement-type grip. In rain or snow, you will soon learn how it got its name, and even the best tires may not get an adequate grip. Walk steep sections first; if you are slipping on foot, chances are your vehicle will slip too.

Slickrock is characterized by ledges and long sections of "pavement." Follow the guidelines for travel over rocks. Refrain from speeding over flat-looking sections, as you may hit an unexpected crevice or water pocket, and vehicles bend easier than slickrock! Turns and ledges can be tight, and vehicles with smaller overhangs and better maneuverability are at a distinct advantage—hence the popularity of the compacts in the slickrock mecca of Moab.

On the steepest sections, engage low range and pick a straight line up or down the slope. Do not attempt to traverse a steep slope sideways.

Steep Uphill Grades. Consider walking the trail to ensure that the steep hill before you is passable, especially if it is clear that backtracking is going to be a problem.

Select 4WD low range to ensure that you have adequate power to pull up the hill. If the wheels begin to lose traction, turn the steering wheel gently from side to side to give the wheels a chance to regain traction.

If you lose momentum, but the car is not in danger of sliding, use the foot brake, switch off the ignition, leave the vehicle in gear (if manual transmission) or park (if automatic), engage the parking brake, and get out to examine the situation. See if you can remove any obstacles, and figure out the line you need to take. Reversing a couple of yards and starting again may allow you to get better traction and momentum.

If, halfway up, you decide a stretch of road is impassably steep, back down the trail. Trying to turn the vehicle around on a steep hill is extremely dangerous; you will very likely cause it to roll over.

Steep Downhill Grades. Again, consider walking the trail to ensure that a steep hill is passable, especially if it is clear that backtracking uphill is going to be a problem.

Select 4WD low range and use first gear to maximize braking assistance from the engine. If the surface is loose and you are losing traction, change up to second or third gear. Do not use the brakes if you can avoid it, but don't let the vehicle's speed get out of control. Feather (lightly pump) the brakes if you slip under braking. For vehicles fitted with ABS, apply even pressure if you start to slip; the ABS helps keep vehicles on line.

Travel very slowly over rock ledges or ruts. Attempt to tackle these diagonally, letting one wheel down at a time.

If the back of the vehicle begins to slide around, gently apply the throttle and correct the steering. If the rear of the vehicle starts to slide sideways, do not apply the brakes.

Mud. Muddy trails are easily damaged, so they should be avoided if possible. But if you must traverse a section of mud, your success will depend heavily on whether you have open-lugged mud tires or chains. Thick mud fills the tighter tread on normal tires, leaving the tire with no more grip than if it were bald. If the muddy stretch is only a few yards long, the momentum of your vehicle may allow you to get through regardless.

If the muddy track is very steep, uphill or downhill, or off camber, do not attempt it. Your vehicle is very likely to skid in such conditions, and you may roll or slip off the edge of the road. Also, check to see that the mud has a reasonably firm base. Tackling deep mud is definitely not recommended unless you have a vehicle-mounted winch—and even then, be cautious, because the winch may not get you out. Finally, check to see that no ruts are too deep for the ground clearance of your vehicle.

When you decide you can get through and have selected the best route, use the following techniques to cross through the mud:

- Avoid making detours off existing tracks to minimize environmental damage.
- Select 4WD low range and a suitable gear; momentum is the key to success, so use a high enough gear to build up sufficient speed.
- Avoid accelerating heavily, so as to minimize wheel spinning and to provide maximum traction.
- Follow existing wheel ruts, unless they are too deep for the clearance of your vehicle.
- To correct slides, turn the steering wheel in the direction that the rear wheels are skidding, but don't be too aggressive or you'll overcorrect and lose control again.
- If the vehicle comes to a stop, don't continue to accelerate, as you will only spin your wheels and dig yourself into a rut. Try backing out and having another go.
- Be prepared to turn back before reaching the point of no return.

Stream Crossings. By crossing a stream that is too deep, drivers risk far more than water flowing in and ruining the interior of their vehicles. Water sucked into the engine's air intake will seriously damage the engine. Likewise, water that seeps into the air vent on the transmission or differential will mix with the lubricant and may lead to serious problems in due course.

Even worse, if the water is deep or fast flowing, it could easily carry your vehicle downstream, endangering the lives of everyone in the vehicle.

Some 4WD manuals tell you what fording depth the vehicle can negotiate safely. If your vehicle's owner's manual doesn't include this information, your local dealer may be able to assist. If you don't know, then avoid crossing through water that is more than a foot or so deep.

The first rule for crossing a stream is to know what you are getting into. You need to ascertain how deep the water is, whether there are any large rocks or holes, if the bottom is solid enough to avoid bogging down the vehicle, and whether the entry and exit points are negotiable. This may take some time and involve getting wet, but you take a great risk by crossing a stream without first properly assessing the situation.

The secret to water crossings is to keep moving, but not too fast. If you go too fast, you may drown the electrics, causing the vehicle to stall midstream. In shallow water (where the surface of the water is below the bumper), your primary concern is to safely negotiate the bottom of the stream, avoiding any rock damage and maintaining momentum if there is a danger of getting stuck or of slipping on the exit.

In deeper water (between 18 and 30 inches), the objective is to create a small bow wave in front of the moving vehicle.

This requires a speed that is approximately walking pace. The bow wave reduces the depth of the water around the engine compartment. If the water's surface reaches your tailpipe, select a gear that will maintain moderate engine revs to avoid water backing up into the exhaust; and do not change gears midstream.

Crossing water deeper than 25 to 30 inches requires more extensive preparation of the vehicle and should be attempted only by experienced drivers.

Snow. The trails in this book that receive heavy snowfall are closed in winter. Therefore, the snow conditions that you are most likely to encounter are an occasional snowdrift that has not yet melted or fresh snow from an unexpected storm. Getting through such conditions depends on the depth of the snow, its consistency, the stability of the underlying surface, and your vehicle.

If the snow is no deeper than about nine inches and there is solid ground beneath it, crossing the snow should not be a problem. In deeper snow that seems solid enough to support your vehicle, be extremely cautious: If you break through a drift, you are likely to be stuck, and if conditions are bad, you may have a long wait.

The tires you use for off-highway driving, with a wide tread pattern, are probably suitable for these snow conditions. Nonetheless, it is wise to carry chains (preferably for all four wheels), and if you have a vehicle-mounted winch, even better.

Sand. As with most off-highway situations, your tires are the key to your ability to cross sand. It is difficult to tell how well a particular tire will handle in sand just by looking at it, so be guided by the manufacturer and your dealer.

The key to driving in soft sand is floatation, which is achieved by a combination of low tire pressure and momentum. Before crossing a stretch of sand, reduce your tire pressure to between 15 and 20 pounds. If necessary, you can safely go to as low as 12 pounds. As you cross, maintain momentum so that your vehicle rides on top of the soft sand without digging in or stalling. This may require plenty of engine power. Avoid using the brakes if possible; removing your foot from the accelerator alone is normally enough to slow or stop. Using the brakes digs the vehicle deep in the sand.

Air the tires back up as soon as you are out of the sand to avoid damage to the tires and the rims. Airing back up requires a high-quality air compressor. Even then, it is a slow process.

In the backcountry of Utah, sandy conditions are commonplace. You will therefore find a good compressor most useful.

Vehicle Recovery Methods

If you do enough four-wheel driving, you are sure to get stuck sooner or later. The following techniques will help you get back on the go. The most suitable method will depend on the equipment available and the situation you are in—whether you are stuck in sand, mud, or snow, or are high-centered or unable to negotiate a hill.

Towing. Use a nylon yank strap of the type discussed in the "Special 4WD Equipment" section on page 21. This type of strap will stretch 15 to 25 percent, and the elasticity will assist in extracting the vehicle.

Attach the strap only to a frame-mounted tow point. Ensure that the driver of the stuck vehicle is ready, take up all but about six feet of slack, then move the towing vehicle away at a moderate speed (in most circumstances this means using 4WD low range in second gear) so that the elasticity of the strap is employed in the way it is meant to be. Don't take off like a bat out of hell or you risk breaking the strap or damaging a vehicle.

Never join two yank straps together with a shackle. If one strap breaks, the shackle will become a lethal missile aimed at one of the vehicles (and anyone inside). For the same reason, never attach a yank strap to the tow ball on either vehicle.

Jacking. Jacking the vehicle allows you to pack under the wheel (with rocks, dirt, or logs) or use your shovel to remove an obstacle. However, the standard vehicle jack is unlikely to be of as much assistance as a high-lift jack. We highly recommend purchasing a good high-lift jack as a basic accessory if you decide that you are going to do a lot of serious, off-highway four-wheel driving. Remember a high-lift jack is of limited use if your vehicle does not have an appropriate jacking point. Some brush bars have two built-in forward jacking points.

Tire Chains. Tire chains can be of assistance in both mud and snow. Cable-type chains provide much less grip than link-type chains. There are also dedicated mud chains with larger, heavier links than on normal snow chains. It is best to have chains fitted to all four wheels.

Once you are bogged down is not the best time to try to fit the chains; if at all possible, try to predict their need and have them on the tires before trouble arises. An easy way to affix chains is to place two small cubes of wood under the center of the stretched-out chain. When you drive your tires up on the blocks of wood, it is easier to stretch the chains over the tires because the pressure is off.

Winching. Most recreational four-wheel drivers do not have a winch. But if you get serious about four-wheel driving, this is probably the first major accessory you should consider buying.

Under normal circumstances, a winch would be warranted only for the more difficult 4WD trails in this book. Having a winch is certainly comforting when you see a difficult section of road ahead and have to decide whether to risk it or turn back. Also, major obstacles can appear when you least expect them, even on trails that are otherwise easy.

Owning a winch is not a panacea to all your recovery problems. Winching depends on the availability of a good anchor point, and electric winches may not work if they are submerged in a stream. Despite these constraints, no accessory is more useful than a high-quality, powerful winch when you get into a difficult situation.

If you acquire a winch, learn to use it properly; take the time to study your owner's manual. Incorrect operation can be extremely dangerous and may cause damage to the winch or to your anchor points, which are usually trees.

Navigation by the Global Positioning System (GPS)

Although this book is designed so that each trail can be navigated simply by following the detailed directions provided, nothing makes navigation easier than a GPS receiver.

The global positioning system (GPS) consists of a network of 24 satellites, nearly 13,000 miles in space, in six different orbital paths. The satellites are constantly moving at about 8,500 miles per hour, making two complete orbits around the earth every 24 hours.

Each satellite is constantly transmitting data, including its identification number, its operational health, and the date and time. It also transmits its location and the location of every other satellite in the network.

By comparing the time the signal was transmitted to the time it is received, a GPS receiver calculates how far away each satellite is. With a sufficient number of signals, the receiver can then triangulate its location. With three or more satellites, the receiver can determine latitude and longitude coordinates. With four or more, it can calculate altitude. By constantly making these calculations, it can determine speed and direction. To facilitate these calculations, the time data broadcast by GPS is accurate to within 40 billionths of a second.

The U.S. military uses the system to provide positions accurate to within half an inch. When the system was first established, civilian receivers were deliberately fed slightly erroneous information in order to effectively deny military applications to hostile countries or terrorists—a practice called selective availability (SA). However on May 1, 2000, in response to the growing importance of the system for civilian applications, the U.S. government stopped intentionally downgrading GPS data. The military gave its support to this change once new technology made it possible to selectively degrade the system within any defined geographical area on demand. This new feature of the system has made it safe to have higher-quality signals available for civilian use. Now, instead of the civilian-use signal having a margin of error between 20 and 70 yards, it is only about one-tenth of that.

A GPS receiver offers the four-wheeler numerous benefits:

- You can track to any point for which you know the longitude and latitude coordinates with no chance of heading in the wrong direction or getting lost. Most receivers provide an extremely easy-to-understand graphic display to keep you on track.
- It works in all weather conditions.
- It automatically records your route for easy backtracking.
- You can record and name any location, so that you can relocate it with ease. This may include your campsite, a fishing spot, or even a silver mine you discover!
- It displays your position, allowing you to pinpoint your location on a map.
- By interfacing the GPS receiver directly to a portable computer, you can monitor and record your location as you travel (using the appropriate map software) or print the route you took.

However, remember that GPS units can fail, batteries can go flat, and tree cover and tight canyons can block the signals. Never rely entirely on GPS for navigation. Always carry a compass for backup when you are going to be traveling in very remote areas.

Special 4WD Equipment

Tires

When 4WD touring, you will likely encounter a wide variety of terrain: rocks, mud, talus, slickrock, sand, gravel, dirt, and bitumen. The immense variety of tires on the market includes many specifically targeted at one or another of these types of terrain, as well as tires designed to handle a range of terrain adequately.

Every four-wheel driver seems to have his or her own preference when it comes to tire selection, but most people undertaking the 4WD trails in this book will need tires that can handle all of the above types of terrain adequately.

The first requirement is to select rugged, light-truck tires rather than passenger-vehicle tires. Check the size data on the sidewall: it should have "LT" rather than "P" before the number.

Among light-truck tires, you must choose between tires that are designated "all-terrain" and more-aggressive, wider-tread mud tires. Either type will be adequate, especially on rocks, gravel, talus, or dirt. Although mud tires have an advantage in muddy conditions and soft snow, all-terrain tires perform better on slickrock, in sand, and particularly on ice and paved roads.

When selecting tires, remember that they affect not just traction but also cornering ability, braking distances, fuel consumption, and noise levels. It pays to get good advice before making your decision.

Global Positioning System Receivers

GPS receivers have come down in price considerably in the past few years and are rapidly becoming indispensable navigational tools. Many higher-priced cars now offer integrated GPS receivers, and within the next few years, receivers will become available on most models.

Battery-powered, hand-held units that meet the needs of off-highway driving currently range from less than $100 to a little over $300 and continue to come down in price. Some high-end units feature maps that are incorporated in the display, either from a built-in database or from interchangeable memory cards. Currently, only a few of these maps include 4WD trails.

If you are considering purchasing a GPS unit, keep the following in mind:

- Price. The very cheapest units are likely outdated and very limited in their display features. Expect to pay from $125 to $300.
- The number of channels, which indicates the number of satellites that the unit tracks concurrently. Many older units have

only one channel that switches from one satellite to another to collect the required information. Modern units have up to 12 channels that are each dedicated to tracking one satellite. This provides greater accuracy, faster start-up (because the unit can acquire the initial data it needs much more rapidly), and better reception under difficult conditions, such as when located in a deep canyon or in dense foliage.

■ The number of routes and the number of sites (or "waypoints") per route that can be stored in memory. For off-highway use, it is important to be able to store plenty of waypoints so that you do not have to load coordinates into the machine as frequently. Having plenty of memory also ensures that you can automatically store your present location without fear that the memory is full.

■ Waypoint storage. The better units store up to 500 waypoints and 20 reversible routes of up to 30 waypoints each. Also consider the number of characters a GPS receiver allows you to use to name waypoints. When you try to recall a waypoint, you may have difficulty recognizing names restricted to only a few characters.

■ Automatic route storing. Most units automatically store your route as you go along and enable you to display it in reverse to make backtracking easy.

■ The display. Compare the graphic display of one unit with another. Some are much easier to decipher or offer more alternative displays.

■ The controls. GPS receivers have many functions, and they need to have good, simple controls.

■ Vehicle mounting. To be useful, the unit needs to be placed where it can be read easily by both the driver and the navigator. Check that the unit can be conveniently located in your vehicle. Different units have different shapes and different mounting systems. Be careful to locate the GPS out of the way of the passenger-side airbag.

■ Position-format options. Different maps use different grids, and you want to be able to display the same format on your GPS unit as on the map you are using, so that cross-referencing is simplified. There are a number of formats for latitude and longitude, as well as the Universal Transverse Mercator (UTM) grid, which is used on some maps.

After you have selected a unit, a number of optional extras are also worth considering:

■ A cigarette lighter electrical adapter. Important because GPS units eat batteries!

■ A vehicle-mounted antenna, which will improve reception under difficult conditions. (The GPS unit can only "see" through the windows of your vehicle; it cannot monitor satellites through a metal roof.) Having a vehicle-mounted antenna also means that you do not have to consider reception when locating the receiver in your vehicle.

■ An in-car mounting system. If you are going to do a lot of touring using the GPS, consider attaching a bracket on the dash rather than relying on a Velcro mount.

■ A computer-link cable. Data from your receiver can be downloaded to your PC; or if you have a laptop computer, you can monitor your route as you go along, using one of a number of inexpensive map software products on the market.

We used a Garmin 45 and a Garmin 45 XL receiver to take the GPS positions included in this book. These Garmin units are now outdated, but both have served us well for the past six years in our travels throughout the United States and around the world and we recommend Garmin GPS products to our readers.

Yank Straps

Yank straps are industrial-strength versions of the flimsy tow straps carried by the local discount store. They are made of heavy nylon, are 20 to 30 feet long and 2 to 3 inches wide, are rated to at least 20,000 pounds, and have looped ends.

Do not use tow straps with metal hooks in the ends (the hooks can become missiles in the event the strap breaks free). Likewise, never join two yank straps together using a shackle.

CB Radios

If you are stuck, injured, or just want to know the conditions up ahead, a citizen's band (CB) radio can be invaluable.

CB radios are relatively inexpensive and do not require an FCC license. Their range is limited, especially in very hilly country, as their transmission patterns basically follow lines of sight. Range can be improved using single sideband (SSB) transmission, an option on more expensive units. Range is even better on vehicle-mounted units that have been professionally fitted to ensure that the antenna and cabling are matched appropriately.

Winches

There are three main options when it comes to winches: manual winches, removable electric winches, and vehicle-mounted electric winches.

If you have a full-size 4WD vehicle—which can weigh in excess of 7,000 pounds when loaded—a manual winch is of limited use without a lot of effort and considerable time. However, a manual winch is a very handy and inexpensive accessory if you have a small 4WD. Typically, manual winches are rated to pull about 5,500 pounds.

Electric winches can be mounted to your vehicle's trailer hitch to enable them to be removed, relocated to the front of your vehicle (if you have a hitch installed), or moved to another vehicle. Although this is a very useful feature, a winch is heavy, so relocating one can be a two-person job. Consider that 5,000-pound-rated winches weigh only about 55 pounds, while 12,000-pound-rated models weigh around 140 pounds. Therefore, the larger models are best permanently front-mounted. Unfortunately, this position limits their ability to winch the vehicle backward.

When choosing between electric winches, be aware that they are rated for their maximum capacity on the first wind of the cable around the drum. As layers of cable wind onto the drum, they increase its diameter and thus decrease the maximum load the winch can handle. This decrease is significant: a winch rated to pull 8,000 pounds on a bare drum may only handle 6,500 pounds on the second layer, 5,750 pounds on the third layer, and 5,000 pounds on the fourth. Electric winches also draw a high level of current and may necessitate upgrading the battery in your 4WD or adding a second battery.

There is a wide range of mounting options—from a simple, body-mounted frame that holds the winch to heavy-duty winch bars that replace the original bumper and incorporate brush bars and mounts for auxiliary lights.

If you buy a winch, either electric or manual, you will also need quite a range of additional equipment so that you can operate it correctly:

- at least one choker chain with hooks on each end,
- winch extension straps or cables,
- shackles,
- a receiver shackle,
- a snatch block,
- a tree protector,
- gloves.

Grill/Brush Bars and Winch Bars

Brush bars protect the front of the vehicle from scratches and minor bumps; they also provide a solid mount for auxiliary lights and often high-lift jacking points. The level of protection they provide depends on how solid they are and on whether they are securely mounted onto the frame of the vehicle. Lighter models attach in front of the standard bumper, but the more substantial units replace the bumper. Prices range from about $150 to $450.

Winch bars replace the bumper and usually integrate a solid brush bar with a heavy-duty winch mount. Some have the brush bar as an optional extra to the winch bar component. Manufacturers such as Warn, ARB, and TJM offer a wide range of integrated winch bars. These are significantly more expensive, starting at about $650.

Remember that installing heavy equipment on the front of the vehicle may necessitate increasing the front suspension rating to cope with the additional weight.

Portable Air Compressors

Most portable air compressors on the market are flimsy models that plug into the cigarette lighter and are sold at the local discount store. These are of very limited use for four-wheel driving. They are very slow to inflate the large tires of a 4WD vehicle; for instance, to reinflate from 15 to 35 pounds typically takes about 10 minutes for each tire. They are also unlikely to be rated for continuous use, which means that they will overheat and cut off before completing the job. If you're lucky, they will start up again when they have cooled down, but this means that you are unlikely to reinflate your tires in less than an hour.

The easiest way to identify a useful air compressor is by the price—good ones cost $200 and over. Many of the quality units feature a Thomas-brand pump and are built to last. Another good unit is sold by ARB. All these pumps draw between 15 and 20 amps and thus should not be plugged into the cigarette lighter socket but attached to the vehicle's battery with clips. The ARB unit can be permanently mounted under the hood. Quick-Air makes a 10-amp compressor that can be plugged into the cigarette lighter socket and performs well.

Auxiliary Driving Lights

There is a vast array of auxiliary lights on the market today, and selecting the best lights for your purpose can be a confusing process.

Auxiliary lights greatly improve visibility in adverse weather conditions. Driving lights provide a strong, moderately wide beam to supplement headlamp high beams, giving improved lighting in the distance and to the sides of the main beam. Fog lamps throw a wide-dispersion, flat beam; and spots provide a high-power, narrow beam to improve lighting range directly in front of the vehicle. Rear-mounted auxiliary lights provide greatly improved visibility for backing up.

For off-highway use, you will need quality lights with strong mounting brackets. Some high-powered off-highway lights are not approved by the Department of Transportation.

Packing Checklist

Before embarking on any 4WD adventure, whether a lazy Sunday drive on an easy trail or a challenging climb over rugged terrain, be prepared. The following checklist will help you gather the items you need.

Essential

- ❒ Rain gear
- ❒ Small shovel or multipurpose ax, pick, shovel, and sledgehammer
- ❒ Heavy-duty yank strap
- ❒ Spare tire that matches the other tires on the vehicle
- ❒ Working jack and base plate for soft ground
- ❒ Maps
- ❒ Emergency medical kit, including sun protection and insect repellent
- ❒ Bottled water
- ❒ Blankets or space blankets
- ❒ Parka, gloves, and boots
- ❒ Spare vehicle key
- ❒ Jumper leads
- ❒ Heavy-duty flashlight
- ❒ Multipurpose tool, such as a Leatherman™
- ❒ Emergency food—high-energy bars or similar

Worth Considering

- ❒ Global Positioning System (GPS) receiver
- ❒ Cell phone
- ❒ A set of light-truck, off-highway tires and matching spare
- ❒ High-lift jack
- ❒ Additional tool kit
- ❒ CB radio
- ❒ Portable air compressor
- ❒ Tire gauge
- ❒ Tire-sealing kit
- ❒ Tire chains
- ❒ Handsaw and ax
- ❒ Binoculars
- ❒ Firearms
- ❒ Whistle
- ❒ Flares
- ❒ Vehicle fire extinguisher
- ❒ Gasoline, engine oil, and other vehicle fluids
- ❒ Portable hand winch
- ❒ Electric cooler

If Your Credit Cards Aren't Maxed Out

- ❒ Electric, vehicle-mounted winch and associated recovery straps, shackles, and snatch blocks
- ❒ Auxiliary lights
- ❒ Locking differential(s)

Trails in the Central Region

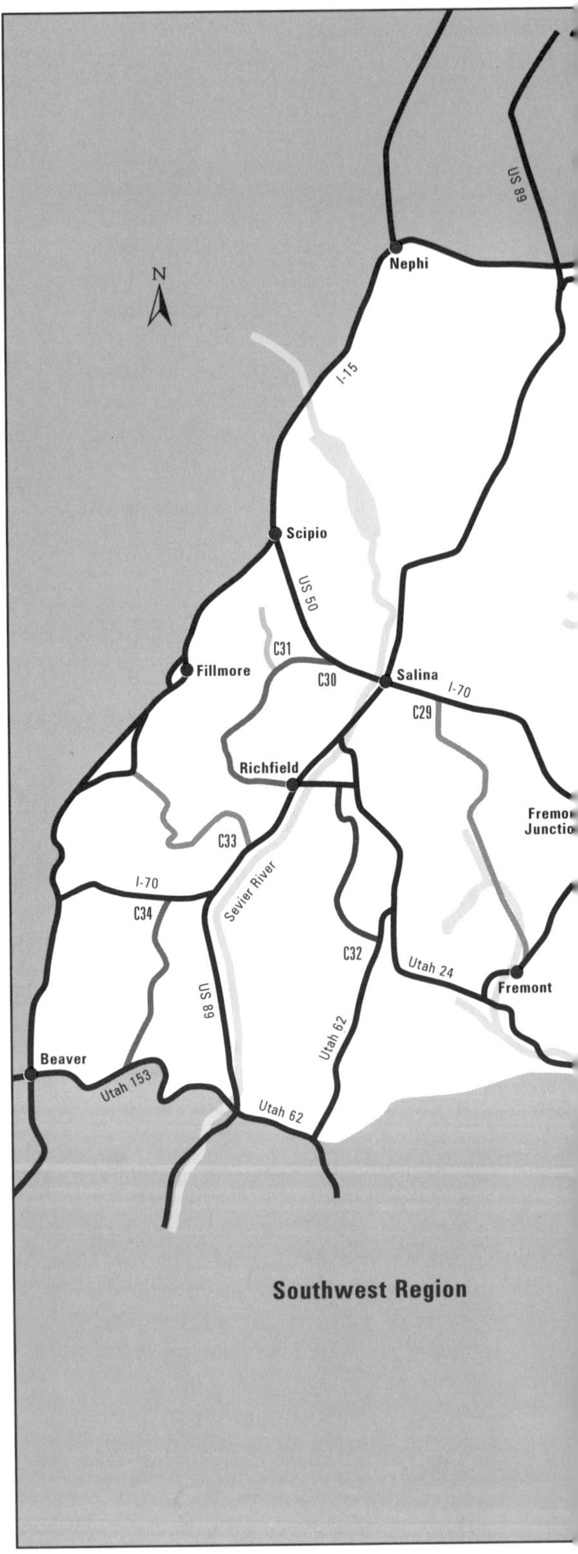

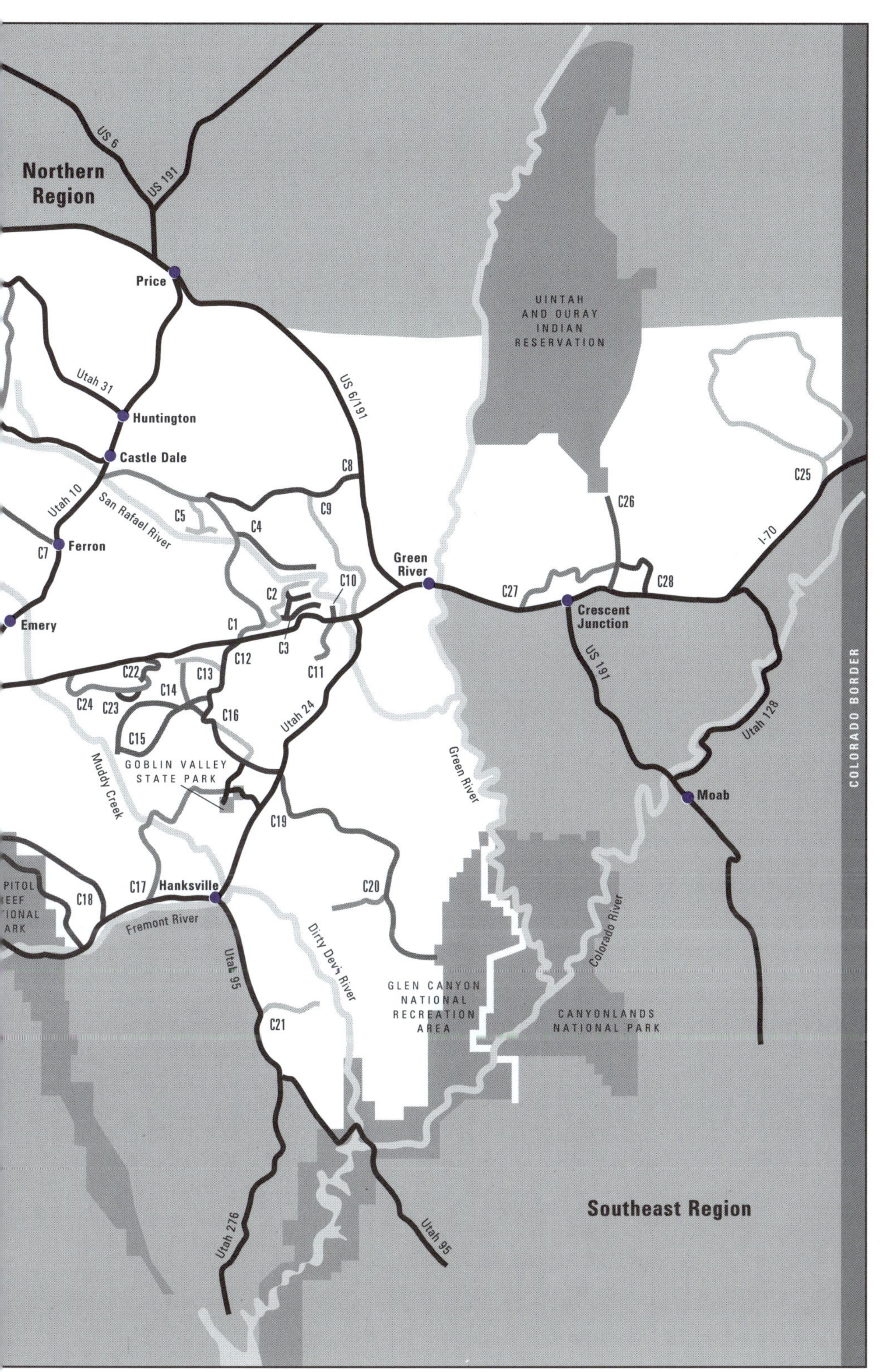
Northern Region
US 6
US 191
Price
Utah 31
Huntington
Castle Dale
US 6/191
UINTAH AND OURAY INDIAN RESERVATION
C8
C25
C26
Utah 10
San Rafael River
C5
C9
C4
I-70
C7
Ferron
Green River
C10
C2
C27
C28
Crescent Junction
Emery
C1
C3
C12
C11
US 191
C22
C13
C14
C24
C23
C16
Utah 24
C15
Utah 128
COLORADO BORDER
Green River
Muddy Creek
GOBLIN VALLEY STATE PARK
Moab
C19
C20
C17
Hanksville
C18
Fremont River
Colorado River
Utah 95
Dirty Devil River
GLEN CANYON NATIONAL RECREATION AREA
CANYONLANDS NATIONAL PARK
C21
Southeast Region
Utah 276
Utah 95

CENTRAL REGION TRAIL #1

Buckhorn Wash Trail

STARTING POINT I-70, exit 129
FINISHING POINT Utah 10, 1.5 miles north of Castle Dale
TOTAL MILEAGE 43 miles
UNPAVED MILEAGE 43 miles
DRIVING TIME 2 hours
ELEVATION RANGE 5,100–6,700 feet
USUALLY OPEN Year-round
DIFFICULTY RATING 1
SCENIC RATING 8
REMOTENESS RATING +0

Special Attractions

- Panels of petroglyphs.
- Dinosaur footprint.
- Matt Warner rock inscription.
- Easy, scenic canyon road that serves as the backbone to other trails.

History

Originally, parts of the Buckhorn Wash Trail were established by the Denver & Rio Grande Western Railroad Company in an effort to build a railroad from Green River to Huntington. When the grade of the planned route exceeded early calculations, the incomplete railroad was abandoned. Many sections of the rail bed have since been washed out by floods.

In 1921, oil companies decided to expand the road by building it through Buckhorn Wash. The Civilian Conservation Corps (CCC) rebuilt the road in the 1930s and also improved the nearby road to Temple Mountain. In 1938, the CCC also constructed the swinging bridge across the San Rafael River.

Although the trail is only a little over a hundred years old, the actual path of Buckhorn Wash has a history that dates back millions of years. Originally, Buckhorn Wash was cut by an early path of the Huntington River, which has since been diverted to its present location. Inside the Navaho sandstone canyon of Buckhorn Wash, the rock walls contain evidence of ancient sand dunes, indicating the region once had a climate comparable to the Sahara Desert. Dinosaurs once roamed central Utah and many traces of their existence can still be found. Along this trail, you can see a dinosaur footprint measuring 12 by 14 inches embedded in sandstone.

About 10,000 years ago, long after that dinosaur left its mark, humans began to inhabit the area. Evidence of this early Desert Archaic culture is literally written on the canyon walls in the form of pictographs and petroglyphs. Scholars refer to this ancient rock art as Barrier Canyon style. These early peoples survived as hunters and gatherers, and it is thought that rock art may have played some role in their spiritual beliefs. Over the years, these pictures have suffered damage from people shooting at or writing on them. However, the BLM has undertaken major repairs to preserve these pictures.

A couple of miles from the rock art, you can see a different kind of inscription on the rocks: one scratched out by outlaw Matt Warner. One of the Wild West's toughest criminals, Warner was involved in many robberies both by himself and with his friend Butch Cassidy. He eventually went straight after serving three and a half years in prison and went on to

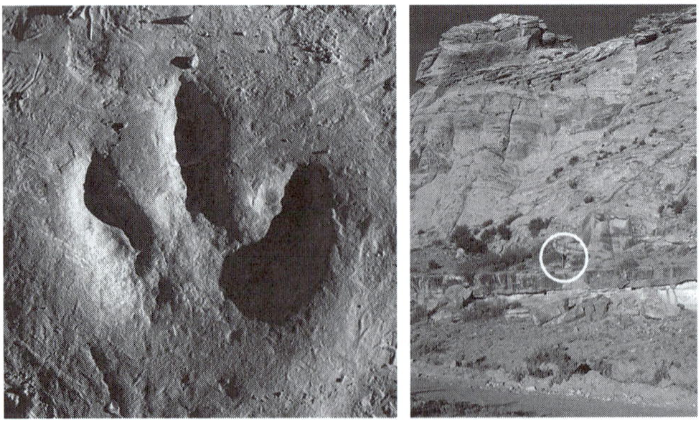

Left: The dinosaur footprint. Right: The location of the footprint viewed from the parking area across the road

The swinging bridge across the San Rafael River

become a justice of the peace and night marshal of Green River. The inscription, which includes his name (spelled "Mat") and the date, is a short distance from the trail about 30 feet up a cliff.

Cassidy himself rode through Buckhorn Draw with his partner Elza Lay while making an escape after the 1897 Castle Gate payroll robbery. As the story goes, Cassidy and Lay had long since passed through the area when the two posses chasing them met up in Buckhorn Draw. Mistaking each other for the band of outlaws, both posses opened fire. No one was killed in the exchange, but the delay allowed Cassidy and Lay to ride comfortably ahead to their hideout in Robbers Roost.

Description

The Buckhorn Wash Trail begins as a well-maintained, two-lane country road, which leaves I-70 at exit 129, and remains an easy, 1-rated trail throughout; navigation is straightforward. Initially, it parallels I-70 through the typical pinyon and juniper of this high desert country. In good weather, this graded gravel road can be traveled by a passenger car.

The trail crosses many washes, most of which are crossed by paved fords to prevent erosion. While you must negotiate some sections of powder-fine sand, none are deep enough to pose any serious problem. After 5.6 miles, you reach the turnoff for Central #2: Swasey's Leap Trail.

The trail passes by the appropriately named Bottleneck Peak about three-quarters of a mile before the San Rafael River crossing, where it then runs along Buckhorn Wash. After the bridge, Central #4: Mexican Bend Trail branches off to the right. Cottonwoods dot the area as the wash meanders along the canyon floor. Sheer cliffs, broken by many little side canyons, rise above both sides of the trail.

While in the wash, the trail approaches a panel of Indian rock art, Matt Warner's inscription, and finally the dinosaur footprint. The footprint can be especially difficult to find; it sits about 20 feet above the road on a rock ledge off to the right. There is a small area to the left where you can park your vehicle and hike up to the ancient footprint. There is no defined trail that leads to the footprint, so it may take a bit of looking around to find it. If it seems to elude you, look under a sandstone slab. People often use a rock to cover the track in order to protect it from vandalism and weathering. After you remove the rock to see the footprint, please be sure to replace it before you leave.

As the trail continues along the wash, it intersects with Central #8: Green River Cutoff and Central #5: Wedge Overlook Trail. The latter trail overlooks what is known as Utah's "Little Grand Canyon" and offers a view a thousand feet above the wandering San Rafael River. The trail reaches Utah 10 in another 12.4 miles, the last 5 or 6 miles of which run mainly through saltbrush and shaley mounds.

Current Road Information

Emery County Road Department
120 West Highway 29
Castle Dale, UT 84513
(435) 381-2550

BLM Price Field Office
125 South 600 West
Price, UT 84501
(435) 636-3600

Central Trail #1: Buckhorn Wash Trail

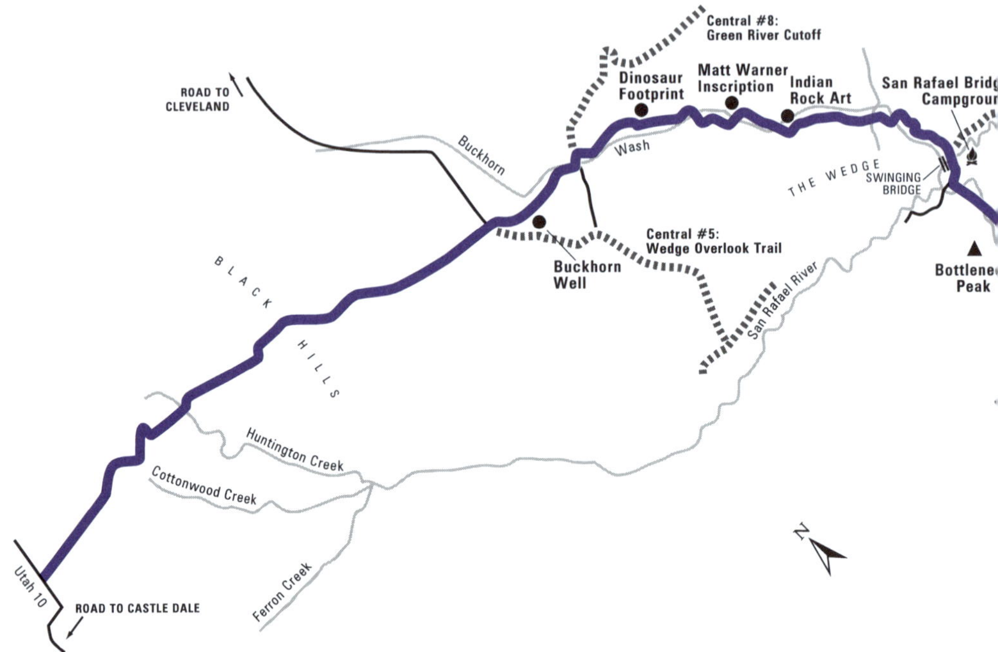

Map References

BLM San Rafael Desert, Huntington
USGS 1:24,000 The Wickiup, Drowned Hole Draw, Bottleneck Peak, Bob Hill Knoll, Buckhorn Reservoir, Hadden Holes
1:100,000 San Rafael Desert, Huntington
Maptech CD-ROM: Central/San Rafael
Trails Illustrated, #712
Utah Atlas & Gazetteer, pp. 39, 38
Utah Travel Council #5; #3
Other: Recreation Map of the San Rafael Swell and San Rafael Desert

Route Directions

▼ 0.0 On the north side of I-70, exit 129, zero trip meter at the intersection of the exit/entry ramps and the underpass road. Cross cattle guard and proceed along frontage road. Follow BLM sign to Buckhorn Draw, Wedge Overlook, and Buckhorn Pictograph Panel.

5.6 ▲ Turn left at signed intersection to Green River and Salina. Trail ends at I-70; turn east for Green River, west for Salina.

GPS: N 38°52.88' W 110°39.52'

▼ 0.8 SO Track on left.
4.8 ▲ SO Track on right.

▼ 0.9 SO Track on left.
4.7 ▲ SO Track on right.

▼ 2.0 SO Cattle guard.
3.5 ▲ SO Cattle guard.

▼ 3.4 SO Track on right to I-70 underpass to Jerry's Flat.
2.1 ▲ SO Track on left.

GPS: N 38°53.98' W 110°36.28'

▼ 5.0 SO Fenced sinkhole on right.
0.5 ▲ SO Fenced sinkhole on left.

▼ 5.6 SO Track on right is Central #2: Swasey's Leap Trail. Zero trip meter.

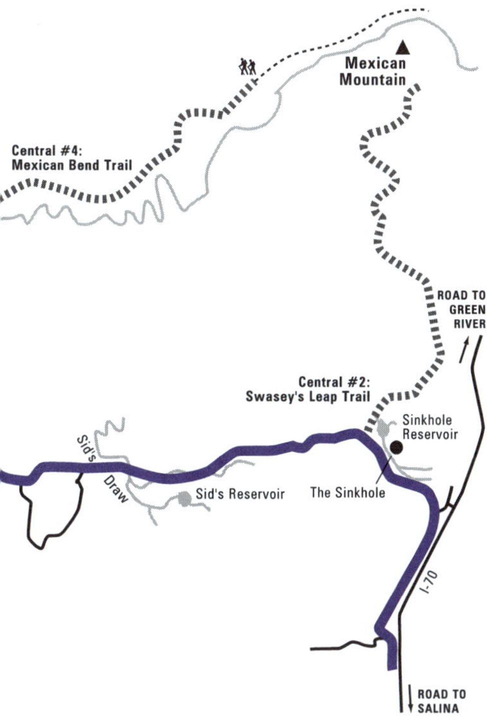

0.0 ▲ Continue straight.
GPS: N 38°55.76′ W 110°36.03′

▼ 0.0 Continue along main road.
13.3 ▲ SO Track on left is Central #2: Swasey's Leap Trail. Zero trip meter.

▼ 4.1 SO Cross through wash.
9.2 ▲ SO Cross through wash.

▼ 4.9 SO Cross ford through wash.
8.4 ▲ SO Cross ford through wash.

▼ 5.9 SO Track on left reconnects with trail in 0.3 miles.
7.4 ▲ SO Track on right.

▼ 7.2 SO Track on left.
6.1 ▲ SO Track on right reconnects with trail in 0.3 miles.

▼ 9.4 SO Track on left.
3.8 ▲ SO Track on right.

▼ 10.5 SO Cross ford through wash.
2.7 ▲ SO Cross ford through wash.

▼ 11.8 SO Cross ford through wash.
1.4 ▲ SO Cross ford through wash.

▼ 12.2 SO Cross ford through wash.
1.1 ▲ SO Cross ford through wash.

▼ 12.4 SO Bottleneck Peak on left.
0.9 ▲ SO Bottleneck Peak on right.

▼ 12.8 SO Track on left marked "corrals." This relatively short track splits and ends at nonmotorized trails.
0.5 ▲ SO Track on right marked "corrals." This relatively short track splits and ends at nonmotorized trails.

▼ 13.1 SO Intersection. San Rafael Bridge Campground on right.
0.2 ▲ SO Intersection. San Rafael Bridge Campground on left.
GPS: N 39°04.77′ W 110°40.00′

▼ 13.2 SO Swinging bridge on left. Cross San Rafael River on contemporary bridge.
0.1 ▲ SO Swinging bridge on right. Cross San Rafael River on contemporary bridge.

▼ 13.3 SO Track on right is Central #4: Mexican Bend Trail. Zero trip meter and cross cattle guard.
0.0 ▲ Continue along main road.
GPS: N 39°04.98′ W 110°39.81′

▼ 0.0 Continue along main road.
9.4 ▲ SO Cross cattle guard and zero trip meter. Track on left is Central #4: Mexican Bend Trail.

▼ 1.0 SO Cross ford.
8.3 ▲ SO Cross ford.

▼ 1.9 SO Cross ford.
7.4 ▲ SO Cross ford.

▼ 3.7 SO Large panel of Indian art nearly 100 feet long; parking area on right.
5.6 ▲ SO Large panel of Indian art nearly 100

feet long; parking area on left.

GPS: N 39°07.43' W 110°41.59'

▼ 4.6 SO Public toilet on right.
4.7 ▲ SO Public toilet on left.

▼ 4.8 SO Cross ford.
4.5 ▲ SO Cross ford.

▼ 5.2 SO Matt Warner inscription on right. Look for small unmarked pull-off area. Inscription is about 30 feet high on a rock wall to the right.
4.2 ▲ SO Matt Warner inscription on left. Look for small unmarked pull-off area. Inscription is about 30 feet high on a rock wall to the left.

GPS: N 39°08.24' W 110°42.16'

▼ 5.7 SO Cross bridge.
3.6 ▲ SO Cross bridge.

▼ 6.3 SO Cross ford.
3.1 ▲ SO Cross ford.

▼ 7.0 SO Pull-off area on right and trail to pictographs. Then cross cattle guard.
2.3 ▲ SO Cross cattle guard. Then pull-off area on left and trail to pictographs.

GPS: N 39°09.29' W 110°43.19'

▼ 7.7 SO Cross ford.
1.7 ▲ SO Cross ford.

▼ 7.8 SO Pull-off area on left and trail to dinosaur footprint on right.
1.6 ▲ SO Pull-off area on right and trail to dinosaur footprint on left.

GPS: N 39°09.61' W 110°43.71'

▼ 9.0 SO Cross bridge.
0.4 ▲ SO Cross bridge.

THE AGE OF THE DINOSAURS

Between 245 and 65 million years ago, Utah's landscape was covered with lush ferns and giant conifers. Enormous herbivores like the brontosaurus, stegosaurus, and diplodocus roamed the countryside as did the smaller, carnivorous allosaurus (Utah's official state fossil). Now, only titanic fossilized bones remain.

Allosaurus, the official fossil of Utah

In 1859, the Macomb Expedition found the first of these prehistoric bones in Utah. Today, dinosaur remains can be seen mainly in and among the rocks known as the Morrison Formation. This formation spreads throughout eastern Utah and Colorado and extends north to the Canadian border. It is known as one of the richest deposits of dinosaur fossils in the world.

Probably the most famous fossil quarry in Utah is Dinosaur National Monument. Here visitors can watch as paleontologists uncover real dinosaur bones. It was in this area that Earl Douglass first discovered the remains of an apatosaurus (a large herbivore similar to a brontosaurus or diplodocus). This fossil deposit has about 2,000 exposed bones in the quarry face for scientists to study and visitors to see. Utah's other major quarry is centrally located near Cleveland. The Cleveland-Lloyd Dinosaur Quarry is a more remote site from which scientists actively remove fossils for further study. It is here where most of the allosaurus remains have been found. Besides these two main sites, smaller deposits of dinosaur fossils from the Age of the Dinosaurs can be found scattered throughout the eastern and southern parts of the state.

▼ 9.4 TL T-intersection. Central #8: Green River Cutoff on right. Zero trip meter and turn left.

0.0 ▲ Continue south.

GPS: N 39°10.27' W 110°45.03'

▼ 0.0 Continue northwest toward Castle Dale.

2.3 ▲ TR Intersection. Central #8: Green River Cutoff is straight ahead. Zero trip meter and turn right.

▼ 0.1 SO Cross bridge.

2.2 ▲ SO Cross bridge.

▼ 0.3 SO Track on left is cutoff to Central #5: Wedge Overlook Trail in 1.5 miles.

2.0 ▲ SO Track on left is cutoff to Central #5: Wedge Overlook Trail in 1.5 miles.

GPS: N 39°10.08' W 110°45.27'

▼ 2.2 SO Buckhorn Well on left (small cinder-block building and tank).

0.1 ▲ SO Buckhorn Well on right (small cinder-block building and tank).

▼ 2.3 SO Buckhorn Flat Well Junction. Central #5: Wedge Overlook Trail on left; right goes to Cleveland. Zero trip meter.

0.0 ▲ Continue southeast.

GPS: N 39°10.54' W 110°47.40'

▼ 0.0 Continue toward Castle Dale.

12.4 ▲ SO Buckhorn Flat Well Junction. Central #5: Wedge Overlook Trail on right; left goes to Cleveland. Zero trip meter.

▼ 0.7 SO Cattle guard.

11.7 ▲ SO Cattle guard.

▼ 2.4 SO Multiple tracks on left.

10.0 ▲ SO Multiple tracks on right.

▼ 3.9 SO Track on right.

8.5 ▲ SO Track on left.

▼ 4.4 SO Track on left.

8.0 ▲ SO Track on right.

▼ 6.4 SO Cross ford through wash.

6.0 ▲ SO Cross ford through wash.

▼ 7.2 SO Track on right, then cattle guard.

5.2 ▲ SO Cattle guard, then track on left.

GPS: N 39°13.02' W 110°54.67'

▼ 7.4 SO Cross over bridge.

5.0 ▲ SO Cross over bridge.

▼ 7.8 SO Track on left.

4.6 ▲ SO Track on right.

▼ 8.6 SO Track on right to overlook on Oil Well Dome.

3.9 ▲ SO Track on left to overlook on Oil Well Dome.

▼ 8.7 SO Cattle guard.

3.8 ▲ SO Cattle guard.

▼ 9.4 SO Track on left.

3.1 ▲ SO Track on right.

▼ 12.4 Cattle guard, then trail ends at Utah 10, 1.5 miles north of Castle Dale.

0.0 ▲ On Utah 10, 1.5 miles north of Castle Dale, turn east onto dirt road. Sign reads, "Buckhorn Draw, Wedge Overlook & Pictograph Panel." Zero trip meter and cross cattle guard. Pass corrals on right.

GPS: N 39°13.23' W 110°59.80'

CENTRAL REGION TRAIL #2

Swasey's Leap Trail

STARTING POINT Central #1: Buckhorn Wash Trail, 5.6 miles from I-70

FINISHING POINT Fence line at walking trail to site of Swasey's Leap

TOTAL MILEAGE 12.5 miles

UNPAVED MILEAGE 12.5 miles

DRIVING TIME 1 hour

ELEVATION RANGE 5,000–6,600 feet

USUALLY OPEN Year-round

DIFFICULTY RATING 3

SCENIC RATING 8

REMOTENESS RATING +0

A view of the old stock bridge built to straddle the span of Swasey's Leap

Special Attractions

- Scenic, seldom-used 4WD spur trail.
- The legend of Swasey's Leap.

History

In the late 1800s, the Swasey family (sometimes spelled Swazy) settled in central Utah on a homestead near Cottonwood Creek. The Swasey boys soon became known throughout the region as good-natured, hard-working cowboys. One day, while working near Black Box with his brother, Sid Swasey came upon a 14-foot-wide canyon that fell nearly 60 feet to the river below. His brother wagered him 75 head of cattle he couldn't jump across the chasm on his saddlehorse. As the story goes, Sid made the jump and won the bet.

Soon after, a bridge of cottonwood logs was constructed across the canyon to enable herds of grazing sheep to cross.

Description

As the Swasey's Leap Trail branches off of Central #1: Buckhorn Wash Trail, the road becomes noticeably less traveled and soon rates a difficulty level of 2. The spur trail crosses flat-topped mesas and grasslands of pinyon and juniper. In many places the classic terrain looks like it was plucked from any number of Hollywood Westerns.

After 4.4 miles, you reach the intersection of Central #3: Black Dragon Wash Trail, which is a loop trail that intersects again at the 8.8-mile mark. At this point, the road deteriorates and becomes a 3-rated trail until it finishes at the boundary of the Mexican Mountain Study Area.

At the end of the driving trail, you can hike another 2 miles along a very scenic, old 4WD trail to the area where Sid Swasey jumped his horse across the canyon. The entire area offers spectacular views of the San Rafael River and the rock formations around the edge of the canyon.

Current Road Information

Emery County Road Department
120 West Highway 29
Castle Dale, UT 84513
(435) 381-2550

BLM Price Field Office
125 South 600 West
Price, UT 84501
(435) 636-3600

A view of the San Rafael River near Swasey's Leap

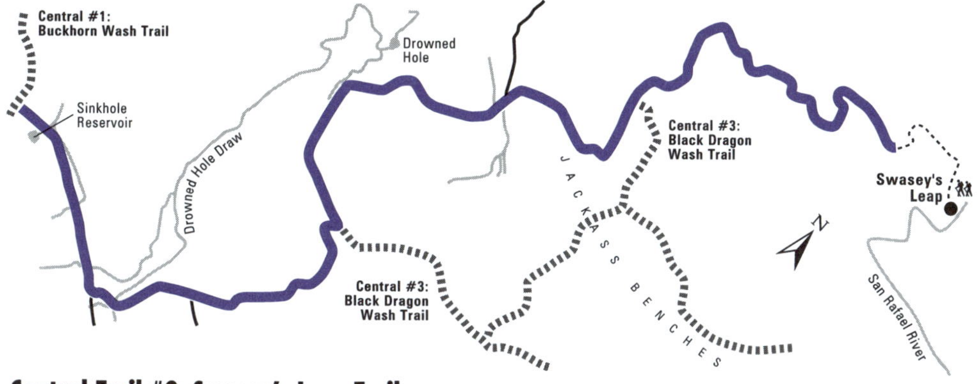

Central Trail #2: Swasey's Leap Trail

Map References

BLM San Rafael Desert
USGS 1:24,000 Drowned Hole Draw, Spotted Wolf Canyon
1:100,000 San Rafael Desert
Maptech CD-ROM: Central/San Rafael
Trails Illustrated, #712
Utah Atlas & Gazetteer, p. 39
Utah Travel Council #5
Other: Recreation Map of the San Rafael Swell and San Rafael Desert

Route Directions

▼ 0.0 On Central #1: Buckhorn Wash Trail, 5.6 miles from I-70, zero trip meter and proceed east along side road.
8.8 ▲ Trail ends at Central #1: Buckhorn Wash Trail; turn left for I-70, right for Castle Dale.
GPS: N 38°55.76' W 110°36.03'

▼ 1.1 SO Cross through wash, then cattle guard.
7.7 ▲ SO Cattle guard, then cross through wash.

▼ 1.5 SO Cross through wash.
7.3 ▲ SO Cross through wash.

▼ 1.7 BL Road forks. Right loops back to Buckhorn Wash Trail and to an I-70 underpass with access to Jerry's Flat.
7.1 ▲ BR Track on left is alternate loop to Buckhorn Wash Trail.
GPS: N 38°55.01' W 110°34.47'

▼ 1.9 SO Cross through wash.
6.9 ▲ SO Cross through wash.

▼ 4.4 BL Road forks. Straight is Central #3: Black Dragon Wash Trail.
4.4 ▲ BR Track on left is Central #3: Black Dragon Wash Trail.
GPS: N 38°56.45' W 110°32.95'

▼ 7.2 SO Cross through wash, then track on left.
1.6 ▲ SO Track on right, then cross through wash.
GPS: N 38°57.87' W 110°32.39'

▼ 8.3 SO Cross through wash.
0.4 ▲ SO Cross through wash.

▼ 8.8 BL Fork in road. Sign on left reads, "Swazys Leap and Lower Black Box." Right is Central #3: Black Dragon Wash Trail. Zero trip meter.
0.0 ▲ BR Proceed southwest along the main road to Central #1: Buckhorn Wash Trail. Track on left is Central #3: Black Dragon Wash. Zero trip meter.
GPS: N 38°58.43' W 110°31.41'

▼ 0.0 Continue toward Swasey's Leap.
▼ 3.5 SO Wilderness study area boundary.
GPS: N 38°59.35' W 110°29.36'

▼ 3.7 End of trail. Park and hike along old, 2-mile trail to Swasey's Leap.
GPS: N 38°59.29' W 110°29.17'

Black Dragon Wash Trail

STARTING POINT Central #2: Swasey's Leap Trail
FINISHING POINT Central #2: Swasey's Leap Trail
TOTAL MILEAGE 12.5 miles
UNPAVED MILEAGE 12.5 miles
DRIVING TIME 1 hour
ELEVATION RANGE 4,700–6,200 feet
USUALLY OPEN Year-round
DIFFICULTY RATING 5
SCENIC RATING 8
REMOTENESS RATING +1

Special Attractions

- Provides an alternative return route from Swasey's Leap.
- Scenic views from Jackass Benches.
- Varied scenery along a moderately difficult 4WD road.
- Little-used, mostly unmapped trail in the midst of many heavily used backcountry roads.

Description

The Black Dragon Wash Trail is a loop trail off of Central #2: Swasey's Leap Trail, which connects to Central #1: Buckhorn Wash Trail. The majority of the trail does not appear on any map as it runs through some very scenic but seldom traveled countryside. The main attractions of this trail are its two spurs, which branch off to dead ends.

After 1.1 miles, you reach the first spur trail, which crosses Jackass Benches and offers some spectacular views into the canyon to the north. The striking, distinct sedimentary layers of the canyon wall clearly display the geological history of the area, moving from the yellow-browns at the bottom to the vivid reds at the top. The road surface along this spur is varied; there are a few rocky patches and a couple of short sections of shelf road.

A view of the early part of the spur along Black Dragon Wash

After 2.3 miles, you reach the second spur trail, which penetrates into the high-walled canyon along Black Dragon Wash. Ironically enough, while this part of the trail feels extremely remote, at times you are no more than a quarter mile from the traffic barreling down I-70. The road here becomes somewhat more difficult as it encounters a couple of narrow, off-camber sections of shelf road. A narrow ridgeline that can be quite rocky may also present you with a bit of a challenge. The road eventually connects through, in about 2 miles, to the end of Central #10: Black Dragon Pictographs Trail; however it becomes badly washed out and is more easily hiked than driven. This part of the road goes beyond the difficulty level of this book, but skilled drivers with short-wheelbase SUVs might be able to pass through.

Once you return from the second spur trail, the main trail continues another 2.2 miles to the junction with Central #2: Swasey's Leap Trail.

A view from the Jackass Benches spur trail

Current Road Information

Emery County Road Department
120 West Highway 29
Castle Dale, UT 84513
(435) 381-2550

BLM Price Field Office
125 South 600 West
Price, UT 84501
(435) 636-3600

Map References

BLM San Rafael Desert (incomplete)
USGS 1:24,000 Drowned Hole Draw, Spotted Wolf Canyon (incomplete)
1:100,000 San Rafael Desert (incomplete)
Maptech CD-ROM: Central/San Rafael
Trails Illustrated, #712
Utah Atlas & Gazetteer, p. 39
Utah Travel Council #5 (incomplete)
Other: Recreation Map of the San Rafael Swell and San Rafael Desert

Route Directions

▼ 0.0 On Central #2: Swasey's Leap Trail, 8.8 miles from Central #1: Buckhorn Wash Trail, zero trip meter and take right fork.
GPS: N 38°58.43' W 110°31.41'

▼ 1.1 BL Fork in road. Sign reads, "Sulphur Springs (6) Road ends (4)." Turn left on spur road to Sulphur Springs and Jackass Benches. Zero trip meter.
GPS: N 38°57.83' W 110°30.90'

First Leg: Jackass Benches

▼ 0.0 Head east on spur trail along Jackass Benches.
▼ 0.3 SO Cross through wash.
▼ 1.4 SO Cross large wash.
▼ 2.6 SO Cross through wash
GPS: N 38°57.86' W 110°28.61'

▼ 3.5 UT Road ends at closure fence. Wilderness study area ahead. Return to main trail and zero trip meter.
GPS: N 38°57.96' W 110°27.76'

Continuation of Main Trail

▼ 0.0 TL Continue south.
▼ 1.2 TL Intersection. Turn left on spur road to Black Dragon Wash. Zero trip meter.
GPS: N 38°56.84' W 110°31.08'

Central Trail #3: Black Dragon Wash Trail

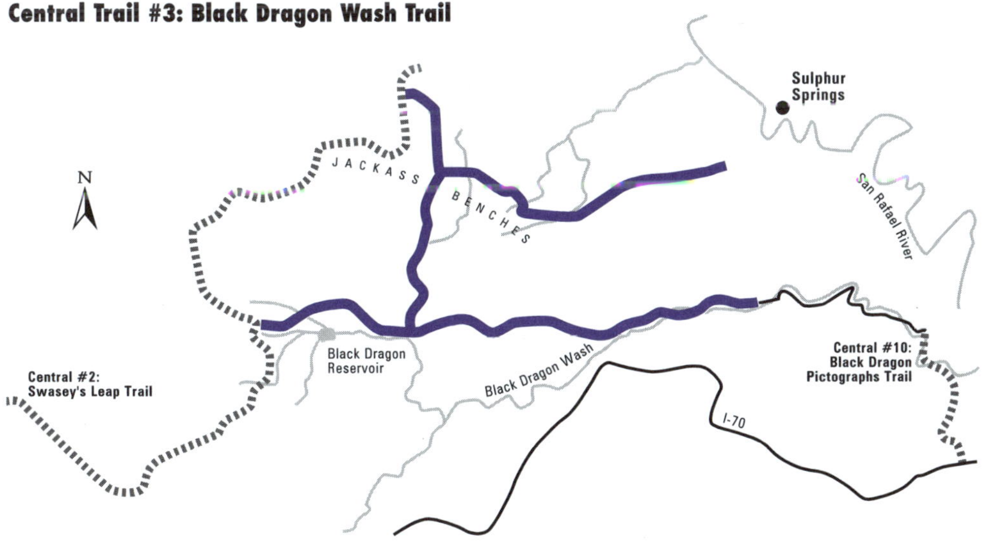

Second Leg: Black Dragon Wash

▼ 0.0 Continue east.
▼ 1.3 SO Cross through wash.
▼ 2.4 SO Stone pillar formation up on left.
▼ 4.3 SO Cross Black Dragon Wash, then a tight squeeze against the canyon wall.

GPS: N 38°56.78' W 110°27.40'

▼ 4.5 UT Spur trail finishes. Track is badly washed out ahead. Return to main trail and zero trip meter.

GPS: N 38°56.84' W 110°27.24'

Continuation Of Main Trail

▼ 0.0 SO Continue west.
▼ 2.2 End at Central #2: Swasey's Leap Trail, 4.4 miles from Central #1: Buckhorn Wash Trail. Turn left for I-70, right for Swasey's Leap.

GPS: N 38°56.45' W 110°32.95'

CENTRAL REGION TRAIL #4

Mexican Bend Trail

STARTING POINT Central #1: Buckhorn Wash Trail, near Swinging Bridge
FINISHING POINT Gate to the wilderness study area
TOTAL MILEAGE 13.8 miles
UNPAVED MILEAGE 13.8 miles
DRIVING TIME 1.25 hours (one-way)
ELEVATION RANGE 4,700–5,500 feet
USUALLY OPEN Year-round
DIFFICULTY RATING 2
SCENIC RATING 8
REMOTENESS RATING +0

Special Attractions

- Numerous good camping spots beside the San Rafael River.
- Short hike to the Black Box section of the San Rafael River; a deep, narrow sandstone canyon.

A view down into the Black Box

History

By the mid to late 1800s, the trail past Mexican Bend was already well known to sheepherders and early explorers. Outlaws also passed through the area on their long rides between hideouts, cattle rustling ventures, and bank robberies.

In the spring of 1897, Mexican Bend was the scene of a daylong standoff between the outlaw Joe Walker and a posse led by Sheriff Ebeneezer Tuttle. Walker was camped at Mexican Bend with three horses recently stolen from the Whitmore Ranch. The posse had been following him from Price, past Cleveland, and into the San Rafael Swell. As the lawmen came around Mexican Bend, they saw Walker cooking dinner. The lawmen immediately took cover behind large boulders, and the standoff began. As Sheriff Tuttle and two of his men tried to gain a closer position on the outlaw, they were met with a volley from Walker. The shots hit the barrel of one man's gun and struck the sheriff in the thigh. Unable to move, Tuttle had to wait until the next day for his posse to rescue him, as the men were too frightened of the dead-shot outlaw to risk leaving their cover. Walker escaped in the night, and Tuttle and his men went back to Price to lick their wounds.

Joe Walker is thought to have returned to Mexican Bend a month later. In April 1897, Butch Cassidy and Elza Lay were making their getaway from the Castle Gate payroll robbery to their hideout in Robbers Roost by way of Buckhorn Draw and Mexican Bend. Walker supposedly assisted them by cutting the telephone and telegraph lines to Price and providing them with a fresh group of horses.

Description

From Central #1: Buckhorn Wash Trail, the Mexican Bend Trail breaks off to the southeast and follows the Mexican Mountain Road. This spur trail is relatively easy, though a couple of rocky sections and wash crossings warrant the 2 rating.

At the start, there are a number of buff-colored sandstone mounds, which are often used by mountain bikers. Past these, the terrain changes to iron red cliffs, which dominate the scenery on the north side for the bulk of the trail.

A drive on the Mexican Bend Trail is considerably enhanced by an exploration of its many side roads. A few lead to overlooks of the San Rafael, while others wind down to the river. There are also a number of extremely good backcountry camping spots located about a quarter mile off the main trail. Some of the most scenic can be found tucked away among the cottonwood trees that flourish on the banks of the river.

One of the area's most striking geological features is the Black Box, where the San Rafael River has cut an extremely narrow canyon through the oldest exposed rock in Emery County. The lower portion is made up of 250-million-year-old Coconino sandstone. The trail intersects with a short, 500-yard hiking trail to the Upper Black Box Overlook. From here you can approach the edge and look down about 60 feet into this narrow and intimidating canyon, where the river silently makes its way through the darkness below.

The Mexican Bend Trail comes to an end at a gate marking the boundary of the Mexican Mountain Wilderness Study Area. While it was once possible to drive all the way out to the bend, today the trail is closed to vehicles before Mexican Mountain. From the gate, you can hike about 1.5 miles farther along the old 4WD trail to the start of Mexican Bend. As you continue around the bend, the valley widens, allowing easy access to the river. The hiking trail passes many cottonwoods around Mexican Bend, and it's not hard to imagine that they once provided a shady retreat for outlaws and their horses as they passed through this otherwise rugged terrain.

A view of the distinctive layers of sedimentary rock vividly exposed in this area

Central Trail #4: Mexican Bend Trail

Current Road Information

Emery County Road Department
120 West Highway 29
Castle Dale, UT 84513
(435) 381-2550

BLM Price Field Office
125 South 600 West
Price, UT 84501
(435) 636-3600

Map References

BLM Huntington
USGS 1:24,000 Bottleneck Peak, Devils Hole, Mexican Mt.
1:100,000 Huntington
Maptech CD-ROM: Central/San Rafael
Trails Illustrated, #712
Utah Atlas & Gazetteer, p. 39
Utah Travel Council #3
Other: Recreation Map of the San Rafael Swell and San Rafael Desert

Route Directions

▼ 0.0 On Central #1: Buckhorn Wash Trail, 18.9 miles from I-70 and just past the swinging bridge over the San Rafael River, zero trip meter and proceed southeast along Mexican Mountain Road. Pass message board.

GPS: N 39°04.98' W 109°39.81'

▼ 0.5 SO Track on right.
▼ 0.6 SO Track on right.
▼ 0.8 SO Track on right to river.

GPS: N 39°04.78' W 110°39.18'

▼ 1.3 SO Track on left to corral.
▼ 1.5 SO Track on right.
▼ 1.6 SO Track on left; track on right to overlook.

GPS: N 39°04.55' W 110°38.39'

▼ 1.8 SO Track on right, then wash; track on right.

GPS: N 39°04.41' W 110°38.28'

▼ 2.0 SO Track on right to river, campsites, and picnic spots among the cottonwoods.
▼ 2.2 SO Track on right.
▼ 2.4 SO Track on right.

GPS: N 39°04.07' W 110°37.73'

▼ 2.7 SO Track on right to numerous campsites along the river among the cottonwoods.

GPS: N 39°03.48' W 110°37.62'

▼ 3.0 SO Cross through wash.
▼ 3.9 SO Cross through wash.
▼ 4.3 BL Track on right to a nice river overlook.

GPS: N 39°02.97' W 110°36.36'

▼ 4.9 SO Track on left.
▼ 5.0 SO Cross through Red Canyon Wash.
▼ 6.1 SO Cross through wash.
▼ 7.1 SO Cross through gate and close behind you.

GPS: N 39°01.93' W 110°34.07'

▼ 7.4 SO Cross through White Horse Canyon Wash.
▼ 8.1 SO Upper Black Box Trail on right.

GPS: N 39°01.33' W 110°33.87'

▼ 9.0 SO Cross through wash.

▼ 9.6 SO Track on right.

GPS: N 39°00.73′ W 110°32.80′

▼ 10.1 SO Upper Black Box Trail on right.

GPS: N 39°00.79′ W 110°32.26′

▼ 11.4 SO Cross through gate.

▼ 13.8 Trail ends at gate into wilderness study area. From here, hike down along the old 4WD trail 1.5 miles to Mexican Bend.

GPS: N 39°00.92′ W 110°29.31′

CENTRAL REGION TRAIL #5

Wedge Overlook Trail

STARTING POINT Central #1: Buckhorn Wash Trail, 2.3 miles from junction with Central #8: Green River Cutoff

FINISHING POINT Wedge Overlook and rim spur trails

TOTAL MILEAGE 10.3 miles

UNPAVED MILEAGE 10.3 miles

DRIVING TIME 1 hour

ELEVATION RANGE 5,700–6,200 feet

USUALLY OPEN Year-round

DIFFICULTY RATING 1

SCENIC RATING 9

REMOTENESS RATING +0

Special Attractions

- Many spectacular viewpoints into the Little Grand Canyon of the San Rafael River.
- Easy spur trail off of Central #1: Buckhorn Wash Trail.
- Many backcountry campsites.

Description

Initially, the Wedge Overlook Trail runs along a wide, maintained gravel road that travels through rolling brush country. After half a mile, a track on the right offers riverside access to Fuller Bottom Draw. The main trail continues toward the Wedge, and after a couple of miles the countryside turns into pleasant grassland dotted with pinyon and juniper. The trail offers numerous side roads that lead to plenty of good camping spots.

At the Wedge Overlook, take some time to admire Utah's "Little Grand Canyon." This remarkable canyon has been formed over the centuries as the San Rafael River has cut its way through the sandstone of the San Rafael Swell. It's this dramatic, stunning overlook that warrants the trail's scenic 9 rating.

From the overlook, spur trails lead in either direction along the canyon rim. At times, a large number of side trails leading to camping spots and overlooks can make navigation difficult. Just stick to the main trail as you wind through the pinyon and juniper around the rim.

The San Rafael River viewed from the overlook at the end of the trail

The "parking spot" at the end of the trail

Of the two rim roads, the shorter, eastern one is easier; a passenger car could easily drive it in good weather. A peninsula, jutting out above the canyon, marks the end of the eastern side trail. This is an excellent spot to view the river on either side below or to park your SUV for a dramatic photo.

Current Road Information

Emery County Road Department
120 West Highway 29
Castle Dale, UT 84513
(435) 381-2550

BLM Price Field Office
125 South 600 West
Price, UT 84501
(435) 636-3600

Map References

BLM Huntington
USGS 1:24,000 Buckhorn Reservoir, Sids Mt., Bottleneck Peak
1:100,000 Huntington
Maptech CD-ROM: Central/San Rafael
Trails Illustrated, #712
Utah Atlas & Gazetteer, pp. 39, 38
Utah Travel Council #3
Other: Recreation Map of the San Rafael Swell and San Rafael Desert

Route Directions

▼ 0.0		From Central #1: Buckhorn Wash Trail, 2.3 miles from junction with Central #8: Green River Cutoff, zero trip meter and turn toward signs for Wedge Overlook. **GPS: N 39°10.54' W 110°47.40'**
▼ 0.5	BL	Track on right to Fuller Bottom Draw.
▼ 1.0	SO	Cattle guard.
▼ 2.1	SO	Information board and track on left to

Central Trail #5: Wedge Overlook Trail

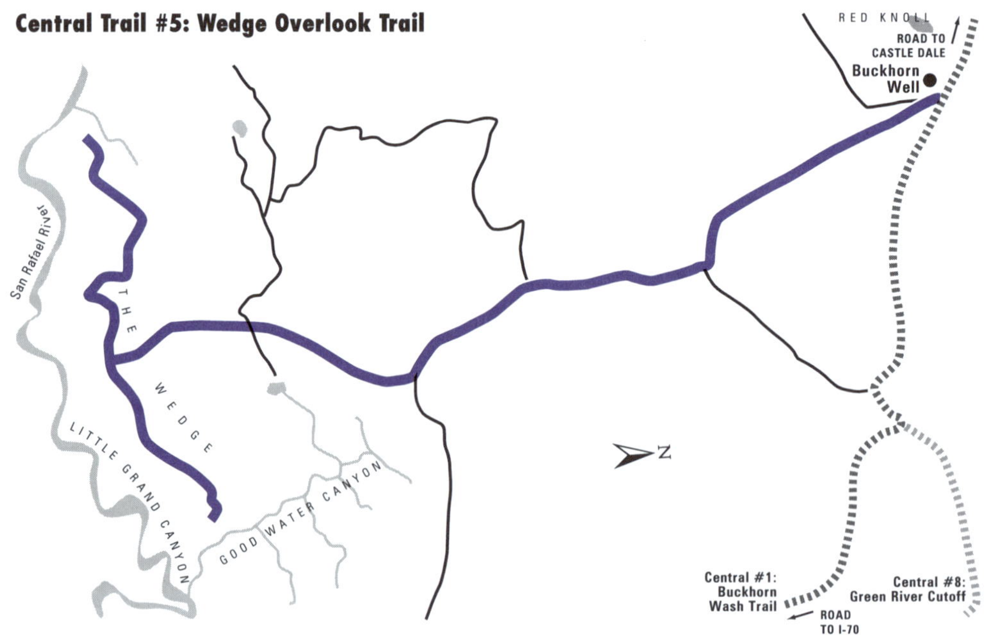

Central #1: Buckhorn Wash Trail.
GPS: N 39°09.10' W 110°46.16'

▼ 3.2 SO Track on right.
▼ 4.3 SO Information board and track on left.
GPS: N 39°07.40' W 110°45.39'

▼ 5.4 SO Tracks on left and right.
▼ 6.5 TR Wedge Overlook. Spur tracks along rim on left and right. Zero trip meter and follow 4WD trail west around the rim.
GPS: N 39°05.58' W 110°45.48'

First Leg: Western Rim

▼ 0.0 Proceed along the western rim.
▼ 2.3 End of western rim trail. Return to main overlook and zero trip meter.
GPS: N 39°05.43' W 110°47.12'

Second Leg: Eastern Rim

▼ 0.0 Continue along the eastern rim.
▼ 0.7 SO Large rock peninsula sticking out above the San Rafael Valley provides a great photo opportunity.
GPS: N 39°05.72' W 110°44.89'

▼ 1.5 End of the eastern rim spur.
GPS: N 39°06.41' W 110°44.44'

CENTRAL REGION TRAIL #6

Upper Joe's Valley Trail

STARTING POINT Utah 29, 18.8 miles from Utah 10
FINISHING POINT Utah 31
TOTAL MILEAGE 20.7 miles
UNPAVED MILEAGE 20.2 miles
DRIVING TIME 2.5 hours
ELEVATION RANGE 7,000–9,100 feet
USUALLY OPEN May to November
DIFFICULTY RATING 4
SCENIC RATING 9
REMOTENESS RATING +0

Potters Ponds

Special Attractions

- Joe's Valley Reservoir.
- Scenic Potters Ponds.

History

On June 20, 1963, the president of the Emery Water Conservancy District, O. Eugene Johansen, addressed the crowd gathered for the groundbreaking ceremony of the Joe's Valley Dam. In his speech, Johansen recalled the three Joes who make up a significant portion of the history of Joe's Valley.

As the story goes, "Indian Joe" was rescued by white settlers when they saw him being mistreated by other Indians. In return for their kindness, Joe joined up with the settlers and helped them in many ways. The second Joe was Joe Swasey, an early settler in Emery County who built many of the first fences in the region. Swasey and his family were among the first white explorers of the San Rafael Swell, and they left their names on many features in the area (such as Rods Valley, Swasey's Leap, and Swasey's Cabin). Finally, "Pete Joe," or Peter Johansen, was an early settler who acquired most of the local ranchlands in the early 1900s.

Any one of these Joes could be the man behind the valley's name, though no one seems to know for sure exactly how or when the valley was discovered and named. However, it must have been one of the earlier known sites in the region, since it was one of the only named features on an 1878 map created by explorer John Wesley Powell.

In 1933, Joe's Valley was the site of a Civilian Conservation Corps camp. A group of young men looking for work during the Great Depression made their way to the valley to work on a reforestation project. Thirty years later, the 195-foot-high, 740-foot-wide Joe's Valley Dam was completed, which created Joe's Valley Reservoir. The reservoir is currently the largest lake in Emery County and is a favorite among fishing enthusiasts, as it holds some of the largest brown and rainbow trout in the region.

Description

Upper Joe's Valley Trail begins on Utah 29, 18.8 miles northwest of its junction with Utah 10 in Castle Dale (coming from the south, you can take a shortcut on Utah 57 to Utah 29). As the paved Utah 29 approaches Joe's Valley Reservoir, it runs through some very picturesque country. The reservoir supports quite a lot of wildlife, ranging from birds and small animals to the elusive mountain lion. The reservoir also serves as a recreational area for fishing, hiking, and camping. As well as the developed campgrounds at Joe's Valley Reservoir, there are a number of backcountry camping spots along the trail, especially from Potters Ponds to the end of the trail. During hunting season, the upper reaches of the trail near Miller Flat Reservoir are particularly popular.

A potentially muddy spot likely to be rutted even when dry

Upper Joe's Valley Trail begins at FR 014, a dirt road that heads north from the reservoir off Utah 29. The maintained, two-lane country road climbs gently, passing through the mature cottonwoods along Joe's Creek.

As you enter some very scenic ranchland, the road narrows to a wide, easy single lane that's still graded and maintained. After 2.1 miles, you turn onto FR 038 and pass a number of good places to camp or picnic beside the creek. Lined with cottonwoods, aspens, and junipers, the trail makes a perfect autumn drive to view the colors, which change to a radiant gold.

After the bridge, at the 4.3-mile mark, the road gets a bit more rough and warrants a 2 rating. Some points are quite rocky or rutted; be careful in wet weather as the ruts turn into deep mud holes. Some intermittent rocky sections can become considerably more difficult than the rest of the trail and rate a difficulty level of 4.

After about 8 miles from the start, there is a 2-mile stretch of very pretty ponds. The final and largest ones—known as Potters Ponds—come near the 10-mile mark and can be reached by driving a short side trail to the left.

After Potters Ponds, the trail reconnects with FR 014 and continues north 10.8 miles to end at Utah 31. From here, continue north 4.8 miles to reach Central #7: Skyline Drive Trail, or continue north 9.5

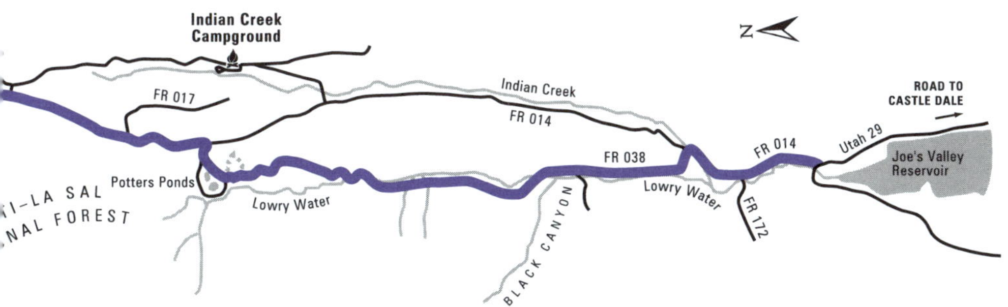

Central Trail #6: Upper Joe's Valley Trail

miles to reach Northern #14: Clear Creek Ridge Trail, which can be found in *4WD Trails: Northern Utah.*

Current Road Information

Manti–La Sal National Forest
Ferron Ranger District
98 South State Street
Ferron, UT 84523
(435) 384-2372

Map References

BLM Manti, Nephi
USFS Manti–La Sal National Forest: Ferron Ranger District
USGS 1:24,000 Joe's Valley Reservoir, South Tent Mt., Rilda Canyon, Candland Mt., Huntington Reservoir
1:100,000 Manti, Nephi
Maptech CD-ROM: Central/San Rafael
Utah Atlas & Gazetteer, pp. 38, 46
Utah Travel Council #3

Route Directions

▼ 0.0 On Utah 29, 10.0 miles from Utah 10 at Joe's Valley Reservoir, turn north onto FR 014 and zero trip meter.
7.1 ▲ End at Utah 29 near Joe's Valley Reservoir; turn southeast for Utah 10.
GPS: N 39°19.21' W 111°16.53'

▼ 0.5 SO Cross cattle guard onto unpaved road.
6.6 ▲ SO Cross cattle guard onto paved road.

▼ 1.1 BR Fork in road. FR 172 on left.
6.0 ▲ SO FR 172 enters on right.

▼ 1.2 SO Cattle guard.
5.9 ▲ SO Cattle guard.

▼ 1.8 SO Cattle guard.
5.3 ▲ SO Cattle guard.

▼ 2.1 BL Fork in road; bear left onto FR 038. Upper Joe's Valley is straight ahead.
5.0 ▲ BR Road is now FR 014.
GPS: N 39°20.89' W 111°16.17'

▼ 4.0 SO Cross over bridge, then FR 174 on left.
3.1 ▲ SO FR 174 on right, then cross over bridge.
GPS: N 39°22.28' W 111°16.37'

▼ 4.3 SO Cross bridge.
2.8 ▲ SO Cross bridge.

▼ 4.9 SO FR 2211 to Black Canyon on left.
2.2 ▲ SO FR 2211 to Black Canyon on right.
GPS: N 39°23.07' W 111°16.49'

▼ 7.0 SO Cross over creek.
0.1 ▲ SO Cross over creek.

▼ 7.1 SO Cross bridge and zero trip meter.
0.0 ▲ Continue along main trail.
GPS: N 39°24.94' W 111°16.16'

▼ 0.0 Continue along main trail.
2.8 ▲ SO Cross bridge and zero trip meter.

▼ 1.6 BR Track on left.
1.2 ▲ BL Track on right.
GPS: N 39°26.12' W 111°15.87'

▼1.6-2.1 SO Pass series of ponds on right.
0.6-1.1 ▲ SO Pass series of ponds on left.

▼ 2.3 SO Cross under high-voltage transmission wires.
0.5 ▲ SO Cross under high-voltage transmission wires.

▼ 2.3 SO Track on left.
0.4 ▲ SO Track on right.

▼ 2.8 TR Intersection. Turn left on FR 271 to reach Potters Ponds in 0.5 miles. Zero trip meter and turn right to continue on main route.
0.0 ▲ Continue along main route.
GPS: N 39°26.92' W 111°15.46'

▼ 0.0 Continue along main route.
8.4 ▲ TL Intersection. To follow main route, turn left and zero trip meter. Straight is FR 271, which leads to Potters Ponds in 0.5 miles.

▼ 0.1 TL T-intersection. Turn left on FR 014 to continue on main trail. Turn right to return to Joe's Valley Reservoir.
8.3 ▲ TR Turn right onto FR 038. FR 014 continues straight to Joe's Valley Reservoir.
GPS: N 39°26.90' W 111°15.37'

▼ 1.5 SO FR 017 on right.
6.9 ▲ SO FR 017 on left.

▼ 2.2 SO FR 020 on left.
6.2 ▲ SO FR 020 on right.

▼ 3.7 SO Track to corral on right.
4.6 ▲ SO Track to corral on left.

▼ 4.0 SO Cross over Paradise Creek.
4.4 ▲ SO Cross over Paradise Creek.

▼ 4.2 BR FR 193 on left.
4.1 ▲ BL FR 193 on right.

▼ 4.9 SO Road on right.
3.4 ▲ BR Road on left.
GPS: N 39°30.69' W 111°14.91'

▼ 5.1 SO Tracks on left and right are FR 231.
3.3 ▲ SO Tracks on left and right are FR 231.

▼ 6.3 SO Cross bridge.
2.0 ▲ SO Cross bridge.

▼ 6.6 SO Track on right to Miller Flat Reservoir.
1.7 ▲ SO Track on left to Miller Flat Reservoir.

▼ 7.6 SO FR 201 on right.
0.8 ▲ SO FR 201 on left.

▼ 8.2 SO Cross bridge.
0.1 ▲ SO Cross bridge.

▼ 8.4 SO On right is left fork of Huntington Creek National Recreation Trail and public toilets. Zero trip meter.
0.0 ▲ Continue south.
GPS: N 39°33.29' W 111°14.46'

▼ 0.0 Continue north.
2.4 ▲ SO On left is left fork of Huntington Creek National Recreation Trail and public toilets. Zero trip meter.

▼ 0.6 SO Cross over Rolfson Creek.
1.8 ▲ SO Cross over Rolfson Creek.

▼ 0.9 SO FR 269 on left.
1.5 ▲ SO FR 269 on right.

▼ 1.9 SO Cross over Lake Creek.
0.5 ▲ SO Cross over Lake Creek.

▼ 2.0 SO FR 089 on right, then cross creek.
0.4 ▲ SO Cross creek, then FR 089 on left.

▼ 2.1 SO Track on right, then track on left.
0.3 ▲ SO Track on right, then track on left.
GPS: N 39°34.78' W 111°14.99'

▼ 2.4 Seasonal gate, then trail ends at Utah 31; turn right for Huntington, left for Fairview.
0.0 ▲ On Utah 31, between Huntington and Cleveland Reservoirs, zero trip meter and turn south onto FR 014.
GPS: N 39°34.97' W 111°15.03'

CENTRAL REGION TRAIL #7

Skyline Drive Trail

STARTING POINT Utah 31, 4.8 miles south of Northern #14: Clear Creek Ridge Trail
FINISHING POINT Ferron
TOTAL MILEAGE 71.8 miles
UNPAVED MILEAGE 67.6 miles
DRIVING TIME 4 hours
ELEVATION RANGE 6,000–10,900 feet
USUALLY OPEN June to November
DIFFICULTY RATING 3
SCENIC RATING 8
REMOTENESS RATING +1

Special Attractions

- Spectacular views over miles of countryside as you cross the Wasatch Plateau, which reaches an altitude of nearly 11,000 feet.
- Varied driving conditions through a forested high-mountain setting.
- Abundant wildlife.

History

Throughout the 1930s, the Civilian Conservation Corps (CCC) made a number of improvements and restorations to Utah's many natural and historical landscapes. In 1933, the CCC came to Emery County and began work in Joe's Valley (for more on Joe's Valley, see Central #6: Upper Joe's Valley Trail). By summer 1935, CCC Company 959 had moved to Gooseberry and begun work on Skyline Drive between the Orangeville-Ephraim and Huntington-Fairview Roads. Upon the completion of the road, 5,000 people turned up for the dedication and ensuing celebration.

In autumn 1935, Company 959 moved to a year-round camp in Ferron and began construction on the road up Ferron Canyon. The route below follows a section of this road before coming to an end in Ferron.

Description

The highest road in Sanpete County, Skyline Drive runs along the dividing line between the Great Basin and the Colorado Plateau. At the start of the trail just off Utah 31, there is an overlook that provides an excellent view west into Sanpete Valley.

The trail is generally wide and allows for passing. There are some areas where water drainage has eroded the sides, making the road more narrow; but these sections are relatively short and present little if any obstacle. In the middle of the trail, a more difficult section is rough and rutted in spots, with potholes large enough to make you keep your speed in check.

For most of its length, Skyline Drive travels near the treeline, initially passing a few stands of aspen before running through large groves of Engelmann spruce. Views from Skyline Drive are truly spectacular, as the landscape combines alpine meadows with distant scenery. Raptors are frequently seen

A view of Ferron Reservoir

One of the sections of the trail that can become very boggy

along this trail riding the air currents in search of prey.

Continue along to the west of the North and South Tent Mountains, which stand at 11,230 and 11,285 feet respectively. Just before you reach Horseshoe Flat, the road improves considerably and warrants a 1 difficulty rating. For a number of sections, the road narrows along short lengths of shelf road and travels past interesting rock formations. Just after the summit, the trail runs along a mile stretch of smooth shelf road.

A mile and a half past the summit, you turn east on the maintained, gravel FR 022 to Ferron. Many side tracks split off from the main road, but none are large enough to present any navigational difficulties.

At Ferron Canyon, the trail follows a switchback down around the end and runs along the canyon floor next to the meandering Ferron Creek. After coming out of the canyon, proceed into the town of Ferron on Canyon Road; the trail ends at Utah 10 (State Street). If you are beginning the trail in Ferron, head north on Utah 10 (State Street) and follow the sign to Millsite State Park on Canyon Road.

Current Road Information

Manti–La Sal National Forest
Sanpete Ranger District
150 South Main Street
Ephraim, UT 84627
(435) 384-2372

Manti–La Sal National Forest
Ferron Ranger District
98 South State Street
Ferron, UT 84523
(435) 384-2372

Map References

BLM Nephi, Manti
USFS Manti–La Sal National Forest: Sanpete and Ferron Ranger Districts
USGS 1:24,000 Huntington Reservoir, South Tent Mt., Spring City, Danish Knoll, Ferron Reservoir, Ferron Canyon, Flagstaff Peak, Ferron
1:100,000 Nephi, Manti
Maptech CD-ROM: Central/San Rafael
Utah Atlas & Gazetteer, pp. 38, 46
Utah Travel Council #3

Route Directions

▼ 0.0 On Utah 31 at Sanpete Valley Overlook, zero trip meter and proceed south on FR 150. Follow signs to South Skyline Drive and Great Western Trail.
8.0 ▲ Trail ends at Utah 31. Turn left for Fairview, right for Huntington.
GPS: N 39°37.03' W 111°18.63'

▼ 0.4-0.5 SO Overlook of Huntington Reservoir to the east.
7.5-7.6 ▲ SO View of Huntington Reservoir to the east.

▼ 0.8 SO FR 067 on right.
7.1 ▲ SO FR 067 on left.

▼ 1.7 SO Track on left.
6.3 ▲ SO Track on right.

▼ 2.0 SO Broad views west across valley.

6.0 ▲ SO Broad views west across valley.

▼ 2.5 SO Lake Canyon Hiking Trail on left.
5.5 ▲ SO Lake Canyon Hiking Trail on right.

▼ 5.0 SO Rough track on right.
3.0 ▲ SO Rough track on left.

▼ 6.0 SO Cattle guard.
2.0 ▲ SO Cattle guard.

▼ 8.0 SO Track on right (FR 037) to Mount Pleasant. Zero trip meter.
0.0 ▲ Continue along Skyline Drive.
GPS: N 39°31.06' W 111°18.13'

▼ 0.0 Continue along Skyline Drive.
8.5 ▲ SO Track on left (FR 037) to Mount Pleasant. Zero trip meter.

▼ 1.5 SO Track on right.
7.0 ▲ BL Track enters on left.

▼ 1.8 SO Pass under high-voltage wires.
6.7 ▲ SO Pass under high-voltage wires.

▼ 3.6 SO Track on left is FR 271 to Bacon Rind Canyon.
4.9 ▲ SO Track on right is FR 271 to Bacon Rind Canyon.

▼ 4.8 SO Track on left.
3.6 ▲ SO Track on right.

▼ 6.4 BR Track on left.
2.0 ▲ SO Track on right.

▼ 7.4 SO Track on left.
1.1 ▲ SO Track on right.

▼ 8.5 BL Track on right is FR 036 to Spring City. Zero trip meter.
0.0 ▲ Continue north along Skyline Drive.
GPS: N 39°25.86' W 111°21.39'

▼ 0.0 Continue south along Skyline Drive.
11.5 ▲ BR Intersection. Track on left is FR 036 to Spring City. Zero trip meter.

▼ 0.1 SO Alternative entry to FR 036 on right.
11.4 ▲ SO FR 036 on left.

▼ 0.2 SO Track on left.
11.2 ▲ SO Track on right.

▼ 0.9 BR Track on left.
10.6 ▲ SO Track on right.

▼ 2.0 SO FR 279 on right.
9.4 ▲ SO FR 279 on left.

▼ 3.1 SO Track on left.
8.3 ▲ SO Track on right.

▼ 3.3 SO Track on left.
8.1 ▲ SO Track on right.

▼ 3.5 SO FR 054 on left.
8.0 ▲ SO FR 054 on right.

▼ 4.2 SO FR 286 on left.
7.2 ▲ SO FR 286 on right.

▼ 7.0 SO Tracks on left and right.
4.5 ▲ SO Tracks on right and left.

▼ 9.4 SO Track on right.
2.1 ▲ SO Track on left.

▼ 10.1 SO Track on right to radio tower.
1.4 ▲ SO Track on left to radio tower.

▼ 11.5 BR Intersection. Left is Utah 29 (FH8) and connects with Central #6: Upper Joe's Valley Trail. Zero trip meter.
0.0 ▲ Continue along Skyline Drive.
GPS: N 39°19.36' W 111°26.53'

▼ 0.0 Continue along Skyline Drive.
15.5 ▲ BL Fork in road. Right is Utah 29 (FH8) and connects with Central #6: Upper Joe's Valley Trail. Zero trip meter.

▼ 0.9 BL Road forks. Follow sign toward Manti. Right goes to Ephraim.
14.6 ▲ SO Road to Ephraim on left.

▼ 1.4 SO FR 346 on right through fence line. Follow sign to Snow Lake and Manti Canyon Road.

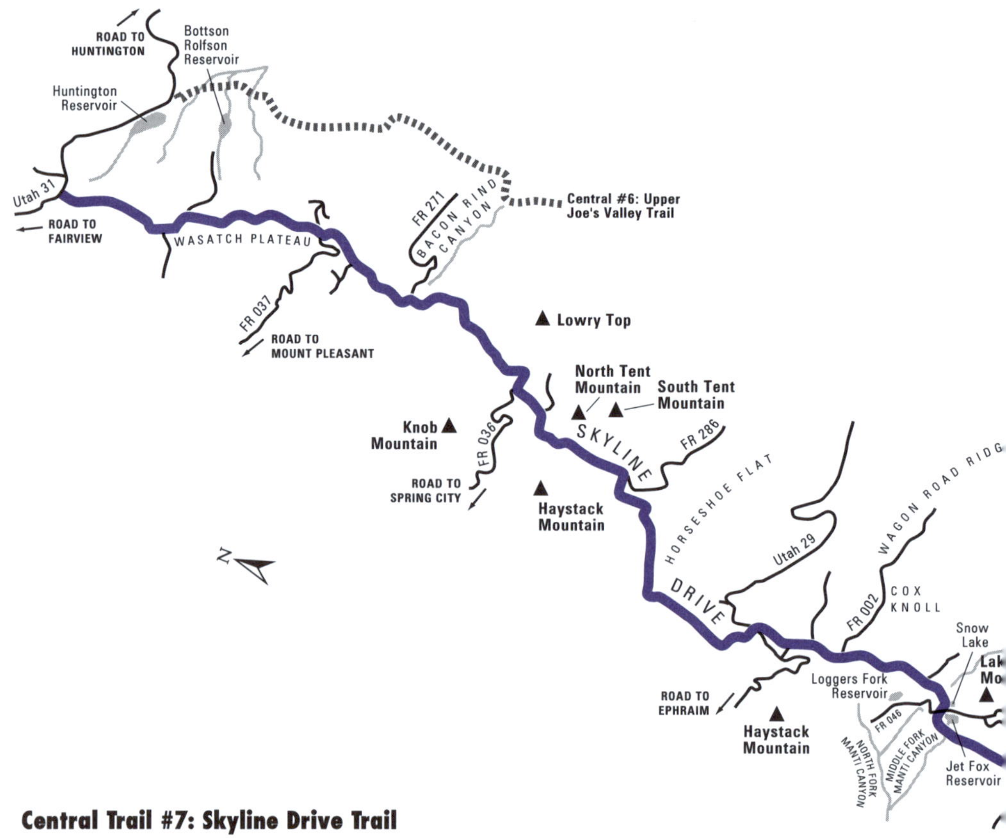

Central Trail #7: Skyline Drive Trail

14.1 ▲ SO FR 346 on left through fence line. Follow sign to Huntington.

▼ 1.6 SO Road on left.
13.8 ▲ SO Road on right.

▼ 1.9 SO Road on left.
13.6 ▲ SO Road on right.

▼ 2.1 SO FR 002 on left to Wagon Road Ridge and Cox Knoll.
13.4 ▲ SO FR 002 on right to Wagon Road Ridge and Cox Knoll.

▼ 3.9 SO Track on right.
11.6 ▲ SO Track on left.

▼ 4.6 BR Track on left is FR 003 to Buck Ridge.
10.8 ▲ BL Track on right is FR 003 to Buck Ridge.
GPS: N 39°15.50' W 111°26.68'

▼ 4.8 SO Track on left is FR 004 to Trail Ridge.
10.7 ▲ SO Track on right is FR 004 to Trail Ridge.

▼ 5.5 SO Track on left to Lake Mountain.
9.9 ▲ SO Track on right to Lake Mountain.

▼ 5.7 SO Snow Lake on left.
9.8 ▲ SO Snow Lake on right.

▼ 5.8 SO Track on right.
9.7 ▲ SO Track on left.

▼ 6.0 SO FR 046 on right to Lowry Fork Trail, Loggers Fork Reservoir, and North Fork Manti Canyon. Road on left to Cove Lake and Cove Creek.
9.5 ▲ SO FR 046 on left. Road to Cove Lake and Cove Creek on right.

▼ 6.2 SO Cattle guard.
9.3 ▲ SO Cattle guard.

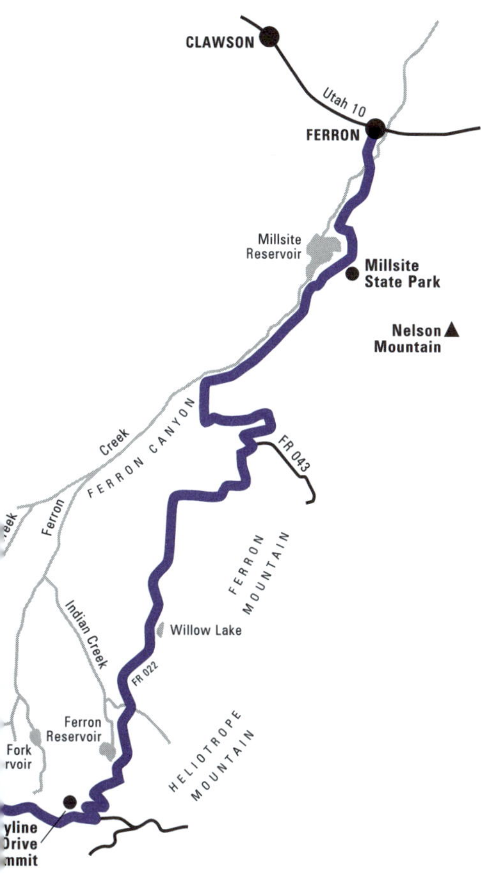

▼ 6.4 SO FR 196 and FR 197 on right.
9.0 ▲ SO FR 196 and FR 197 on left.

▼ 7.4 SO Cattle guard. Then FR 207 on right.
8.1 ▲ SO FR 207 on left. Then cattle guard.

▼ 9.1 SO FR 045, Manti Canyon Road, on right (12 miles to Manti).
6.4 ▲ SO FR 045, Manti Canyon Road, on left (12 miles to Manti).

▼ 9.2 SO Cross over drainage and FR 133 on right. Cattle guard.
6.3 ▲ SO Cattle guard. FR 133 on left. Cross over drainage.

▼ 9.5 SO FR 061 on left.
6.0 ▲ SO FR 061 on right.

▼ 10.2 SO Cattle guard. FR 231 on right.
5.3 ▲ SO FR 231 on left. Cattle guard.

▼ 11.7 BR Road on left.
3.7 ▲ SO Road on right.

▼ 12.8 BR Two roads on left.
2.6 ▲ BL Two roads on right.

▼ 13.9 SO Skyline Drive summit. Elevation 10,897 feet.
1.6 ▲ SO Skyline Drive summit. Elevation 10,897 feet.

▼ 15.0 BR FR 327 on left on switchback.
0.5 ▲ BL FR 327 on right. Continue on switchback.

▼ 15.5 UT At intersection make a U-turn toward Ferron on FR 022. Zero trip meter.
0.0 ▲ Continue on Skyline Drive.
GPS: N 39°08.38' W 111°29.03'

▼ 0.0 Continue toward Ferron.
14.7 ▲ UT At intersection make a U-turn to the right. Zero trip meter.

▼ 0.9 SO Road on left (rejoins main road after a short distance).
13.8 ▲ BL Road on right (rejoins main road after a short distance).

▼ 1.5 SO Road on right.
13.1 ▲ SO Road on left.

▼ 2.6 SO Road on left is FR 025 to Ferron Reservoir.
12.1 ▲ SO Road on right is FR 025 to Ferron Reservoir.

▼ 2.7 SO Road to reservoir on left.
12.0 ▲ SO Road to reservoir on right.

▼ 3.0 SO Road to reservoir on left.
11.7 ▲ BL Road to reservoir on right.

▼ 3.2 BR Duck Fork Road on left.
11.5 ▲ BL Duck Fork Road on right.

▼ 3.9 SO Cattle guard and FR 070 on right.
10.8 ▲ SO FR 070 on left. Cattle guard.

▼ 4.3 SO Cross over Little Horse Creek.
10.3 ▲ SO Cross over Little Horse Creek.

▼ 7.4 SO Willow Lake on right.
7.3 ▲ SO Willow Lake on left.
GPS: N 39°08.14' W 111°22.90'

▼ 8.4 SO FR 085 on left.
6.2 ▲ SO FR 085 on right.

▼ 10.5 SO Cattle guard.
4.2 ▲ SO Cattle guard.

▼ 14.7 SO Left on FR 279 leads 0.3 miles to Ferron Canyon Overlook. Then FR 043 on right to 12 Mile Flat, Horse Creek, and Wrigley Springs Reservoir. Zero trip meter.
0.0 ▲ Continue along main road.
GPS: N 39°07.04' W 111°17.41'

▼ 0.0 Continue on main road.
13.6 ▲ SO FR 043 on left to 12 Mile Flat, Horse Creek, and Wrigley Springs Reservoir. Then FR 279 on right leads 0.3 miles to Ferron Canyon Overlook. Zero trip meter.

▼ 3.0 SO Cross ford over Stevens Creek.
10.6 ▲ SO Cross ford over Stevens Creek.

▼ 4.1 SO Cross through creek.
9.5 ▲ SO Cross through creek.

▼ 7.5 SO Cattle guard.
6.1 ▲ SO Cattle guard.

▼ 13.4 SO Ferron Ranger Station, Manti-La Sal National Forest, on right.
0.2 ▲ SO Ferron Ranger Station, Manti-La Sal National Forest, on left.

▼ 13.6 Trail ends at State Street (Utah 10) and Canyon Road in Ferron.
0.0 ▲ On Utah 10 (State Street) in Ferron, zero trip meter and proceed west along Canyon Road.
GPS: N 39°05.30' W 111°07.85'

CENTRAL REGION TRAIL #8

Green River Cutoff

STARTING POINT Unmarked dirt road off US 6/191, about 17 miles north of I-70
FINISHING POINT Central #1: Buckhorn Wash Trail
TOTAL MILEAGE 27.8 miles
UNPAVED MILEAGE 27.3 miles
DRIVING TIME 1.5 hours
ELEVATION RANGE 4,800–6,200 feet
USUALLY OPEN Year-round
DIFFICULTY RATING 1
SCENIC RATING 7
REMOTENESS RATING +0

Special Attractions

- Picturesque entrance to this route through a narrow, boulder-strewn canyon.
- Historic region includes part of the Spanish Trail and the original route of the Denver & Rio Grande Western Railroad.
- Easy backcountry road offering alternative access to Central #1: Buckhorn Wash Trail from either Price or Green River.

History

The Green River Cutoff crosses or briefly runs along two of Utah's historic routes: The Spanish Trail and the original route of the Denver & Rio Grande Western (D&RGW) Railroad. It is often difficult to find the specific route of the Spanish Trail as it is now

A patch of the deep, powder-fine sand along the Green River Cutoff

The start of the canyon at the eastern end of the trail

mostly worn away. However, it did go through much the same area as the Green River Cutoff trail. The original D&RGW railbed is a bit more defined (though still worn away) and crosses paths with the Green River Cutoff in a couple places.

Description

The start of the Green River Cutoff is unmarked; the road branches west off US 6/191 between mileposts 283 and 284. The trail follows a wide, two-lane maintained country road with a gravel surface. Though a 1-rated trail, in wet weather it can become impassable. The only parts that might pose a problem in dry weather are thick sections of powder-fine dust that create huge clouds and block your vision if a car passes. Navigation is straightforward throughout, as all the side roads are much smaller.

Initially, the trail moves through rolling grasslands. It then enters a narrow, rock-strewn canyon with huge boulders on either side of the road. After 11.7 miles, you reach the intersection with Central #9: Tidwell Draw Trail. The scenery changes around the wide grasslands of Chimney Rock Flat, as the flatland spreads out around the foot of the towering Chimney Rock, which rises over 700 feet high. The road continues through grassland and varying stands of pinyon and juniper. The trail ends at Central #1: Buckhorn Wash Trail, 14.7 miles from Castle Dale.

Current Road Information

Emery County Road Department
120 West Highway 29
Castle Dale, UT 84513
(435) 381-2550

BLM Price Field Office
125 South 600 West
Price, UT 84501
(435) 636-3600

Map References

BLM Huntington
USGS 1:24,000 Cliff, Dry Mesa, Chimney Rock, Bob Hill Knoll
1:100,000 Huntington
Maptech CD-ROM: Central/San Rafael
Trails Illustrated, #712
Utah Atlas & Gazetteer, p. 39
Utah Travel Council #3
Other: Recreation Map of the San Rafael Swell and San Rafael Desert

Route Directions

▼ 0.0 On US 6/191 between mile markers 283 and 284, approximately 17 miles north of I-70, zero trip meter and proceed west on unmarked dirt road. Cross cattle guard. Yellow sign reads, "Roads May Be Impassable Due to Storms."
11.7 ▲ Trail ends at US 6/191; turn right for Green River, left for Price.
GPS: N 39°11.74' W 110°20.27'

▼ 0.9 TL T-intersection. Turn left on old paved road.
10.8 ▲ TR Turn right toward US 6/191.
GPS: N 39°12.26' W 110°21.07'

▼ 1.2 SO Cross under railway overpass.
10.5 ▲ SO Cross under railway overpass.

▼ 1.4 TR Turn right onto unpaved road.
10.3 ▲ TL Turn left onto paved road.
GPS: N 39°11.84' W 110°21.24'

▼ 2.1 SO Cattle guard.
9.6 ▲ SO Cattle guard.

Central Trail #8: Green River Cutoff

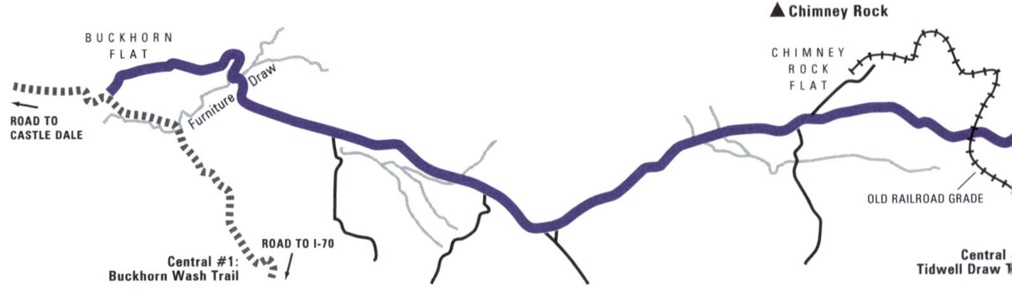

▼ 3.2 SO Track on left.
8.5 ▲ SO Track on right.

▼ 5.0 SO Cattle guard.
6.7 ▲ SO Cattle guard.

▼ 5.9 SO Track on right.
5.8 ▲ SO Track on left.

▼ 6.4 SO Cross over wash.
5.3 ▲ SO Cross over wash.

▼ 7.4 SO Track on right.
4.3 ▲ SO Track on left.

GPS: N 39°10.47' W 110°25.12'

▼ 7.5 SO Track on right.
4.2 ▲ SO Track on left.

▼ 7.8 SO Track on right.
3.9 ▲ SO Track on left.

▼ 8.5 SO Track on left.
3.2 ▲ SO Track on right.

GPS: N 39°10.17' W 110°25.87'

▼ 10.5 SO Cattle guard.
1.2 ▲ SO Cattle guard.

▼ 11.0 SO Track on left.
0.7 ▲ SO Track on right.

▼ 11.7 SO Track on left is Central #9: Tidwell Draw Trail to Smith's cabin. Track on right. Zero trip meter.
0.0 ▲ Continue along main road.

GPS: N 39°10.76' W 110°29.00'

▼ 0.0 Continue along main road.
8.2 ▲ SO Track on right is Central #9: Tidwell Draw Trail to Smith's cabin. Track on left. Zero trip meter.

▼ 1.0 SO Cross old railroad grade.
7.2 ▲ SO Cross old railroad grade.

GPS: N 39°10.61' W 110°30.00'

▼ 3.5 SO Chimney Rock on right, across Chimney Rock Flat.
4.7 ▲ SO Chimney Rock on left, across Chimney Rock Flat.

▼ 3.7 SO Track on right.
4.5 ▲ SO Track on left.

▼ 4.0 SO Two tracks on left.
4.2 ▲ SO Two tracks on right.

▼ 6.2 SO Track on left.
2.0 ▲ SO Track on right.

▼ 7.5 SO Bridge over wash.
0.7 ▲ SO Bridge over wash.

▼ 8.0 SO Track on left.
0.2 ▲ SO Track on right.

▼ 8.2 SO Track on left was a portion of the Spanish Trail. Zero trip meter.
0.0 ▲ Continue along main road.

GPS: N 39°08.93' W 110°37.35'

▼ 0.0 Continue along main road.

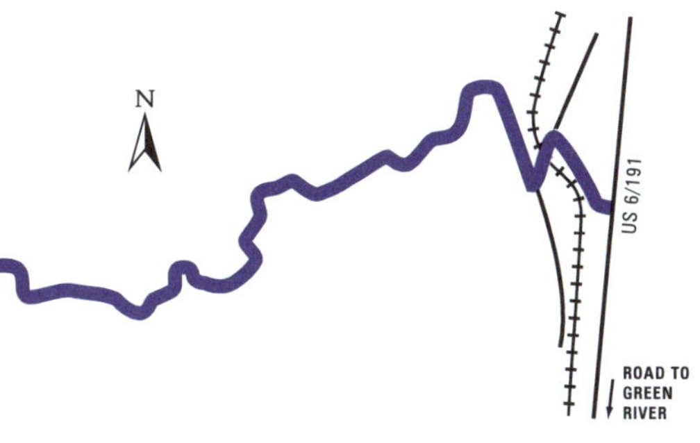

7.9 ▲ SO Track on right was a portion of the Spanish Trail. Zero trip meter.

▼ 0.6 SO Cattle guard and track on right.
7.3 ▲ SO Track on left and cattle guard.

▼ 1.1 SO Track on left.
6.8 ▲ SO Track on right.

▼ 2.9 SO Track on right and corral.
5.0 ▲ SO Track on left and corral.

▼ 4.5 SO Track on left.
3.4 ▲ SO Track on right.

▼ 5.5 SO Cross Furniture Draw. Old bridge foundation on right.
2.4 ▲ SO Cross Furniture Draw. Old bridge foundation on left.
GPS: N 39°10.66′ W 110°42.92′

▼ 5.6 SO Cross cattle guard.
2.3 ▲ SO Cross cattle guard.

▼ 5.8 SO Road on right.
2.1 ▲ SO Road on left.

▼ 6.6 SO Descend into Buckhorn Flat.
1.3 ▲ SO Leave Buckhorn Flat.

▼ 7.7 SO Buckhorn corral on left.
0.2 ▲ SO Buckhorn corral on right.

▼ 7.8 SO Cattle guard.
0.1 ▲ SO Cattle guard.

▼ 7.9 Sign reads: "Castle Dale straight; Buckhorn Wash Pictograph Panel and San Rafael Bridge Recreational site to the left." Then trail ends at Central #1: Buckhorn Wash Trail; turn left to I-70, straight to Utah 10.
0.0 ▲ On Central #1: Buckhorn Wash Trail, 14.7 miles from Utah 10, zero trip meter and proceed east into Buckhorn Flat.
GPS: N 39°10.27′ W 110°45.03′

CENTRAL REGION TRAIL #9

Tidwell Draw Trail

STARTING POINT Central #8: Green River Cutoff, 11.7 miles from US 6/191
FINISHING POINT I-70, exit 147
TOTAL MILEAGE 23.8 miles
UNPAVED MILEAGE 23.8 miles
DRIVING TIME 2.5 hours
ELEVATION RANGE 4,400–5,300 feet
USUALLY OPEN Year-round
DIFFICULTY RATING 3
SCENIC RATING 8
REMOTENESS RATING +0

Special Attractions

- Smith's cabin.
- Historic, varied, and seldom-used trail.

History

After they were married in 1933, Wayne and Betty Smith settled down to start a ranch in the San Rafael Swell. They chose a site near a spring, which would supply them with the water necessary for survival. However, artificial seismic activity in the region, caused by drilling for water, destroyed the natural spring. Wayne and Betty later moved to Green River. Today at Smith's cabin, there are several ranch buildings and corrals still standing. Though some of the cabins and cattle yards are currently in various states of decay, enough is left of this scenic ranch to give you a good feel of frontier life in the San Rafael Swell.

A good portion of the trail follows the

Smith's cabin and ranch buildings

original Denver & Rio Grande Western (D&RGW) railbed through Emery County. Thinking this line would become part of the shortest route across the continent, the D&RGW built this section of railbed from Green River toward Buckhorn Flat in the early 1880s. However, the company decided to postpone plans for a transcontinental line and focus its efforts on Salt Lake City and the Wasatch Front. It wasn't until after they had spent over $200,000 on the railbed that D&RGW's senior management realized that this route through Emery County was still under construction. Realizing the mistake, they quickly abandoned the railbed and fired the project's unfortunate head surveyor.

Description

The Tidwell Draw Trail begins on Central #8: Green River Cutoff, 11.7 miles from US 6/191. The area is typical of San Rafael country, with various rock formations, canyons, and rolling grasslands dotted with sage, pinyon, and juniper.

Overall, the trail is rather easy, as it moves across a number of sandy patches. However, a couple of stream crossings, slickrock areas, and eroded sandy sections provide an added element of difficulty. After Smith's cabin, the trail evens out and the difficulty rating drops to a 1.

The trail's high scenic rating is mainly due to its history in connection with the remains of the D&RGW railroad, the Spanish Trail, and Smith's cabin. The trail more or less follows the path of the old railbed for the first 15 miles or so.

Toward the end of the trail, the few remains of an old mining district lie in Buckmaster Draw. You can still see some foundations, mines, and tailings dumps, and the ground itself remains scarred from what was most likely open mining. The trail finishes at I-70.

Current Road Information

Emery County Road Department
120 West Highway 29
Castle Dale, UT 84513
(435) 381-2550

BLM Price Field Office
125 South 600 West
Price, UT 84501
(435) 636-3600

Map References

BLM Huntington, San Rafael Desert (incomplete)
USGS 1:24,000 Dry Mesa, Mexican Mt., Desert, Jessies Twist, Spotted Wolf Canyon
1:100,000 Huntington, San Rafael Desert (incomplete)
Maptech CD-ROM: Central/San Rafael
Trails Illustrated, #712
Utah Atlas & Gazetteer, p. 39
Utah Travel Council #3; #5
Other: Recreation Map of the San Rafael Swell and San Rafael Desert

Route Directions

▼ 0.0 On Central #8: Green River Cutoff, 11.7 miles from US 6/191, turn south onto dirt track.
4.3 ▲ Trail ends at Central #8: Green River Cutoff; turn right for US 6/191, left for Central #1: Buckhorn Wash Trail.
GPS: N 39°10.76' W 110°29.00'

▼ 0.1 BR Fork in road.
4.2 ▲ BL Fork in road.

▼ 0.3 SO Cross through sandy wash.

4.0 ▲ SO Cross through sandy wash.

▼ 1.1 SO Cross through wash.
3.2 ▲ SO Cross through wash.

▼ 1.7 SO Cross through wash.
2.6 ▲ SO Cross through wash.

▼ 2.1 SO Structures on left include well and stock trough.
2.2 ▲ SO Structures on right include well and stock trough.

GPS: N 39°09.15' W 110°28.34'

▼ 2.3 SO Sign on right notes this was part of the Spanish Trail.
2.0 ▲ SO Sign on left notes this was part of the Spanish Trail.

▼ 2.3 BL Fork in road. Bear left across Cement Crossing.
1.9 ▲ BR Cross Cement Crossing. Road on left.

GPS: N 39°09.03' W 110°28.44'

▼ 2.5 SO Track on right.
1.8 ▲ SO Track on left.

▼ 2.7 SO Cross through rocky wash.
1.6 ▲ SO Cross through rocky wash.

▼ 2.8 SO Culvert on left.
1.4 ▲ SO Culvert on right.

▼ 3.2 SO Cross through wash.
1.1 ▲ SO Cross through wash.

DENVER & RIO GRANDE WESTERN RAILROAD

The story of the Denver & Rio Grande Western Railroad (D&RGW) is one filled with legal maneuverings, near bankruptcies, and questionable buyouts. William Jackson Palmer, president of this Colorado company, originally intended to lay a north-south route along the eastern side of the Colorado Rockies down into Mexico. In 1878, he was beat out by a rival company, the Atchison, Topeka & Santa Fe (AT&SF) Railroad. Disputes between the competitors developed into a heated legal battle, even resulting in physical violence at times. Both companies sent armed construction crews to secure strategic passes along the way. In the end, the courts upheld the AT&SF Railroad's right to build the line into Mexico.

The confusing legal battle also allowed George Gould, son of railroad tycoon Jay Gould, the opportunity to buy into the D&RGW. Together, Palmer and Gould reclaimed some of their railroad lines in Pueblo, Colorado, in a brief but bloody scuffle against the AT&SF and famed gunman Bat Masterson. Gould then turned his attentions westward and pushed for a connection between Denver and Salt Lake City. On July 21, 1881, the company became incorporated in the Territory of Utah under the name Denver & Rio Grande. This allowed the firm to build in the region. Excitement spread through the territory at the prospect of someone breaking the monopoly of the Union Pacific Railroad, something people hoped would cut freight costs and allow for more commerce in the area.

The first tracks were laid between Salt Lake City and Springfield, and west from Denver. The year 1883 saw the long anticipated completion of the railway when the tracks met in Deseret, near Green River. Soon more D&RGW tracks crisscrossed the territory and became the backbone of transportation throughout Utah. However, the company's presence was not always welcome; the very first train to arrive in Salt Lake City did so on a Sunday, much to the chagrin of devout Mormons.

Denver & Rio Grande Western Railroad

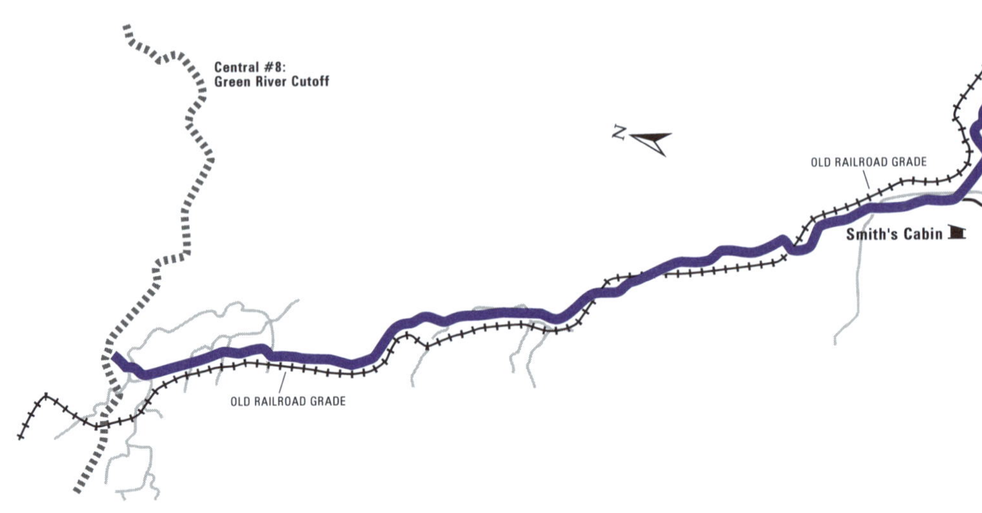

▼ 4.3 SO Cross through gate and close behind you. Zero trip meter.
0.0 ▲ Continue north.

GPS: N 39°07.74' W 110°27.69'

▼ 0.0 Continue south.
7.0 ▲ SO Cross through gate and close behind you. Zero trip meter.

▼ 0.3 SO Track on left.
6.7 ▲ SO Track on right.

▼ 1.0 SO Cross through wash.
5.9 ▲ SO Cross through wash.

▼ 1.8 SO Cross through large wash.
5.1 ▲ SO Cross through large wash.

GPS: N 39°06.31' W 110°26.81'

▼ 2.7 BL Tracks on right.
4.3 ▲ BR Tracks on left.

▼ 3.0 SO Cross through wash.
4.0 ▲ SO Cross through wash.

▼ 3.6 SO Track on right.
3.3 ▲ SO Track on left.

▼ 3.7 SO Track on right.
3.2 ▲ SO Track on left.

▼ 3.9 SO Cross through wash.
3.1 ▲ SO Cross through wash.

▼ 5.4 SO Cross through creek.
1.6 ▲ SO Cross through creek.

GPS: N 39°03.77' W 110°24.89'

▼ 5.8 SO Track on left.
1.2 ▲ SO Track on right.

▼ 7.0 SO Pass through gate and close behind you. Zero trip meter.
0.0 ▲ Continue north.

GPS: N 39°02.82' W 110°24.04'

▼ 0.0 Continue south.
1.2 ▲ SO Pass through gate and close behind you. Zero trip meter.

▼ 0.1 SO Track on right.
1.1 ▲ SO Track on left.

▼ 1.2 TL Pass through gate and close behind you. Then intersection. Track on right is a short side road that goes 0.2 miles to Smith's cabin and buildings. After visiting the cabin, return to this intersection and zero trip meter.
0.0 ▲ Intersection. Turn left (north) onto main trail. Pass through gate and close behind you.

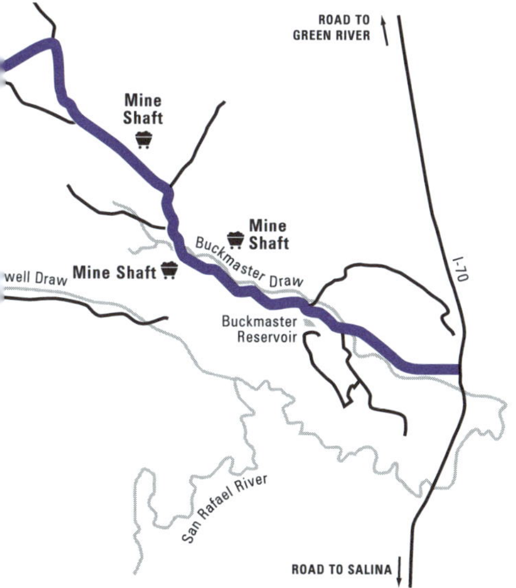

GPS: N 39°01.89' W 110°23.64'

▼ 0.0 Intersection. Continue straight (east) on main trail.

4.3 ▲ TR Intersection. Track ahead is a short side road that goes 0.2 miles to Smith's cabin and buildings. After visiting the cabin, return to this intersection and zero trip meter.

▼ 1.2 SO Pass through gate and close behind you.

3.1 ▲ SO Pass through gate and close behind you.

GPS: N 39°01.97' W 110°22.60'

▼ 2.1 SO Track on left. Old railroad grade crosses.

2.2 ▲ SO Track on right. Old railroad grade crosses.

GPS: N 39°01.88' W 110°21.64'

▼ 3.0 BR Track on left.

1.2 ▲ BL Track on right.

▼ 4.3 TR T-intersection. Turn right to Buckmaster Reservoir. Left goes to US 6/191. Zero trip meter.

0.0 ▲ Continue along road.

GPS: N 39°00.53' W 110°19.94'

▼ 0.0 Proceed toward reservoir.

7.0 ▲ TL Intersection. Take road on left and zero trip meter.

▼ 1.4 SO Track on right.

5.6 ▲ SO Track on left.

▼ 2.3 TR Intersection.

4.7 ▲ TL Intersection.

GPS: N 38°58.95' W 110°21.43'

▼ 3.0 SO Track on right. Then mine shaft visible on left.

3.9 ▲ BR Mine shaft on right. Then track on left.

▼ 5.1 SO Old corral on right.

1.9 ▲ SO Old corral on left.

▼ 6.8 SO Cattle guard.

0.1 ▲ SO Cattle guard.

▼ 7.0 Trail ends at I-70, exit 147; turn left for Green River, right for Salina.

0.0 ▲ Take I-70, exit 147, to intersection of exit ramp and the overpass on the north side of highway; zero trip meter and proceed north. Road becomes unpaved almost immediately.

GPS: N 38°55.48' W 110°22.60'

CENTRAL REGION TRAIL #10

Black Dragon Pictographs Trail

STARTING POINT I-70, 0.3 miles westbound past mile marker 145
FINISHING POINT BLM fence near the Black Dragon pictographs
TOTAL MILEAGE 1.7 miles
UNPAVED MILEAGE 1.7 miles
DRIVING TIME 15 minutes (one-way)
ELEVATION RANGE 4,300–4,400 feet
USUALLY OPEN Year-round
DIFFICULTY RATING 3
SCENIC RATING 9
REMOTENESS RATING +0

Special Attractions

- The famous Black Dragon pictographs.
- The scenic Black Dragon Canyon.
- Short spur trail can be combined with Central #11: Three Fingers Petroglyphs Trail.

History

In Black Dragon Canyon, you will find panels of artwork on the canyon walls in the Barrier Canyon style, which predates the Fremont Indians. While it is difficult to accurately date the paintings, they are at least 1,500 years old. There are two zoo-morphs (representations of animals with human qualities or characteristics), one of which resembles a dragon and the figure to its right resembles a praying dog. At about the same height along the canyon wall to the left are three red-colored, three- to seven-foot-tall pictures that resemble humans with elongated bodies.

Description

The Black Dragon Pictographs Trail is short but interesting and can serve as a quick side trip off of I-70 if you are just passing through. As the trail does not start from a proper exit off the interstate, use caution when slowing down to pull off the road. Do not stop until you are completely off I-70. Heading westbound past mile marker 145, look for a gate about 20 yards off to the side; this marks the beginning of the trail.

Once you're through the gate, you almost immediately pass the track on the left that leads under the freeway culvert to Central #11: Three Fingers Petroglyphs Trail. The Black Dragon trail is easy—and accessible for any vehicle—until near the end, when it becomes more difficult and jumps up to a difficulty level of 3. Here you need a high-clearance vehicle to traverse the rocks and washes of the canyon floor. The scenic canyon and pictographs make the trail very striking and enjoyable.

The road continues past the pictographs into the canyon and eventually connects with Central #3: Black Dragon Wash Trail after about 2 miles. However, this part of the road is badly washed out after about 1.3 miles with rough spots that have steep angles of entry and departure. The road here goes beyond the difficulty level of this book. Skilled drivers might be able to pass through this stretch of road, especially if they have short-wheelbase SUVs. Otherwise, we recommend that you park your vehicle and hike up the canyon.

Current Road Information

Emery County Road Department
120 West Highway 29
Castle Dale, UT 84513
(435) 381-2550

A view of the spectacular canyon you travel through to get to the Black Dragon pictographs

Central Trail #10: Black Dragon Pictographs Trail

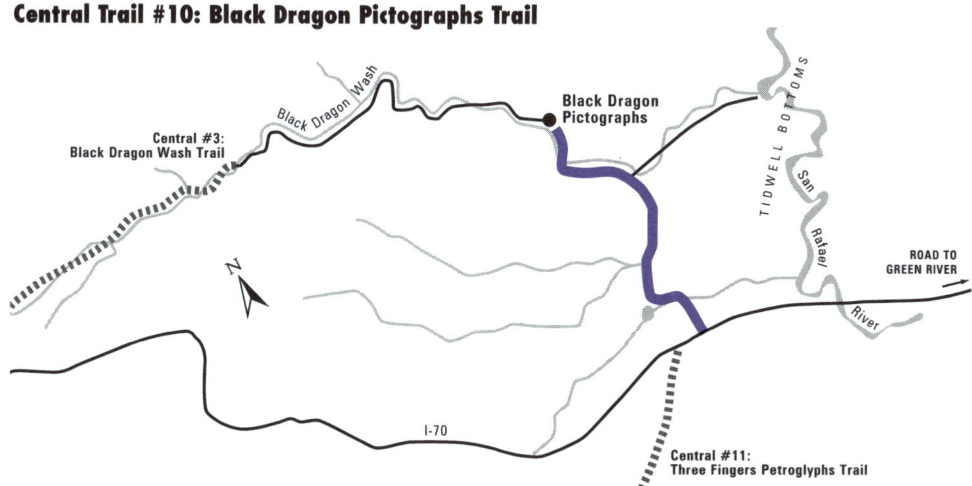

BLM Price Field Office
125 South 600 West
Price, UT 84501
(435) 636-3600

Map References

USGS 1:24,000 Spotted Wolf Canyon
Maptech CD-ROM: Central/San Rafael
Trails Illustrated, #712
Utah Atlas & Gazetteer, p. 39
Other: Recreation Map of the San Rafael Swell and San Rafael Desert

Route Directions

▼ 0.0 Westbound on I-70, 0.3 miles past mile marker 145, pull off highway at a wire gate with a BLM sign. Pass through gate, zero trip meter, and follow the dirt road north. Then pass a track on left that leads under the freeway culvert to Central #11: Three Fingers Petroglyphs Trail.
GPS: N 38°55.54′ W 110°24.99′

▼ 0.1 SO Cross through wash.
▼ 0.6 SO Track on left.
▼ 1.0 BL Fork in road. Bear left following BLM marker for Black Dragon.
GPS: N 38°56.21′ W 110°25.06′

▼ 1.1 SO Track on right. Tracks straight and on left both continue to the pictographs. Track straight on goes through wash.
▼ 1.2 SO Track on right.
▼ 1.7 Trail ends at BLM fence and marker. The Black Dragon pictographs are inside BLM fenced area about 40 feet up, above a talus slope.
GPS: N 38°56.32′ W 110°25.36′

CENTRAL REGION TRAIL #11

Three Fingers Petroglyphs Trail

STARTING POINT I-70, 0.7 miles eastbound past mile marker 144
FINISHING POINT Three Fingers petroglyphs
TOTAL MILEAGE 8 miles
UNPAVED MILEAGE 8 miles
DRIVING TIME 45 minutes (one-way)
ELEVATION RANGE 4,300–4,600 feet
USUALLY OPEN Year-round
DIFFICULTY RATING 5
SCENIC RATING 9
REMOTENESS RATING: +1

Special Attractions

- Three Fingers petroglyphs.
- A short, scenic spur trail that can be combined with Central #10: Black Dragon Pictographs Trail.

A tunnel to the left of the Three Fingers petroglyphs

Description

The trail to the Three Fingers petroglyphs starts out rather easy and remains so until the more difficult final 2 miles. About 0.1 miles from the start, the trail intersects a road to the right that crosses through a culvert under the interstate and connects in 0.2 miles with Central #10: Black Dragon Pictographs Trail. The Three Fingers Trail bears to the left and proceeds along the foot of the San Rafael Reef. The first section of road is periodically graded and runs through a number of wash crossings and sandy spots. This part of the trail is relatively flat but very scenic, with a typical red mesa to the left and the windblown reef on the right.

After about 6 miles, the trail turns right and heads directly for the reef. This is where a few sections of the trail can become considerably more difficult and rate a 5. An awkward wash crossing, a couple of badly washed out narrow sections, and a short but steep descent can all pose potential difficulties. As you approach the reef, the terrain is sporadically dotted with pinyons and junipers. At the end of the trail, you must hike a short distance into the facing canyon to view the petroglyphs, which are on the right-hand side. The main panel is located next to a tunnel, about ten feet up the canyon wall.

Current Road Information

Emery County Road Department
120 West Highway 29
Castle Dale, UT 84513
(435) 381-2550

BLM Price Field Office
125 South 600 West
Price, UT 84501
(435) 636-3600

Central Trail #11: Three Fingers Petroglyphs Trail

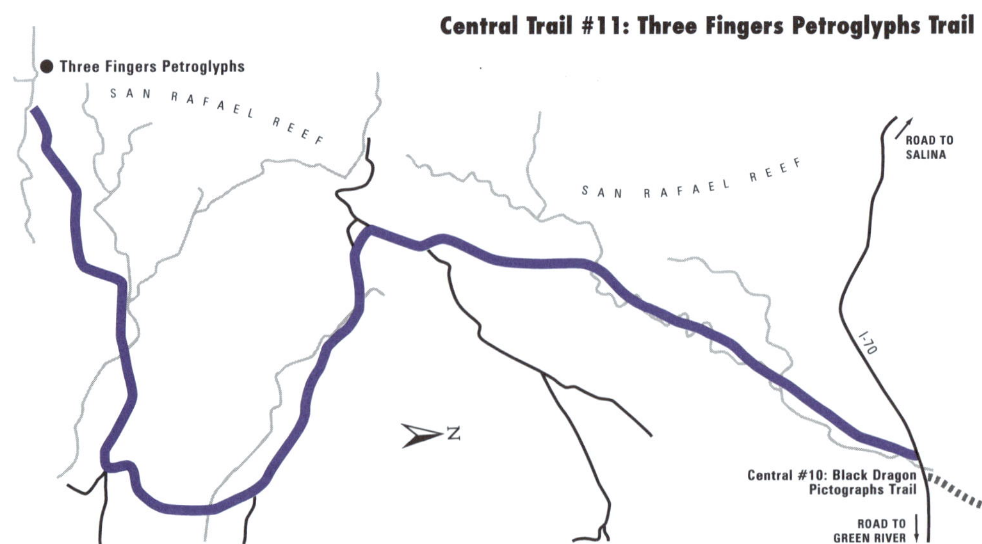

Map References

BLM San Rafael Desert
USGS 1:24,000 Spotted Wolf Canyon, Greasewood Draw
1:100,000 San Rafael Desert
Maptech CD-ROM: Central/San Rafael
Trails Illustrated, #712
Utah Atlas & Gazetteer, p. 39
Other: Recreation Map of the San Rafael Swell and San Rafael Desert

Route Directions

▼ 0.0		Eastbound on I-70, 0.7 miles past mile marker 144, look for unmarked dirt track on right. Pass through gate and close it behind you. Zero trip meter. **GPS: N 38°55.43' W 110°25.05'**
▼ 0.1	BL	Track on right goes through culvert to Central #10: Black Dragon Pictographs Trail.
▼ 0.6	SO	Cross through wash.
▼ 0.9	SO	Cross through wash.
▼ 1.0	SO	Cross through wash.
▼ 1.1	SO	Cross through wash.
▼ 1.3	SO	Cross through wash.
▼ 1.6	SO	Cross through wash.
▼ 1.8	SO	Cross through wash.
▼ 2.1	SO	Cross through wash.
▼ 3.5	SO	Road on right.
▼ 4.9	BR	Bear right at fork in road.

FREMONT INDIANS AND ROCK ART

Fremont petroglyphs

"Fremont" is a collective name given to the scattered groups of Indians who lived throughout the Great Basin. They arrived in Utah around A.D. 100 and were at first primarily nomadic hunter-gatherers. Although they were not quite as advanced as the Anasazi, their contemporaries in southern Utah, the Fremont developed a horticultural system and an elaborate culture evidenced today by excavated ceremonial clay figures and famous rock art. By 750 they had mostly abandoned their nomadic ways and settled in more permanent dwellings. Evidence of pit houses has been discovered, as well as houses built precariously into the sides of cliffs. They also built camouflaged lookout towers high on the top of bluffs, presumably to keep guard over the surrounding land.

Despite their widespread presence in the region and advanced agriculture, the Fremont faded from existence some time after 1250. Like the Anasazi, this culture's disappearance is shrouded in mystery. Most archaeologists believe a period of severe drought probably drove them away, and the survivors were likely absorbed into other, newer cultures. However, their enigmatic story lives on through the art that they left on Utah's canyon walls.

Anthropologists have studied the rock art of eastern Utah for years, and yet we are still left wondering: what does it mean? The majority of the rock art throughout Utah has been attributed to the Fremont Indians, and it comes in two forms: petroglyphs, which are pictures etched into the rock, and pictographs, which are figures painted on the rock. Humans and animals are the typical subjects, and images of hunting parties are very common. A variety of animals such as bighorn sheep, grizzly bears, snakes, and coyotes are represented. Often, hunters of these animals are themselves dressed in the animals' skins. Other rock art includes shapes and designs as well as unexplained symbols that are thought to be a form of picture writing. Some of the figures may relate to the heavens above and act as some sort of calendar. Just remember, when you run across unprotected, unexpected petroglyphs, this rock art is a historic treasure and should be left undisturbed.

GPS: N 38°52.34′ W 110°25.38′

▼ 5.8 TR Take small, unmaintained track on right. Zero trip meter.

GPS: N 38°51.62′ W 110°25.63′

▼ 0.0 Continue along trail. Then bear right, proceeding toward rock reef.

▼ 0.7 SO Cross through sandy wash.

GPS: N 38°51.76′ W 110°26.31′

▼ 1.5 SO/BR Short, steep, narrow downhill section and then bear right.

▼ 1.9 BL Fork in road.

▼ 2.0 BL Fork in road.

▼ 2.2 Road ends. The panels are a short walk farther on the right-hand side of a canyon on the reef wall you are facing.

GPS: N 38°51.46′ W 110°27.80′

CENTRAL REGION TRAIL #12

Temple Mountain Trail

STARTING POINT I-70, exit 129
FINISHING POINT Utah 24
TOTAL MILEAGE 28.3 miles
UNPAVED MILEAGE 22.0 miles
DRIVING TIME 1.25 hours
ELEVATION RANGE 4,900–7,000 feet
USUALLY OPEN Year-round
DIFFICULTY RATING 2
SCENIC RATING 7
REMOTENESS RATING +0

Special Attractions

- Backbone for many other 4WD trails in the area.
- The scenic, white Temple Mountain set against the deep red of the surrounding countryside.
- Access to numerous backcountry campsites.

Description

The Temple Mountain Trail begins at I-70, exit 129, and heads south through rolling grassland. Over the course of the first 14.7 miles, you pass the turnoffs to Central #13: Swasey's Cabin Trail, Central #15: Reds Canyon Trail, and Central #16: Temple Wash and Mining Camp Trail.

After the Reds Canyon turnoff, the canyon country becomes far more dramatic with wonderful views of Temple Mountain. The red road set against the white rock of Temple Mountain makes for a striking contrast and a very scenic drive.

Overall, the road is easy; it is a 1-rated trail through the pinyon-and-juniper-dotted canyon. After Flat Top Mountain, there are numerous mines and backcountry camping spots, especially near the part of the trail that runs along Temple Wash to where the road is paved.

Shortly after the road becomes paved is the turnoff for Goblin Valley State Park (fee required), which has an unusual display of hundreds of sandstone, mudstone, and siltstone "goblins." These unique rock formations have been carved out over millions of years by wind and rain and are thought by many to resemble little goblin-like creatures. This strange collection of pinnacles inhabits the floor of Goblin Valley and was first noted by the region's early cowboys and ranchers. However, the valley remained relatively unknown until the 1950s, when photographs taken by Arthur Chaffin brought widespread publicity to the area and its now-famous goblins.

The trail ends at Utah 24, approximately 24 miles south of I-70.

Current Road Information

Emery County Road Department
120 West Highway 29
Castle Dale, UT 84513
(435) 381-2550

BLM Price Field Office
125 South 600 West
Price, UT 84501
(435) 636-3600

Map References

BLM San Rafael Desert
USGS 1:24,000 The Wickiup, Twin Knolls, San Rafael Knob, Horse

Temple Mountain

Valley, Temple Mt., Old Woman
1:100,000 San Rafael Desert
Maptech CD-ROM: Central/San Rafael
Trails Illustrated, #712
Utah Atlas & Gazetteer, p. 38
Utah Travel Council #5
Other: Recreation Map of the San Rafael Swell and San Rafael Desert

Route Directions

▼ 0.0 On I-70, take exit 129 at ranch. On south side of highway, at intersection of exit ramp and underpass, zero trip meter and proceed south. Cross cattle guard and follow road across Indian Flat.
4.9 ▲ Trail ends at I-70, exit 129; turn right for Green River, left for Salina.
GPS: N 38°52.82' W 110°39.45'

▼ 0.1 BR Follow sign to Goblin Valley, Temple Mountain, and Utah 24.
4.8 ▲ BL Follow sign to I-70.

▼ 1.2 SO The Big Pond on left.
3.7 ▲ SO The Big Pond on right.

▼ 1.8 SO Cross over ditch and enter Paige Flat.
3.1 ▲ SO Cross over ditch.

▼ 3.0 SO Tracks on left and right. Cross cattle guard.
1.9 ▲ SO Cross cattle guard. Tracks on left and right.

▼ 3.8 SO Message board, then track on right goes past State Pond.
1.1 ▲ SO Track on left goes past State Pond.
GPS: N 38°50.61' W 110°42.28'

▼ 4.1 SO Cross through wash.
0.8 ▲ SO Cross through wash.

▼ 4.9 SO Track on right is Central #13: Swasey's Cabin Trail. Zero trip meter. Follow sign to Utah 24.
0.0 ▲ Proceed straight.
GPS: N 38°49.69' W 110°42.44'

▼ 0.0 Proceed straight.
4.9 ▲ SO Track on left is Central #13: Swasey's Cabin Trail. Zero trip meter and follow sign to I-70.

▼ 0.1 SO Track on right.
4.8 ▲ SO Track on left.

▼ 0.3 SO Cross through Georges Draw.
4.6 ▲ SO Cross through Georges Draw.

▼ 1.5 SO Track on left.
3.4 ▲ SO Track on right.

▼ 1.7 SO Cross cattle guard, then track on left.
3.2 ▲ SO Track on right, then cattle guard.

▼ 2.6 SO Track on left to motorcycle trailhead.
2.3 ▲ SO Track on right to motorcycle trailhead.

▼ 3.1 SO Cross through wash.

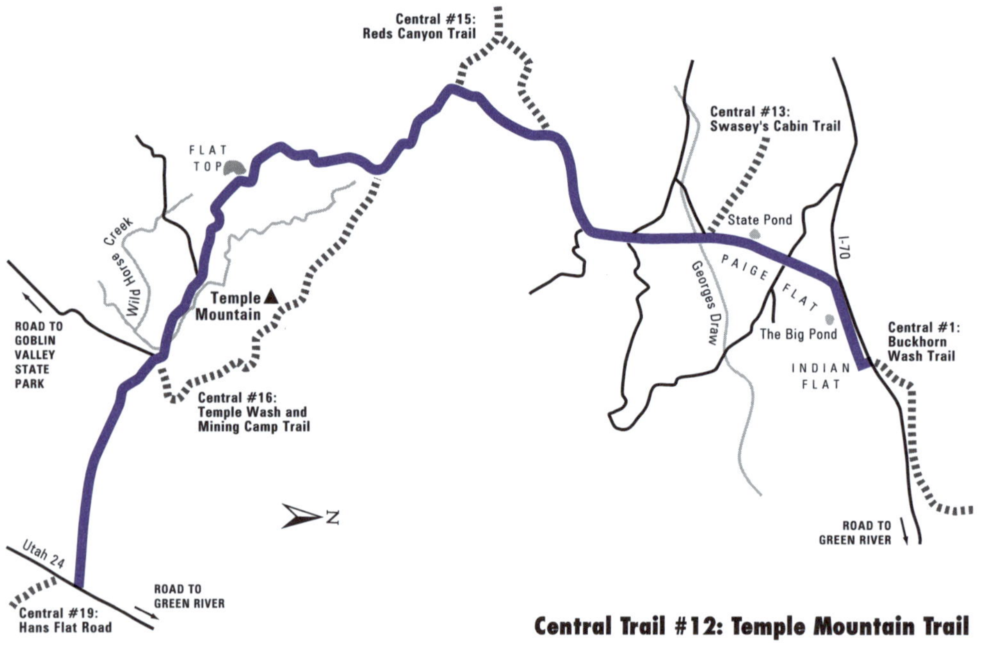

Central Trail #12: Temple Mountain Trail

1.8 ▲ SO Cross through wash.

▼ 4.9 BL Fork in road. Right is Central #15: Reds Canyon Trail. Zero trip meter.
0.0 ▲ Continue along main road.
GPS: N 38°46.63' W 110°44.73'

▼ 0.0 Continue toward Goblin Valley and Temple Mountain.
2.6 ▲ BR Road on left is Central #15: Reds Canyon Trail. Zero trip meter.

▼ 0.7 SO Track on left.
1.9 ▲ SO Track on right.

▼ 0.9 SO Track on right.
1.7 ▲ SO Track on left.

▼ 2.6 BL Intersection. Right is Central #15: Reds Canyon Trail. Zero trip meter.
0.0 ▲ Continue toward 1-70.
GPS: N 38°44.70' W 110°45.76'

▼ 0.0 Continue toward Goblin Valley and Temple Mountain.
2.1 ▲ BR Track on left is Central #15: Reds Canyon Trail. Zero trip meter.

▼ 1.4 SO Track on left.
0.7 ▲ SO Track on right.

▼ 2.1 SO Track on left is Central #16: Temple Wash and Mining Camp Trail. Zero trip meter.
0.0 ▲ Continue toward I-70.
GPS: N 38°43.60' W 110°44.04'

▼ 0.0 Continue toward Utah 24.
8.7 ▲ SO Track on right is Central #16: Temple Wash and Mining Camp Trail. Zero trip meter.

▼ 2.6 SO Track on right.
6.1 ▲ SO Track on left.

▼ 4.4 SO Track on right.
4.3 ▲ SO Track on left.

▼ 5.0 SO Track on right.
3.7 ▲ SO Track on left.

▼ 6.7 SO Track on right to Wild Horse Creek.
2.0 ▲ SO Track on left to Wild Horse Creek.
GPS: N 38°40.04' W 110°41.22'

▼ 7.0 SO Track on left. Note that in this area there are numerous side trails, many to good backcountry campsites. Most have been ignored in these directions.

1.7 ▲ SO Track on right.

▼ 7.3 SO Track on left in wash.
1.4 ▲ SO Track on right in wash.

▼ 7.5 SO Road becomes paved.
1.2 ▲ SO Road becomes unpaved.

▼ 7.7 SO Track on left.
1.0 ▲ SO Track on right.

▼ 8.7 SO Intersection. Right goes to Goblin Valley State Park. Track on left is Central #16: Temple Wash and Mining Camp Trail. Zero trip meter.
0.0 ▲ Continue straight.

GPS: N 38°39.20' W 110°39.23'

▼ 0.0 Continue straight toward Utah 24.
5.1 ▲ SO Intersection. Left goes to Goblin Valley State Park. Track on right is Central #16: Temple Wash and Mining Camp Trail. Zero trip meter.

▼ 5.1 Trail ends at Utah 24; turn left for Green River, right for Hanksville.
0.0 ▲ On Utah 24, about 24 miles south of I-70, zero trip meter and proceed west on paved road.

GPS: N 38°37.84' W 110°33.97'

CENTRAL REGION TRAIL #13

Swasey's Cabin Trail

STARTING POINT Central #12: Temple Mountain Trail, 4.9 miles from I-70
FINISHING POINT Swasey's cabin
TOTAL MILEAGE 7.5 miles
UNPAVED MILEAGE 7.5 miles
DRIVING TIME 30 minutes (one-way)
ELEVATION RANGE 6,800–7,200 feet
USUALLY OPEN Year-round
DIFFICULTY RATING 2
SCENIC RATING 8
REMOTENESS RATING +0

The crevice that divides the cabin from the cave used as a refrigerator

Special Attractions

- Swasey's cabin and spectacular rock formations.
- Part of a network of 4WD trails.

History

Although it only dates back to the 1920s, Swasey's cabin is one of the oldest remaining structures in the desert. Tucked in a remote location, the cabin stands in front of a unique and striking rock formation. When the Swaseys lived there, they used a cool cave behind the house as a year-round meat locker. You can still see the Swasey's "refrigerator," as it has come to be called; simply approach the rock formation behind the cabin and pass through the tight crevice to the rock's left.

Description

Generally, the road to Swasey's cabin is fairly easy, passing along rolling grassland dotted with sagebrush, pinyon, and juniper. A high-clearance vehicle is preferred as the road suffers washouts every now and then.

After 6.7 miles, you reach the intersection with Central #14: Rods Valley Trail, and a little farther on, there are many backcountry campsites near Swasey's cabin. Though the road continues beyond the cabin, it is rec-

An example of the type of erosion that can make the trail less accessible

ommended that you turn around here, as it becomes very narrow and eroded about a half mile ahead. The track running in front of Swasey's cabin continues north around the cliff faces and leads to numerous backcountry campsites. Most of these tracks eventually make their way back to the main Swasey's Cabin Trail.

Current Road Information

Emery County Road Department
120 West Highway 29
Castle Dale, UT 84513
(435) 381-2550

BLM Price Field Office
125 South 600 West
Price, UT 84501
(435) 636-3600

Map References

BLM San Rafael Desert
USGS 1:24,000 Twin Knolls, San Rafael Knob
1:100,000 San Rafael Desert
Maptech CD-ROM: Central/San Rafael
Trails Illustrated, #712
Utah Atlas & Gazetteer, p. 39
Utah Travel Council #5
Other: Recreation Map of the San Rafael Swell and San Rafael Desert

Route Directions

▼ 0.0 On Central #12: Temple Mountain Trail, 4.9 miles from I-70, zero trip meter and turn west onto road marked "Head of Sinbad."
4.4 ▲ Trail ends at Central #12: Temple Mountain Trail; turn left for I-70, right for Utah 24.
GPS: N 38°49.70' W 110°42.44'

▼ 0.5 SO Cross through wash.
3.9 ▲ SO Cross through wash.

▼ 1.0 SO Track on right, then cross cattle guard.
3.4 ▲ SO Cross cattle guard, then track on left.

▼ 2.0 SO Cross through wash. Cattle guard.
2.4 ▲ SO Cattle guard. Then cross through wash.

SAN RAFAEL SWELL GEOLOGY

The San Rafael Swell is a stunning blister of sedimentary rock that rises 800 to 2,000 feet above the surrounding desert landscape. This geological marvel is roughly 50 miles long and 30 miles wide and is pitted with canyons, dotted by buttes, and appears as a jagged reef of sandstone. Sandstone is easily eroded and, because the San Rafael Swell has been violently uplifted, wind and water have stripped away the younger rock formations at the top and left the oldest rock formations exposed. This means that the youngest rock lies at the base, and the oldest (about 250 million years old) lies at the top of the swell.

The dramatic variety in the colors of the landscape throughout the Colorado Plateau region comes from the minor constituents of the rocks. Iron oxides create reds, pinks, and yellows; unoxidized iron particles create greens and blues; and manganese contributes lavender to the land's natural palette. The plateau province is also rich in hydrocarbons, such as petroleums, oil shales, natural gas, and coal. Gilsonite (a type of solid asphalt), potash, uranium, and vanadium have also been mined from the region.

Central Trail #13: Swasey's Cabin Trail

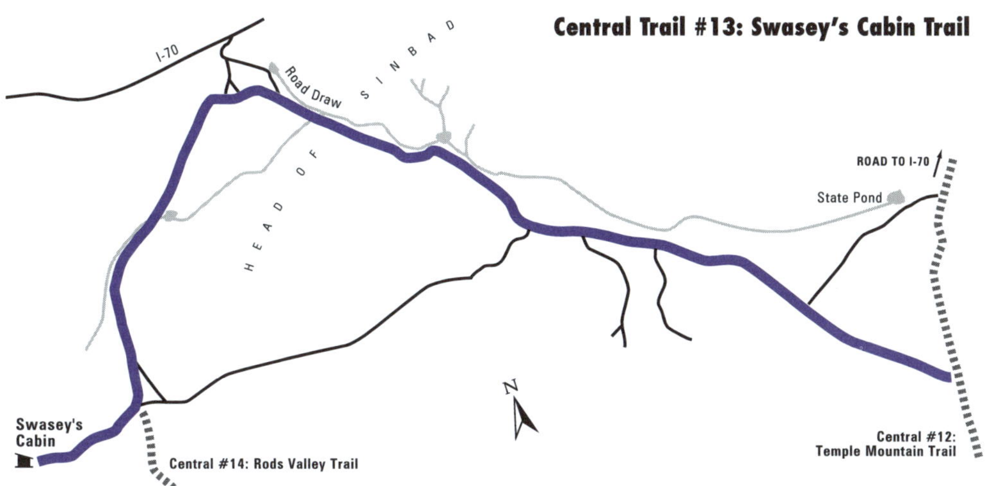

▼ 2.6 BR Tracks on left.
1.7 ▲ BL Tracks on right.
GPS: N 38°50.88' W 110°44.94'

▼ 2.7 SO Cross through large wash.
1.7 ▲ SO Cross through large wash.

▼ 3.6 BR Track on left.
0.8 ▲ BL Track on right.

▼ 3.7 SO Track on left.
0.6 ▲ SO Track on right.

▼ 4.4 SO Track on right to I-70. Zero trip meter.
0.0 ▲ Continue east.
GPS: N 38°51.71' W 110°46.45'

▼ 0.0 Continue west.
2.3 ▲ SO Track on left to I-70. Zero trip meter.

▼ 0.3 SO Track on right.
2.0 ▲ SO Track on left.
GPS: N 38°51.78' W 110°46.80'

▼ 0.9 SO Track and corral on right.
1.4 ▲ SO Another track to corral on left.

▼ 1.0 SO Another track to corral on right.
1.3 ▲ SO Track and corral on left.

▼ 1.1 SO Cattle guard. Then track on right. Stock pond on left.
1.2 ▲ SO Stock pond on right. Track on left. Cross cattle guard.

▼ 1.5 SO Track on right.
0.8 ▲ SO Track on left.
GPS: N 38°51.01' W 110°47.71'

▼ 1.6 SO Tracks on right.
0.7 ▲ SO Tracks on left.

▼ 1.9 SO Track on left.
0.4 ▲ SO Track on right.

▼ 2.0 BL Track on right.
0.3 ▲ BR Track on left.

▼ 2.3 BR Fork in road. Proceed right toward Swasey's cabin. Track on left is Central #14: Rods Valley Trail. Zero trip meter.
0.0 ▲ Continue along main trail.
GPS: N 38°50.37' W 110°47.67'

▼ 0.0 Continue toward Swasey's cabin.
0.8 ▲ SO Track on right is Central #14: Rods Valley Trail. Zero trip meter.

▼ 0.2 SO Track on left.
0.6 ▲ SO Track on right.

▼ 0.7 SO Track on left.
0.1 ▲ SO Track on right.

▼ 0.8 Trail ends at Swasey's cabin.

0.0 ▲ From Swasey's cabin, zero trip meter and return along main trail.
GPS: N 38°50.15' W 110°48.39'

CENTRAL REGION TRAIL #14

Rods Valley Trail

STARTING POINT Central #13: Swasey's Cabin Trail
FINISHING POINT Central #15: Reds Canyon Trail
TOTAL MILEAGE 5.8 miles
UNPAVED MILEAGE 5.8 miles
DRIVING TIME 30 minutes
ELEVATION RANGE 6,700–7,200 feet
USUALLY OPEN Year-round
DIFFICULTY RATING 3
SCENIC RATING 8
REMOTENESS RATING +0

Special Attractions

- Provides an alternative route to connect through to Central #15: Reds Canyon Trail.
- Numerous backcountry camping sites.

History

As the Swasey family (sometimes spelled Swazy) was settling the region in and around the San Rafael Swell in the late 1800s, they became well liked by the local homesteaders, who considered them good-natured, skillful cowboys. Their true home was said to be the open range, and so today they are not linked to any one place, though a number of landforms in central Utah are named after the family or one of its members. Rod Swasey was said to have been so impressed with this scenic valley that he named it after himself.

Description

From Central #13: Swasey's Cabin Trail, Rods Valley Trail heads south through grassland and sagebrush with some scattered pinyon and juniper. The trail crosses a number of washes and passes through a dense area of pinyon and juniper as an interesting mix of red- and buff-colored cliffs rise up on either side.

The 3-rated trail is not one of the more frequently used and has a number of good backcountry camping spots. Both the beginning and end of the trail are relatively easy to drive. A few wash crossings in the middle section tend to be the most difficult. Ending at Central #15: Reds Canyon Trail, Rods Valley Trail finishes as it started—in sagebrush and grassland with only occasional pinyon and juniper.

Current Road Information

Emery County Road Department
120 West Highway 29
Castle Dale, UT 84513
(435) 381-2550

BLM Price Field Office
125 South 600 West
Price, UT 84501
(435) 636-3600

Map References

BLM San Rafael Desert
USGS 1:24,000 San Rafael Knob
1:100,000 San Rafael Desert

Central Trail #14: Rods Valley Trail

A view of Rods Valley

Maptech CD-ROM: Central/San Rafael
Trails Illustrated, #712
Utah Atlas & Gazetteer, p. 39
Other: Recreation Map of the San Rafael Swell and San Rafael Desert

Route Directions

▼ 0.0 On Central #13: Swasey's Cabin Trail, 6.7 miles from Central #12: Temple Mountain Trail, zero trip meter and proceed southeast.

5.8 ▲ Trail ends at Central #13: Swasey's Cabin Trail; turn left for Swasey's cabin, right for Central #12: Temple Mountain Trail.

GPS: N 38°50.37' W 110°47.67'

▼ 0.1 SO Track on right.
5.7 ▲ SO Track on left.

▼ 0.8 SO Track on right.
4.9 ▲ SO Track on left.

▼ 1.2 BR Fork in road through wash.
4.6 ▲ BL Road on right.

▼ 1.6 SO Track on right, then cross through wash.
4.2 ▲ SO Cross through wash, then track on left.

GPS: N 38°49.16' W 110°48.04'

▼ 1.8 SO Pass through gate and close behind you.
3.9 ▲ SO Pass through gate and close behind you.

▼ 2.4 SO Cross through wash.
3.3 ▲ SO Cross through wash.

▼ 3.3 SO Track on right.
2.4 ▲ SO Track on left.

GPS: N 38°47.76' W 110°48.44'

▼ 3.9 SO Cross through wash.
1.8 ▲ SO Cross through wash.

▼ 5.4 SO Pass through gate and close behind you.
0.4 ▲ SO Pass through gate and close behind you.

GPS: N 38°46.22' W 110°47.83'

▼ 5.8 Trail ends at Central #15: Reds Canyon Trail; turn left for Central #12: Temple Mountain Trail, turn right for Reds Canyon.

0.0 ▲ On Central #15: Reds Canyon Trail, 3 miles from northern intersection with Central #12: Temple Mountain Trail, zero trip meter and proceed north. Follow sign that reads, "Rods Valley Road, Swasey Cabin 6."

GPS: N 38°45.96' W 110°47.69'

CENTRAL REGION TRAIL #15

Reds Canyon Trail

STARTING POINT Central #12: Temple Mountain Trail
FINISHING POINT Central #12: Temple Mountain Trail
TOTAL MILEAGE 37.6 miles
UNPAVED MILEAGE 37.6 miles
DRIVING TIME 2.5 hours
ELEVATION RANGE 5,200–7,000 feet
USUALLY OPEN Year-round
DIFFICULTY RATING 3
SCENIC RATING 10
REMOTENESS RATING +0

Special Attractions

- A moderately easy, fun, varied loop drive.
- Driving along Reds Wash through magnificent red canyon scenery.
- Hondoo Arch.
- Numerous old uranium mines.

History

In the 1950s, uranium prospectors came into Reds Canyon looking for a lucky strike. Vernon Pick, a farmer and mechanic from Minnesota with no prospecting experience, was one of them. Though most prospectors quickly abandoned the harsh landscape for easier pickings around Moab, in June 1952, Pick came upon a large deposit of the mineral and staked his claim, the Delta Mine, in this section of the San Rafael Swell.

Pick was determined to make the remote mine a success and soon was pumping out 1,500 tons of ore a month, making the Delta Mine one of the more successful uranium mines in Emery County. In 1954, a wealthy entrepreneur named Floyd Odlum liked the prospects of the Delta Mine and asked its owner to name his price. Pick reportedly asked for and was paid $9 million. Renaming it Hidden Splendor Mine, Odlum made only a fraction of his money back before the ore pinched out. The deal soon became known as Odlum's Hidden Blunder.

The Hidden Splendor Mine had one of the larger deposits in the region; other mines, such as the one on Tomsich Butte, were much smaller. Tomsich was the name of a prospector near Muddy Creek who, along with his dog, drank the poison creek water. Tomsich survived, but his ill-fated dog did not. Eventually, Tomsich and his partner Hannert found uranium on the mountain. They immediately staked claims around the butte and began to mine the ore. However, once the ore tapped out, the mine and some of its machinery were abandoned.

Description

The Reds Canyon Trail is a loop trail that begins and ends on Central #12: Temple Mountain Trail. It sets off through sagebrush and rolling grasslands dotted with pinyon and juniper, where layers of deep red- and buff-colored soil stand out in sharp contrast with each other.

The road's rating of 3 is contingent upon the amount of erosion from recent rain and/or how long it has been since the road

The towering Tomsich Butte (at the rear) along Reds Canyon Trail

Old mines on the south face of Tomsich Butte

was last graded. If graded and dry, the road would rate a 2. However, if there have been recent washouts, the trail could be considerably more difficult, perhaps even impassable without some road repairs.

The road moves through the deep red canyon, traveling in the wash for about 7.5 miles. As you leave the wash, there are some excellent views of Tomsich Butte (also spelled Tomsick), which rises some 700 feet ahead to an elevation of 5,805 feet above sea level. The trail winds around the eastern side of Tomsich Butte along short sections of shelf road before eventually reaching an intersection south of the butte.

For the best view of Hondoo Arch, turn right at this intersection and head down a short, half-mile spur road toward Muddy Creek. The arch is on the left, and mines still sit to the right of the trail along the southern side of Tomsich Butte.

From the Hondoo Arch viewpoint to the end, the trail levels out and becomes a 1-rated road, passing through rolling grassland and sagebrush (used for cattle grazing). Five miles from Hondoo Arch you reach the turnoff for the Hidden Splendor Mine, and after 16.8 miles you meet back up with Central #12: Temple Mountain Trail.

Current Road Information

Emery County Road Department
120 West Highway 29
Castle Dale, UT 84513
(435) 381-2550

BLM Price Field Office
125 South 600 West
Price, UT 84501
(435) 636-3600

Map References

BLM San Rafael Desert
USGS 1:24,000 Twin Knolls, San Rafael Knob, Copper Globe, Tomsich Butte, Horse Valley
1:100,000 San Rafael Desert
Maptech CD-ROM: Central/San Rafael
Trails Illustrated, #712
Utah Atlas & Gazetteer, pp. 38, 39
Utah Travel Council #5
Other: Recreation Map of the San Rafael Swell and San Rafael Desert

Route Directions

▼ 0.0 On Central #12: Temple Mountain Trail, 9.8 miles from I-70, zero trip meter and proceed southeast.
3.0 ▲ Trail ends at Central #12: Temple Mountain Trail; turn left for I-70, right for Utah 24.
GPS: N 38°46.63' W 110°44.73'

▼ 3.0 SO Trail on right is Central #14: Rods Valley Trail. Zero trip meter.
0.0 ▲ Continue along main trail.
GPS: N 38°45.96' W 110°47.69'

▼ 0.0 Continue along main trail.
10.7 ▲ SO Trail on left is Central #14: Rods Valley Trail. Zero trip meter.

▼ 0.6 TR Cross through wash, then turn right at T-intersection. Left returns to Temple Mountain Trail. Follow sign to Reds Canyon and McKay Flat.
10.1 ▲ TL Take track on left. Then cross through wash.
GPS: N 38°45.60' W 110°48.14'

Central Trail #15: Reds Canyon Trail

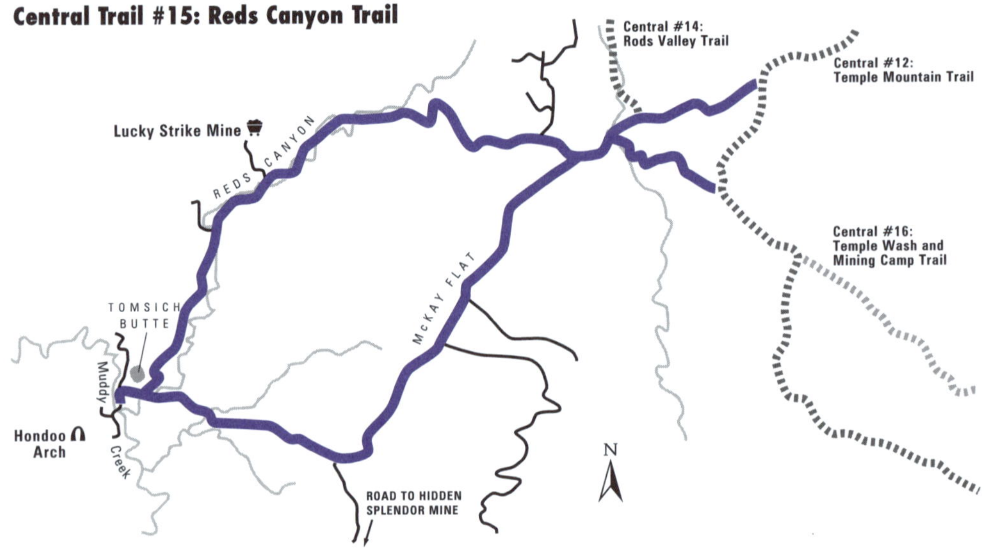

▼ 0.7 SO Cattle guard. Then track on right.
10.0 ▲ SO Track on left. Then cattle guard.

▼ 1.5 SO Track on left to McKay Flat. Continue toward Reds Canyon.
9.1 ▲ SO Track on right to McKay Flat.
GPS: N 38°45.29′ W 110°48.97′

▼ 2.5 SO Track on right.
8.2 ▲ SO Track on left.

▼ 10.7 SO Track on right. Zero trip meter
0.0 ▲ Continue northeast.
GPS: N 38°44.77′ W 110°56.28′

▼ 0.0 Continue southwest.
5.8 ▲ SO Track on left. Zero trip meter.

▼ 5.2 BL Roads on right.
0.6 ▲ BR Roads on left.
GPS: N 38°41.40′ W 110°59.04′

▼ 5.7 BR Fork in road.
0.1 ▲ SO Road on right.

▼ 5.8 TR T-intersection. Zero trip meter. Turn left to head down toward Muddy Creek for the best views of Hondoo Arch. Note: You will return to this point to continue along the main route.
0.0 ▲ Continue along main route.
GPS: N 38°40.98′ W 110°59.21′

▼ 0.0 Continue toward Tomsich Butte.
1.2 ▲ TL Intersection back with the main trail.

▼ 0.2 SO Track on right to mine.
1.0 ▲ SO Track on left to mine.

▼ 0.3 SO Track on right.
0.9 ▲ SO Track on left.

▼ 0.4 BR Track on left.
0.8 ▲ SO Track on right.

▼ 0.6 UT Track on right. View of Hondoo Arch to the left. Return to intersection noted above.
0.6 ▲ UT Track on right. View of Hondoo Arch. Return to intersection noted below.
GPS: N 38°41.05′ W 110°59.88′

▼ 1.2 BR Intersection. Continue along the main trail. Zero trip meter.
0.0 ▲ Continue along route.
GPS: N 38°40.98′ W 110°59.21′

▼ 0.0 Proceed southeast along the main trail.
5.0 ▲ BL Bear left toward Muddy Creek and zero trip meter. This spur to the main trail will provide the best views of

Hondoo Arch as you proceed toward Muddy Creek. Note: You will return to this intersection to continue along the main route.

▼0.1 SO/SO Track on left. Then track on right.
4.9 ▲ SO/BL Track on left. Then bear left at fork in road. Follow sign to Hondoo Arch.

▼ 1.4 SO Cross through wash.
3.6 ▲ SO Cross through wash.

▼ 1.6 SO Cattle guard.
3.4 ▲ SO Cattle guard.
GPS: N 38°40.62' W 110°57.79'

▼ 5.0 BL Track on right to Hidden Splendor Mine. Zero trip meter.
0.0 ▲ Continue west.
GPS: N 38°39.77' W 110°54.37'

▼ 0.0 Continue east.
8.3 ▲ BR Fork in road. Left goes to Hidden Splendor Mine. Zero trip meter.

▼ 3.2 SO Track on right.
5.0 ▲ SO Track on left.

▼ 3.4 SO Track on left.
4.9 ▲ SO Track on right.
GPS: N 38°42.10' W 110°52.21'

▼ 4.0 SO Track on left.
4.2 ▲ SO Track on right.

▼ 4.2 SO Tracks on left.
4.1 ▲ SO Tracks on right.

▼ 4.4 SO Track on right.
3.9 ▲ SO Track on left.

▼ 4.6 SO Cattle guard.
3.7 ▲ SO Cattle guard.
GPS: N 38°43.01' W 110°51.61'

▼ 7.2 SO Track on right.
1.1 ▲ SO Track on left.

▼ 8.3 TR T-intersection. Zero trip meter.
0.0 ▲ Continue southwest.
GPS: N 38°45.27' W 110°48.98'

▼ 0.0 Continue east.
3.5 ▲ TL Intersection. Follow sign to McKay Flat. Zero trip meter.

▼ 0.8 SO Track on left. Then cattle guard.
2.7 ▲ SO Cattle guard. Then track on right.
GPS: N 38°45.59' W 110°48.19'

▼ 0.9 SO Track on left.
2.6 ▲ SO Track on right.

▼ 1.0 SO Cross through wash.
2.5 ▲ SO Cross through wash.

▼ 3.5 Trail ends at Central #12: Temple Mountain Trail; turn right for Utah 24, left for I-70.
0.0 ▲ On Central #12: Temple Mountain Trail, 12.4 miles from I-70, zero trip meter and proceed west. Follow sign to Tan Seep and Reds Canyon.
GPS: N 38°44.70' W 110°45.75'

CENTRAL REGION TRAIL #16

Temple Wash and Mining Camp Trail

STARTING POINT Central #12: Temple Mountain Trail
FINISHING POINT Central #12: Temple Mountain Trail
TOTAL MILEAGE 9.2 miles
UNPAVED MILEAGE 9.2 miles
DRIVING TIME 1.5 hours
ELEVATION RANGE 5,300–6,800 feet
USUALLY OPEN Year-round
DIFFICULTY RATING 4
SCENIC RATING 9
REMOTENESS RATING +1

Special Attractions

- Mines and old mining camp.
- Moderately challenging alternative trail around Temple Mountain.

A building still standing at the mining camp

History

The town of Temple Mountain was first settled just before the turn of the 20th century when prospectors discovered uranium, radium, and vanadium ores at the spot. By 1910, it was a small village. Most of the valuable minerals in the area were exported to France, and it is believed that some of the radium mined in Temple Mountain ended up in the laboratory of Madame Curie and played a part in her famous discovery.

After World War I, the town folded as cheaper sources of uranium were found elsewhere, and it was not until the uranium boom of the 1950s that people returned to the area. At that point, the center of town was moved away from the mine to the mine road's junction with Utah 24. When the uranium boom died in the late 1960s, the town once again did too. In its years of operation, the Temple Mountain district produced more than 2.5 million tons of ore. While there are still several interesting buildings standing in town, note that the mine itself remains radioactive and constitutes a health hazard.

Description

Temple Wash and Mining Camp Trail begins and ends along Central #12: Temple Mountain Trail in the region known as Sinbad Country, so-called because the area's rock formations, cliffs, and canyons bear a resemblance to the exotic scenery described in the *Arabian Nights*.

After a half mile or so, the trail follows an easy shelf road along the side of a canyon with great views straight ahead to Temple Mountain and east over the San Rafael Desert. This 3-rated section is fairly rough and rocky and can be somewhat hard on tires. After about 4 miles, at the base of Temple Mountain, the road becomes considerably rougher as you cross back and forth through the wash. This 4-rated section of the trail also offers remarkable views of Temple Mountain and the very attractive country around it.

After 5.2 miles, you reach the Temple Mountain ghost town and uranium mining operation. You can still see the remains of the old camp, open mine portals, tailings, and other assorted mine structures. Be sure not to go into any of the mine entrances as they are dangerous.

After the ghost town, the trail improves, becoming a 1-rated graded track. The trail descends through a narrow canyon that cuts through the San Rafael Reef on its way to the edge of the San Rafael Desert. For the better part of a mile along the wash, sheer canyon walls crowd in on both sides. The trail ends

A section of trail that squeezes through the narrow canyon

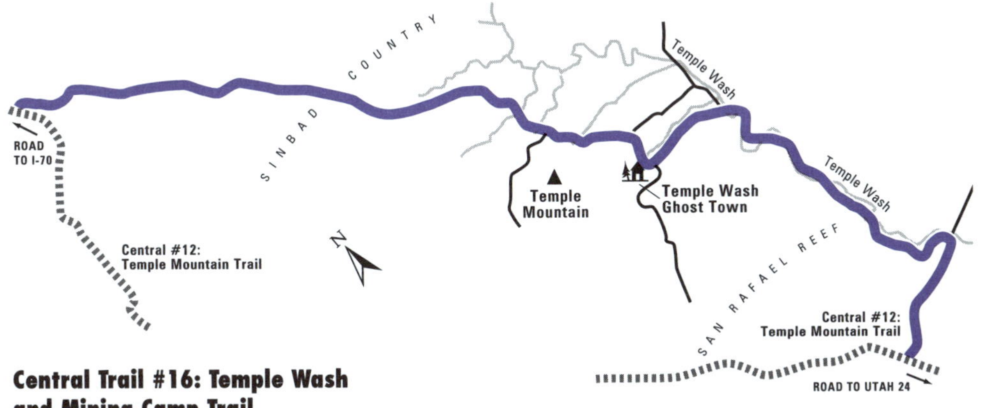

Central Trail #16: Temple Wash and Mining Camp Trail

at Central #12: Temple Mountain Trail at an information board opposite the paved turnoff to Goblin Valley State Park.

Current Road Information

Emery County Road Department
120 West Highway 29
Castle Dale, UT 84513
(435) 381-2550

BLM Price Field Office
125 South 600 West
Price, UT 84501
(435) 636-3600

Map References

BLM San Rafael Desert
USGS 1:24,000 Temple Mt.
1:100,000 San Rafael Desert
Maptech CD-ROM: Central/San Rafael
Trails Illustrated, #712
Utah Atlas & Gazetteer, p. 39
Utah Travel Council #5 (incomplete)
Other: Recreation Map of the San Rafael Swell and San Rafael Desert

Route Directions

▼ 0.0 On Central #12: Temple Mountain Trail, 14.5 miles from I-70, zero trip meter and turn east onto unmarked road.
5.2 ▲ Trail ends at Central #12: Temple Mountain Trail; turn right for I-70, left for Utah 24.
GPS: N 38°43.60′ W 110°44.04′

▼ 0.3 BR Road on left.
4.9 ▲ BL Road on right.

▼ 3.6 SO Cross through wash.
1.5 ▲ SO Cross through wash.
GPS: N 38°41.97′ W 110°40.82′

▼ 3.9 SO Cross through wash.
1.3 ▲ SO Cross through wash.

▼ 4.0 BL Track on right.
1.1 ▲ BR Track on left.
GPS: N 38°41.72′ W 110°40.65′

▼ 4.2 BL Cross through wash. Track on right.
0.9 ▲ BR Track on left. Cross through wash.

▼ 4.5 BL Track on right.
0.6 ▲ BR Intersection. Follow track to the right.
GPS: N 38°41.40′ W 110°40.40′

▼ 5.0 SO Cross through wash.
0.2 ▲ SO Cross through wash.

▼ 5.1 BL Intersection. Road on right, then cross through wash.
0.1 ▲ BR Cross through wash, then road on left.
GPS: N 38°41.15′ W 110°40.03′

▼ 5.2 BL Intersection. Right goes to mines. Then pass Temple Wash ghost town. Zero trip meter at building on left.
0.0 ▲ Cross through wash.

GPS: N 38°41.08' W 110°40.03'

▼ 0.0 Proceed past track on right and continue.
4.0 ▲ BR Temple Wash ghost town. Zero trip meter at building on right. Straight on goes to mines.

▼ 0.6 BR Track on left.
3.3 ▲ BL Track on right.

▼ 0.7 SO Cross through wash twice.
3.3 ▲ SO Cross through wash twice.

▼ 0.8 SO Cross through wash.
3.2 ▲ SO Cross through wash.

▼ 1.1 SO Cross through wash.
2.9 ▲ SO Cross through wash.

GPS: N 38°40.82' W 110°39.16'

▼ 2.5 SO Track on left.
1.5 ▲ SO Track on right.

▼ 2.7 BL Track on right.
1.2 ▲ SO Track on left.

▼ 3.0 BR Intersection. Road on left.
1.0 ▲ BL Road on right.

GPS: N 38°39.64' W 110°38.33'

▼ 3.2 SO Track on right.
0.8 ▲ SO Track on left.

▼ 3.5 SO Cross through wash, then tracks on right.
0.4 ▲ SO Tracks on left, then cross through wash.

▼ 3.6 BL Tracks on right.
0.4 ▲ BR Tracks on left.

▼ 3.9 TR Four-way intersection. Turn right toward message board.
0.1 ▲ TL Four-way intersection.

▼ 4.0 Trail ends at paved intersection with Central #12: Temple Mountain Trail. Go straight for Goblin Valley State Park, left for Utah 24.
0.0 ▲ On Central #12: Temple Mountain Trail, 5.1 miles from Utah 24, zero trip meter and turn north at message board, opposite the paved turnoff to Goblin Valley State Park.

GPS: N 38°39.20' W 110°39.23'

CENTRAL REGION TRAIL #17

Wild Horse Mesa Trail

STARTING POINT Utah 24, 9.7 miles west of Hanksville
FINISHING POINT Goblin Valley State Park
TOTAL MILEAGE 28.9 miles
UNPAVED MILEAGE 28.9 miles
DRIVING TIME 3 hours
ELEVATION RANGE 4,500–5,000 feet
USUALLY OPEN Year-round
DIFFICULTY RATING 3
SCENIC RATING 9
REMOTENESS RATING +1

Special Attractions

- Old timber cabins and springs near Muddy Creek.
- Goblin Valley State Park.
- Desert scenery along Wild Horse Mesa, San Rafael Reef, and Wild Horse Canyon.

History

It is thought that one of the earliest European explorers in the San Rafael Swell was John C. Frémont. His artist's renditions of his travels in 1853 when scouting for a route for the railroad include drawings with striking similarities to Wild Horse Mesa.

One of the landmarks on this trail is Factory Butte, which was originally named Provo Factory by the road exploration teams of the early 1880s, as it reminded them of the Provo Woollen Mills, one of the earliest major industries in Utah.

Like many other regions around Utah, the San Rafael Swell saw its share of uranium exploration. The most famous rags-to-riches story concerns Vernon Pick and the Hidden Splendor Mine, which can be accessed from

The trail looking toward Hunts Craw Gap in the San Rafael Reef

this trail; see Central #15: Reds Canyon Trail for a full description of Pick's legendary strike.

Description

This route crosses the lower parts of the San Rafael Swell and finishes at Goblin Valley State Park. It makes an interesting backcountry access to Goblin Valley and travels through a wide variety of arid desert scenery.

The trail commences on Utah 24, 9.7 miles west of Hanksville. The graded gravel road is unmarked, but the highly distinctive and isolated Factory Butte, with its high sides and sheer cliffs that rise above the Factory Benches, is hard to miss.

The trail leads toward Factory Butte and passes it on its eastern side. After 9.2 miles the trail standard drops from wide, graded gravel to a narrower dirt trail, and it is marked for high-clearance vehicles only. After another 1.4 miles, you crest a slight rise and the trail abruptly disappears! At this point, the trail meets a T-intersection and descends down an escarpment to the east. Ahead is a sheer drop to a claypan. This spot is particularly scenic; you drive over gray shale domes while admiring the tilted pink slabs of the North Caineville Reef in the distance.

The crossing of Muddy Creek is the most difficult portion of the trail. There are often alternative crossings and the creek can be soft and, not surprisingly, muddy. When the trail was surveyed, the upstream crossing was easiest, but this may change. Immediately after the creek crossing, a track on the left heads north to the Hidden Splendor Mine.

Shortly after Muddy Creek, the trail passes by a spring in a thicket of tamarisk and the remains of a two-story wooden cabin. There are animal sheds and corrals and a second cabin a little farther on, but the story behind the cabins is unknown.

From the cabins, the trail climbs onto Little Wild Horse Mesa and then drops down to enter the canyon. It travels for a couple of miles in the wash of Little Wild Horse Creek before exiting the canyon to the

A two-story cabin along the trail

north and turning east to parallel the San Rafael Reef. After passing the popular hiking trail for Little Wild Horse and Bell Canyons, 10.4 miles after Muddy Creek, the trail follows a sandy track along the wide, grassy valley to finish at Goblin Valley State Park.

This trail is impassable in wet weather; the clay on the Factory Benches becomes incredibly greasy and it is impossible to get any traction at all. There is also the danger of sudden flash flooding in Little Wild Horse Canyon. There are some pretty backcountry campsites here, but camping is not advised in the canyon.

Current Road Information

BLM Price Field Office
125 South 600 West
Price, UT 84501
(435) 636-3600

Map References

BLM Hanksville, San Rafael Desert (incomplete)
USGS 1:24,000 Town Point, Factory Butte, Hunt Draw, Little Wild Horse Mesa, Goblin Valley
1:100,000 Hanksville, San Rafael (incomplete)
Maptech CD-ROM: Moab/Canyonlands; Central/San Rafael
Utah Atlas & Gazetteer, pp. 28, 29
Utah Travel Council #5
Other: Recreation Map of the San Rafael Swell and San Rafael Desert (incomplete)
Recreation Map of the Henry Mountains Area (incomplete)

Route Directions

▼ 0.0 From Utah 24, 9.7 miles west of Hanksville, zero trip meter and turn north on unmarked graded gravel road toward Factory Butte.
9.2 ▲ Trail ends at Utah 24. Turn right for Capitol Reef National Park, left for Hanksville.
GPS: N 38°22.03' W 110°53.50'

▼ 0.7 SO Track on left.
8.5 ▲ SO Track on right.

▼ 1.4 SO Track on left.
7.8 ▲ SO Track on right.

▼ 1.7 SO Cross over Neilson Wash. Factory Butte is to the left.
7.5 ▲ SO Cross over Neilson Wash. Factory Butte is to the right.

▼ 2.3 SO Cross over wash.
6.9 ▲ SO Cross over wash.

▼ 3.6 SO Dam on left, then track on right.
5.6 ▲ SO Track on left, then dam on right.

▼ 5.8 SO Track on right.
3.4 ▲ SO Track on left.

▼ 6.6 SO Track on right.
2.6 ▲ SO Track on left.

▼ 7.1 SO Track on right.
2.1 ▲ SO Track on left.

▼ 7.8 SO Cross through wash.
1.4 ▲ SO Cross through wash.

▼ 8.4 SO Cross through Coal Mine Wash.
0.8 ▲ SO Cross through Coal Mine Wash.

▼ 9.2 BL Trail becomes narrow, dirt road. Larger track on right. Zero trip meter.
0.0 ▲ Continue on wider gravel road.
GPS: N 38°29.17' W 110°55.14'

▼ 0.0 Continue on narrower trail.
4.2 ▲ SO Larger track on left. Zero trip meter.

▼ 1.4 TR T-intersection—caution! Steep drop ahead. North Caineville Reef is ahead. Trail winds down shelf road on right.
2.8 ▲ TL Turn left near the top of shelf road.

▼ 2.7 SO Descend to cross over creek.
1.5 ▲ SO Cross over creek and ascend short shelf road.

▼ 4.1 SO Cross bed of Muddy Creek, multichanneled and surrounded by tamarisks.

Central Trail #17: Wild Horse Mesa Trail

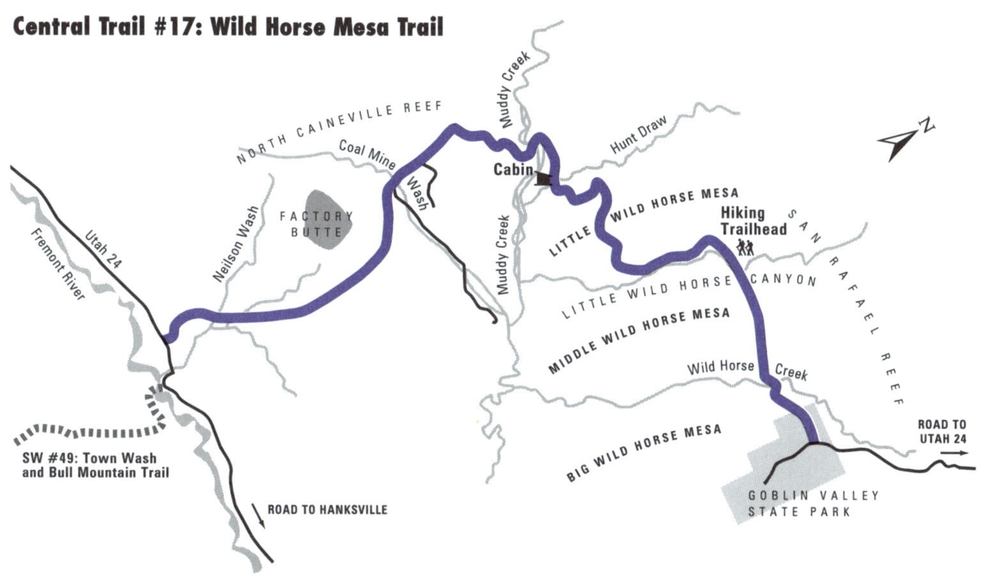

0.1 ▲ SO Cross bed of Muddy Creek, multichanneled and surrounded by tamarisks.

▼ 4.2 BL Two options to ford Muddy Creek's main channel; upstream is generally easier. Both can be soft on approach and exit, but have firmer bottoms. Zero trip meter after crossing.

0.0 ▲ Continue along trail.

GPS: N 38°31.90' W 110°54.14'

▼ 0.0 Continue northeast alongside Muddy Creek.

10.4 ▲ SO Two options to ford Muddy Creek's main channel; upstream crossing is generally easier. Both can be soft on approach and exit, but have firmer bottoms. Zero trip meter before crossing.

▼ 0.1 SO Track on left to Hidden Splendor Mine, then rejoin downstream crossing.

10.3 ▲ SO Track on left is first creek crossing, then track on right to Hidden Splendor Mine.

GPS: N 38°31.93' W 110°54.25'

▼ 0.4 SO Cross through wash.

10.0 ▲ SO Cross through wash.

▼ 1.2 SO Cross through wash, then track on right goes to old two-story wooden cabin, spring, and animal yards.

9.2 ▲ SO Track on left goes to old two-story wooden cabin, spring, and animal yards, then cross through wash.

GPS: N 38°31.95' W 110°53.17'

▼ 1.6 SO Cross through Hunt Draw.

8.8 ▲ SO Cross through Hunt Draw.

▼ 2.6 SO Track on left.

7.8 ▲ SO Track on right.

▼ 3.2 SO Cross through wash.

7.2 ▲ SO Cross through wash.

GPS: N 38°32.77' W 110°52.09'

▼ 3.7 SO Cross through wash.

6.7 ▲ SO Cross through wash.

▼ 4.3 SO Cross through wash.

6.1 ▲ SO Cross through wash.

▼ 4.5 SO Cross through wash.

5.9 ▲ SO Cross through wash.

▼ 4.6 SO Cross through wash.

5.8 ▲ SO Cross through wash.

GPS: N 38°32.43' W 110°50.90'

▼ 5.3 SO Small rocky steps descend to cross a

series of washes in the next 0.3 miles.
5.1 ▲ SO End of series of washes and rocky section.

GPS: N 38°32.59′ W 110°50.27′

▼ 5.5 BL Track on right.
4.9 ▲ BR Track on left.

GPS: N 38°32.45′ W 110°50.17′

▼ 5.6 SO End of series of washes and rocky section.
4.8 ▲ SO Small rocky steps and a series of washes in the next 0.3 miles.

▼ 6.0 SO Track on right to spring.
4.4 ▲ SO Track on left to spring.

GPS: N 38°32.41′ W 110°49.75′

▼ 6.4 SO Track on left.
4.0 ▲ SO Track on right.

▼ 6.5 SO Track winds down into Little Wild Horse Canyon.
3.9 ▲ SO Track leaves Little Wild Horse Canyon.

▼ 6.8 SO Enter Little Wild Horse Canyon creek wash.
3.6 ▲ SO Exit Little Wild Horse Canyon creek wash.

GPS: N 38°32.89′ W 110°49.54′

▼ 8.6 SO Exit narrow part of canyon.
1.8 ▲ SO Entering narrow part of Little Wild Horse Canyon.

▼ 10.4 SO Trail exits wash. Little Wild Horse Canyon and Bell Canyon hiking trail and parking area on left. Zero trip meter.
0.0 ▲ Continue along wash.

GPS: N 38°34.97′ W 110°48.13′

▼ 0.0 Continue on graded road.
5.1 ▲ SO Little Wild Horse Canyon and Bell Canyon hiking trail and parking area on right. Zero trip meter. Trail enters Little Wild Horse Canyon creek wash.

▼ 0.4 SO Track on right.
4.7 ▲ SO Track on left.

▼ 0.7 SO Cross through wash.
4.4 ▲ SO Cross through wash.

▼ 1.9 SO Track on right.
3.2 ▲ SO Track on left.

▼ 2.8 SO Cross through wash.
2.3 ▲ SO Cross through wash.

▼ 3.1 SO Cross through Wild Horse Canyon creek wash.
2.0 ▲ SO Cross through Wild Horse Canyon creek wash.

GPS: N 38°34.57′ W 110°44.68′

▼ 3.4 SO Track on right.
1.7 ▲ SO Track on left.

▼ 3.6 SO Cattle guard. Entering Goblin Valley State Park.
1.5 ▲ SO Cattle guard. Leaving Goblin Valley State Park.

GPS: N 38°34.70′ W 110°43.98′

▼ 5.1 Trail ends at T-intersection with paved road. Turn right to enter Goblin Valley, left for Utah 24.
0.0 ▲ On Goblin Valley Road, 10.5 miles from Utah 24, turn west onto graded dirt road, following the sign for Muddy Creek, and zero trip meter.

GPS: N 38°34.99′ W 110°42.56′

CENTRAL REGION TRAIL #18

Cathedral Valley Trail

STARTING POINT Utah 24, 2.6 miles east of Capitol Reef National Park
FINISHING POINT Caineville, Utah 24
TOTAL MILEAGE 55.1 miles
UNPAVED MILEAGE 55.1 miles
DRIVING TIME 7 hours
ELEVATION RANGE 4,500–6,900 feet
USUALLY OPEN: Year-round
DIFFICULTY RATING 2
SCENIC RATING 10
REMOTENESS RATING +1

Cathedral Valley Overlook with yuccas in the foreground

Special Attractions

- Desert viewpoints of Lower and Upper South Desert Overlooks.
- Historic Morrell cabin.
- Desert scenery in Cathedral Valley in Capitol Reef National Park.

History

Cathedral Valley was named in 1945 by Charles Kelly, the first superintendent of Capitol Reef National Park, and Frank Beckwith because they thought the valley's large monoliths looked like gothic cathedrals. John Frémont's 1853 expedition passed through the valley.

Morrell's cabin, a small log cabin in Cathedral Valley, was originally built by Paul Christensen on Thousand Lake Mountain to the west. The Christensen family lived there every summer for 20 years, working a sawmill on Lake Creek. Then in the late 1930s, Lesley Morrell bought the cabin and moved it piece by piece to Cathedral Valley and carefully reconstructed it. Here, cowboys used the cabin during roundups and when moving cattle from summer to winter pastures. The property was incorporated into Capitol Reef National Park in 1970 and is listed on the National Register of Historic Places.

Other pioneers have given their names to features around Cathedral Valley. Hartnet Draw is named for David Hartnet, who was the first to use this route to travel from Fremont to Caineville. His rough road was used to transport freight between Caineville and the northern areas of Wayne County. The present-day Cathedral Valley Trail follows the lower reaches of this original pioneer road down Caineville Wash. Hartnet's road passed Willow Spring and Rock Water Spring before ascending Polk Creek to Thousand Lake Mountain. Pete Ackland, an early cattle rancher in the area, gave his name to springs in Hartnet Draw.

Caineville, at the end of the trail, is a onetime ghost town that now struggles to survive. It was settled in the early 1880s by Mormon pioneers, who planted a variety of crops. Sorghum was the most successful; as well as being used as a sweetener, it was boiled down to produce a potent liquor,

Old drilling equipment along the trail

A spectacular vantage point for intrepid backcountry travelers

which was sold to local cattlemen and miners or exchanged for lumber and hard goods. One project unique to Caineville was the growing of silk! Acting under the directive of the church, the pioneers imported silkworms and mulberry bushes, but the attempt was never successful and was soon abandoned.

Like the neighboring ghost town of Giles, Caineville suffered frequent flooding by the Fremont River, and by 1910 the town was abandoned. Today, Caineville has a few residents, who live mainly in more modern housing. Most of the original townsite is derelict or gone.

Description

This long route travels through remote areas of Capitol Reef National Park and BLM land north of Caineville. The route is normally suitable for a 2WD high-clearance vehicle in good weather. Long stretches of sand, some minor rough sections, and the Fremont River crossing make it unsuitable for passenger vehicles.

The route commences 2.6 miles east of Capitol Reef National Park on Utah 24. There is a small sign that reads "river ford" and a gate, which may be closed but not locked. Half a mile from the start is the ford over the Fremont River. It is a long crossing at an angle; bear slightly downstream to exit on the far bank approximately 50 yards downriver. The ford itself has a firm bottom and unless the river is in flood or running high, it should be negotiable by high-clearance vehicles.

The entire trail is graded dirt road. The early sections can be sandy, especially as the trail runs along the Blue Hills and dips down to cross several washes. After 8.6 miles, the trail winds through the spectacular Bentonite Hills, whose purple hues are formed from volcanic ash. This section of the trail is impassable in wet weather.

After 13.4 miles, you reach the first of the two South Desert overlooks, with the immense Jailhouse Rock in the middle, in Capitol Reef National Park. This one is at the end of a 1.1-mile spur trail and a short walk. There used to be an old vehicle trail that continued down from this viewpoint, but unfortunately it's only for foot and pack travel these days.

About 2 miles farther, the trail enters Capitol Reef National Park and travels through the Hartnet Exclosure (established 1983) and Hartnet Draw. Camping in the park is restricted to the free primitive campground at Cathedral Valley. There are many hiking trails to overlooks and points of interest along the route. One of the best is the Upper South Desert Overlook, where a short hike around the rim and then a scramble up to the high point yields surreal views over the South Desert far below. Just past this spot is another good viewpoint, the Cathedral Valley Overlook, which looks down on the trail and the famous monoliths. The Cathedral Campground is a quarter mile farther.

The trail then winds down some easy switchbacks into Cathedral Valley. Another short hike leads to the historic Morrell cabin, set against a backdrop of red rock buttes, and farther along other short spurs lead to the Temples of the Sun and Moon, Entrada sandstone towers rising abruptly from the valley floor. After this, the trail leaves Cathedral Valley and enters Caineville Wash. Finally, the trail follows alongside the Caineville Reef before finishing at Utah 24 at the small settlement of Caineville.

There are great views for almost the entire trail. At many points the Henry Mountains are visible to the southeast, the Waterpocket Fold to the southwest, the Caineville Mesas to the south, and Thousand Lake Mountain to the west.

Current Road Information

BLM Henry Mountain Field Station
PO Box 99
Hanksville, UT 84734
(435) 542-3461

Capitol Reef National Park
HC-70 Box 15
Torrey, UT 84775
(435) 425-3791

Map References

BLM Loa, Salina
USGS 1:24,000 Caineville, Fruita, Fruita NW, Cathedral Mt., Solomon's Temple, Caine Springs
1:100,000 Loa, Salina
Maptech CD-ROM: Escalante/Dixie National Forest; Central/San Rafael
Trails Illustrated, #213
Utah Atlas & Gazetteer, p. 28
Utah Travel Council #5
Other: Capitol Reef National Park Recreation Map of the Henry Mountains Area (incomplete)

Route Directions

▼ 0.0 On Utah 24, 2.6 miles east of Capitol Reef National Park, turn northeast on graded dirt road at the sign for "river ford." Pass through gate and zero trip meter.
0.5 ▲ Pass through gate, then trail ends at Utah 24. Turn right for Capitol Reef National Park, left for Hanksville.

GPS: N 38°16.50' W 111°05.34'

▼ 0.4 TL Pass through gate and turn left. Track on right to corral.
0.1 ▲ TR Turn right, then pass through gate. Track on left to corral.

▼ 0.5 BR Ford Fremont River; bear right downstream for approximately 50 yards to exit. Zero trip meter on far bank.
0.0 ▲ Continue toward Utah 24.

GPS: N 38°16.49' W 111°04.76'

▼ 0.0 Continue away from river.
8.1 ▲ BR Zero trip meter on bank, then ford Fremont River; bear right upstream for approximately 50 yards to exit.

▼ 0.1 SO Track on left is old upper ford crossing (not used).
8.0 ▲ SO Track on right is old upper ford crossing (not used).

▼ 0.2 SO Cross through wash.
7.9 ▲ SO Cross through wash.

▼ 2.1 SO Track on right.
6.0 ▲ SO Track on left.

▼ 2.2 SO Cattle guard.
5.9 ▲ SO Cattle guard.

▼ 2.3 SO Cross through wash. Many wash crossings in the next 4.1 miles.
5.8 ▲ SO Cross through wash.

▼ 2.8 SO Track on right.
5.3 ▲ SO Track on left.

▼ 4.8 SO Cross through wash, then track on right.
3.3 ▲ SO Track on left, then cross through wash.

GPS: N 38°19.29' W 111°06.09'

▼ 6.4 SO Old drilling rig on right.
1.7 ▲ SO Old drilling rig on left. Many wash crossings in the next 4.1 miles.

GPS: N 38°20.34' W 111°07.16'

▼ 8.1 SO Marker post for Bentonite Hills. Zero trip meter.

0.0 ▲ Continue southeast.

GPS: N 38°21.67' W 111°07.65'

▼ 0.0 Continue northwest.

4.8 ▲ SO Marker post for Bentonite Hills. Zero trip meter.

▼ 0.6 SO Track on right to Guys Reservoir.

4.2 ▲ SO Track on left to Guys Reservoir.

GPS: N 38°22.25' W 111°07.78'

▼ 1.2 BL Track on right to Rock Water Spring.

3.6 ▲ BR Track on left to Rock Water Spring.

GPS: N 38°22.57' W 111°08.09'

▼ 2.4 SO Track on left.

2.4 ▲ SO Track on right.

▼ 4.6 SO Cross through wash.

0.2 ▲ SO Cross through wash.

▼ 4.8 SO Cross through wash, then track on left to Lower South Desert Overlook (1.1 miles). Zero trip meter.

0.0 ▲ Continue toward Utah 24.

GPS: N 38°24.13' W 111°11.08'

▼ 0.0 Continue toward Capitol Reef National Park.

2.2 ▲ SO Track on right to Lower South Desert Overlook (1.1 miles). Zero trip meter, then cross through wash.

▼ 0.5 SO Cross through wash.

1.7 ▲ SO Cross through wash.

▼ 0.7 SO Cattle guard.

1.5 ▲ SO Cattle guard.

▼ 0.9 SO Cross through wash.

1.3 ▲ SO Cross through wash.

▼ 2.0 SO Cross through wash.

0.2 ▲ SO Cross through wash.

▼ 2.2 SO Entering Capitol Reef National Park. Zero trip meter.

0.0 ▲ Continue away from Capitol Reef National Park.

GPS: N 38°25.54' W 111°11.19'

▼ 0.0 Continue into Capitol Reef National Park.

3.5 ▲ SO Leaving Capitol Reef National Park. Zero trip meter.

▼ 0.3 SO Exclosure on right.

3.2 ▲ SO Exclosure on left.

▼ 1.1 SO Hiking trail on right to Lower Cathedral Valley Overlook.

2.4 ▲ SO Hiking trail on left to Lower Cathedral Valley Overlook.

GPS: N 38°25.82' W 111°12.28'

▼ 2.1 SO Hartnet Exclosure on left.

1.4 ▲ SO Hartnet Exclosure on right.

▼ 2.9 SO Cross through wash.

0.6 ▲ SO Cross through wash.

▼ 3.3 SO Cross through Hartnet Draw.

0.2 ▲ SO Cross through Hartnet Draw.

▼ 3.4 SO Cross through Hartnet Draw.

0.1 ▲ SO Cross through Hartnet Draw.

▼ 3.5 SO Cross through Hartnet Draw. Ackland Spring immediately after wash on right. Zero trip meter.

0.0 ▲ Continue southeast.

GPS: N 38°26.73' W 111°14.46'

▼ 0.0 Continue northwest. Many wash crossings in next 5 miles.

7.3 ▲ SO Ackland Spring on left, then cross through Hartnet Draw. Zero trip meter.

▼ 5.0 SO Trail climbs out of canyon.

2.3 ▲ SO Trail enters canyon, many wash crossings in next 5 miles.

▼ 6.7 SO Track on left to Upper South Desert Overlook.

0.6 ▲ SO Track on right to Upper South Desert Overlook.

GPS: N 38°28.45' W 111°21.14'

▼ 7.0 SO Track on right to Cathedral Valley Overlook.

Central Trail #18: Cathedral Valley Trail

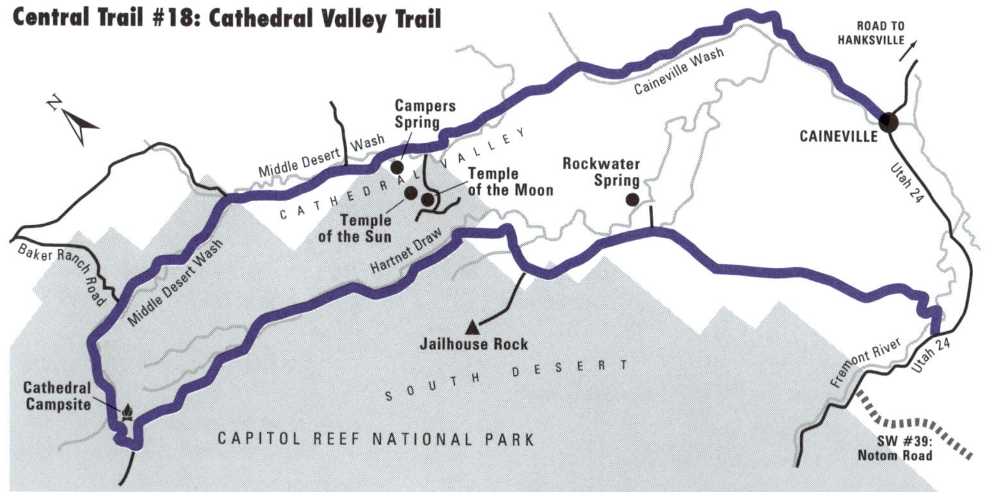

0.3 ▲ SO Track on left to Cathedral Valley Overlook.

GPS: N 38°28.39' W 111°21.50'

▼ 7.3 TR Track ahead to Thousand Lake Mountain. Zero trip meter.

0.0 ▲ Continue toward Cathedral Valley Overlook

GPS: N 38°28.18' W 111°21.78'

▼ 0.0 Continue toward Cathedral Campground.

5.0 ▲ TL Track on right to Thousand Lake Mountain. Zero trip meter.

▼ 0.3 SO Cathedral Campground on left.

4.7 ▲ SO Cathedral Campground on right.

GPS: N 38°28.43' W 111°21.88'

▼ 0.4 SO Descend into Cathedral Valley on wide shelf road.

4.6 ▲ SO End of shelf road.

▼ 1.3 SO Enter Cathedral Valley.

3.7 ▲ SO Exit Cathedral Valley up wide shelf road.

▼ 1.7 SO Small parking area and short hike to Morrell cabin on left.

3.3 ▲ SO Small parking area and short hike to Morrell cabin on right.

GPS: N 38°29.02' W 111°21.65'

▼ 1.8 SO Cross through wash.

3.2 ▲ SO Cross through wash.

▼ 1.9 SO Cross through wash.

3.1 ▲ SO Cross through wash.

▼ 2.3 SO Cathedral Trail hiking trailhead on left.

2.7 ▲ SO Cathedral Trail hiking trailhead on right.

GPS: N 38°29.29' W 111°21.16'

▼ 2.7 SO Enter wash.

2.3 ▲ SO Exit wash.

▼ 2.8 SO Exit wash.

2.2 ▲ SO Enter wash.

▼ 3.3 SO Cross through wash.

1.7 ▲ SO Cross through wash.

▼ 3.5 SO Cross through wash.

1.5 ▲ SO Cross through wash.

▼ 3.8 SO Cross through creek.

1.2 ▲ SO Cross through creek.

▼ 4.6 SO Cross through wash, then cross through fence line.

0.4 ▲ SO Cross through fence line, then cross through wash.

▼ 5.0 SO Track on left is Baker Ranch Road, which goes to I-70. Zero trip meter.

0.0 ▲ Continue toward Cathedral Campground.

GPS: N 38°30.35′ W 111°19.00′

▼ 0.0 Continue toward Utah 24.
4.1 ▲ SO Track on right is Baker Ranch Road, which goes to I-70. Zero trip meter.

▼ 0.1 BL Track on right to Gypsum Sinkholes.
4.0 ▲ SO Track on left to Gypsum Sinkholes.
GPS: N 38°30.34′ W 111°18.88′

▼ 2.2 SO Cross through wash.
1.9 ▲ SO Cross through wash.

▼ 2.5 SO Enter Middle Desert Wash.
1.6 ▲ SO Exit Middle Desert Wash.

▼ 2.6 SO Exit Middle Desert Wash.
1.5 ▲ SO Enter Middle Desert Wash.

▼ 3.1 SO Exclosure on left.
1.0 ▲ SO Exclosure on right.

▼ 3.3 SO Cross through wash.
0.8 ▲ SO Cross through wash.

▼ 3.6 SO Cross through wash.
0.5 ▲ SO Cross through wash.

▼ 4.0 SO Track on left.
0.1 ▲ SO Track on right.
GPS: N 38°29.96′ W 111°14.87′

▼ 4.1 SO Leaving Capitol Reef National Park. Zero trip meter.
0.0 ▲ Continue into Capitol Reef National Park.
GPS: N 38°29.91′ W 111°14.84′

▼ 0.0 Continue toward Caineville.
4.9 ▲ SO Entering Capitol Reef National Park. Zero trip meter.

▼ 0.1 SO Cross through wash.
4.8 ▲ SO Cross through wash.

▼ 0.3 SO Cattle guard, then cross through wash.
4.6 ▲ SO Cross through wash, then cattle guard.

▼ 2.0 SO Cross through wash.
2.9 ▲ SO Cross through wash.

▼ 3.9 SO Cross through wash.
1.0 ▲ SO Cross through wash.

▼ 4.2 SO Campers Spring on right.
0.7 ▲ SO Campers Spring on left.
GPS: N 38°27.94′ W 111°11.10′

▼ 4.9 SO Track on right to the Temple of the Sun and Temple of the Moon. Zero trip meter.
0.0 ▲ Continue toward Capitol Reef National Park.
GPS: N 38°27.57′ W 111°10.50′

▼ 0.0 Continue toward Caineville.
14.7 ▲ SO Track on left to the Temple of the Sun and Temple of the Moon. Zero trip meter.

▼ 0.6 SO Track on left.
14.1 ▲ SO Track on right.

▼ 0.8 SO Cross through wash.
13.9 ▲ SO Cross through wash.

▼ 2.1 SO Track on right.
12.6 ▲ SO Track on left.
GPS: N 38°26.84′ W 111°08.54′

▼ 2.2 SO Tracks on right and left.
12.5 ▲ SO Tracks on right and left.

▼ 2.6 SO Cross through wash.
12.1 ▲ SO Cross through wash.

▼ 3.2 SO Cross through two washes.
11.5 ▲ SO Cross through two washes.

▼ 3.6 SO Cross over wash.
11.1 ▲ SO Cross over wash.

▼ 3.7 SO Leaving Cathedral Valley.
11.0 ▲ SO Entering Cathedral Valley.
GPS: N 38°26.18′ W 111°06.92′

▼ 4.5 SO Track on left.
10.2 ▲ SO Track on right.

▼ 4.6 SO Cross through wash. Caineville Mesa

and the Henry Mountains directly ahead.

10.1 ▲ SO Cross through wash.

▼ 4.7 SO Cross through Caineville Wash.

10.0 ▲ SO Cross through Caineville Wash.

▼ 5.4 SO Cross through wash.

9.3 ▲ SO Cross through wash.

▼ 5.8 SO Track on right.

8.9 ▲ SO Track on left.

GPS: N 38°25.21' W 111°05.25'

▼ 6.0 SO Small dam on left.

8.7 ▲ SO Small dam on right.

▼ 6.4 SO Cross through two washes.

8.3 ▲ SO Cross through two washes.

▼ 6.7 SO Cross wash.

8.0 ▲ SO Cross wash.

▼ 6.8 SO Small track on left.

7.9 ▲ SO Small track on right.

▼ 7.0 SO Salt Wash on right.

7.7 ▲ SO Salt Wash on left.

GPS: N 38°24.68' W 111°04.17'

▼ 7.2 SO Willow Seep on right.

7.5 ▲ SO Willow Seep on left.

GPS: N 38°24.59' W 111°04.02'

▼ 7.4 SO Cross through wash.

7.3 ▲ SO Cross through wash.

▼ 8.0 SO Cross through wash.

6.7 ▲ SO Cross through wash.

▼ 8.3 SO Cross through wash.

6.4 ▲ SO Cross through wash.

▼ 8.8 SO Track on left; views east to North and South Caineville Mesas.

5.9 ▲ SO Track on right; views east to North and South Caineville Mesas.

GPS: N 38°24.02' W 111°01.89'

▼ 10.7 SO Track on right.

4.0 ▲ SO Track on left.

▼ 11.7 SO Carl's Reservoir on left.

3.0 ▲ SO Carl's Reservoir on right.

GPS: N 38°22.66' W 111°01.74'

▼ 11.9 SO Cattle guard, then track on right.

2.8 ▲ SO Track on left, then cattle guard.

▼ 12.3 SO Cross through wash, then track on left.

2.4 ▲ SO Track on right, then cross through wash.

▼ 14.4 SO Track on right.

0.3 ▲ SO Track on left.

▼ 14.7 Cross cattle guard, then trail ends at Utah 24 at Caineville. Turn right for Capitol Reef National Park, left for Hanksville.

0.0 ▲ On Utah 24 at Caineville, turn northwest on graded dirt road, following sign for Caineville Wash Road. Zero trip meter.

GPS: N 38°20.06' W 111°01.40'

CENTRAL REGION TRAIL #19

Hans Flat Road

STARTING POINT Utah 24, 18 miles north of Hanksville
FINISHING POINT Hans Flat Ranger Station
TOTAL MILEAGE 42.7 miles
UNPAVED MILEAGE 42.7 miles
DRIVING TIME 3 hours
ELEVATION RANGE 5,000–6,500 feet
USUALLY OPEN Year-round
DIFFICULTY RATING 1
SCENIC RATING 7
REMOTENESS RATING +0

Special Attractions

- Access to Canyonlands National Park Maze District.
- Access to historic Robbers Roost area.
- Remote, lightly traveled route.

A view of the trail with Little Flat Top in the background

Description

The Hans Flat Road is the major access to the remote Maze District of Canyonlands National Park. As a whole, the Maze receives a fraction of the visitors that the more accessible Island in the Sky and Needles District do, but it is no less spectacular. This graded dirt road is open year-round, as it is the primary access for the national park rangers who live at the remote Hans Flat Ranger Station. It may become temporarily impassable after heavy rain or snow. In dry weather it is accessible to passenger vehicles, but all trails within the Maze District, including the Flint Trail, past the ranger station require a high-clearance 4WD.

The route heads east from Utah 24 about 18 miles north of Hanksville. The first features on the trail are the aptly named mesas Little Flat Top and Big Flat Top. The sandy trail then wraps down to the south, passing by Spire Point, and ascends to run along the ridge of Texas Hill. From the hill there are 360-degree views: to the north over the San Rafael Desert, Dugout Wash, and the Sweetwater Reef; to the east all the way to the La Sal Mountains; and of course, to the southwest to the bulk of the Henry Mountains.

After 22.8 miles, a major road heads north to the Horseshoe Canyon Unit of Canyonlands National Park, which is famous for its petroglyph panels. An information board at the junction gives public land information for the unit as well as for other public lands. The trail then enters the broad Antelope Valley and crests Burr Pass, which is unmarked. Central #20: Robbers Roost Spring Trail leaves from here, and this spur trail makes a nice addition to the main route.

The trail finishes at the Hans Flat Ranger Station, which is open all year. Note that camping in the Maze District is limited to designated sites, and at peak times, typically spring and fall, you will almost certainly need advance booking. There are some reasonable sites outside the park, mainly at the Hans Flat end where there are more trees for shelter. Access to the Maze District from the ranger station is via the Flint Trail, a narrow series of switchbacks that are impassable for most of the winter, since snow builds up on the north-facing switchbacks. Alternate access to the Maze District is from Hite Crossing.

There is a good chance of seeing wildlife along this trail, especially pronghorn antelope, coyotes, and various raptors.

Current Road Information

BLM Henry Mountain Field Station
PO Box 99
Hanksville, UT 84734
(435) 542-3461

Canyonlands National Park
Maze District
(435) 259-2652

Map References

BLM San Rafael Desert, Hanksville
USGS 1:24,000 Gilson Butte, The Flat Tops, Point of Rocks East,

Whitbeck Knoll, Robbers Roost Flats, Head Spur
1:100,000 San Rafael Desert, Hanksville
Maptech CD-ROM: Central/San Rafael, Moab/Canyonlands
Trails Illustrated, # 213 (incomplete); #246 (incomplete)
Utah Atlas & Gazetteer, p. 29
Utah Travel Council #5
Other: Canyon Country Off-Road Vehicle Map—Maze Area

Route Directions

▼ 0.0 From Utah 24, 0.3 miles north of mile marker 136 and just south of turn to Goblin Valley State Park, turn southeast on graded dirt road (signed to the Maze) and cross cattle guard. Zero trip meter.
9.0 ▲ Trail ends at Utah 24; turn right for Goblin Valley State Park and Green River, left for Hanksville.
GPS: N 38°37.41' W 110°34.20'

▼ 2.4 SO Track on right to Utah 24, track on left.
6.6 ▲ SO Track on left to Utah 24, track on right.
GPS: N 38°35.30' W 110°33.34'

▼ 2.6 SO Cattle guard.
6.4 ▲ SO Cattle guard.

▼ 6.3 TL Corral on right. Turn left in front of small hill.
2.7 ▲ TR Turn right. Corral on left.
GPS: N 38°31.78' W 110°32.41'

▼ 7.4 SO Track on right.
1.6 ▲ SO Track on left.

▼ 7.6 SO Second entrance to track on right.
1.4 ▲ SO Second entrance to track on left.

▼ 9.0 SO Track on left around base of Little Flat Top. Zero trip meter directly underneath the butte at the cattle guard on slight rise between Little Flat Top and Big Flat Top.
0.0 ▲ Continue toward Utah 24.
GPS: N 38°32.29' W 110°29.42'

▼ 0.0 Continue away from Little Flat Top.
5.7 ▲ SO Zero trip meter directly underneath the butte at the cattle guard on slight rise between Little Flat Top and Big Flat Top. Track on right around base of Little Flat Top.

▼ 0.1 SO Track on left.
5.6 ▲ SO Track on right.

▼ 1.3 SO Track on left.
4.4 ▲ SO Track on right.
GPS: N 38°32.53' W 110°27.88'

▼ 3.1 SO Track on right.
2.6 ▲ SO Track on left.

▼ 3.4 SO Track on right.
2.3 ▲ SO Track on left.

▼ 4.6 SO Track on left. Spire Point on right.
1.1 ▲ SO Track on right. Spire Point on left.
GPS: N 38°30.60' W 110°25.42'

▼ 5.3 SO Track on right.
0.4 ▲ SO Track on left.

▼ 5.7 SO Trail winds up to the top of Texas Hill. Graded dirt road on right to large shed. Zero trip meter.
0.0 ▲ Continue toward Utah 24.
GPS: N 38°29.98' W 110°24.83'

▼ 0.0 Continue south toward Hans Flat Ranger Station.
8.1 ▲ SO Graded dirt road on left to large shed. Trail descends from Texas Hill. Zero trip meter.

▼ 0.3 SO Track on right.
7.8 ▲ SO Track on left.

▼ 2.2 SO Track on left along edge of Sweetwater Reef.
5.9 ▲ SO Track on right along edge of Sweetwater Reef.

▼ 3.9 SO Track on right.

Central Trail #19: Hans Flat Road

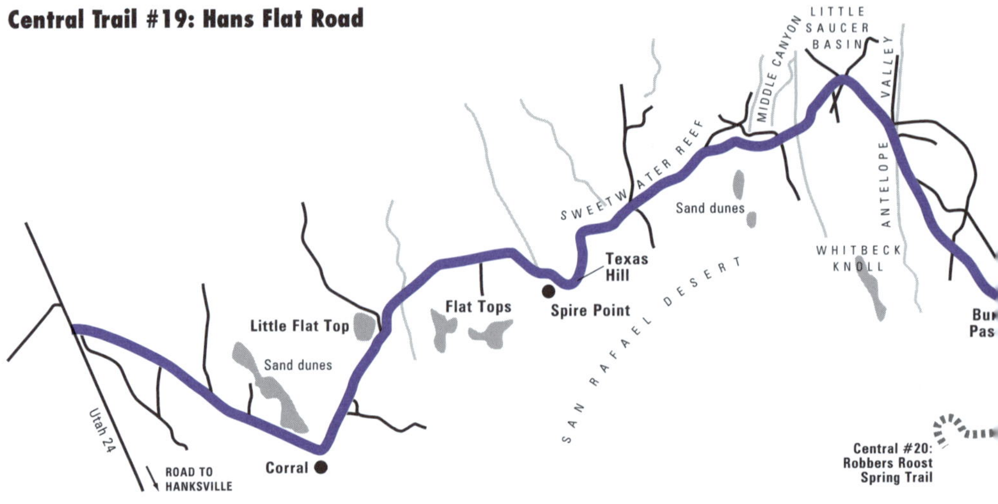

4.2 ▲ SO Track on left.

▼ 6.2 SO Track on right to corral.
1.9 ▲ SO Track on left to corral.
GPS: N 38°28.51' W 110°18.90'

▼ 6.6 SO Track on right.
1.5 ▲ SO Track on left.

▼ 7.8 SO Track on right and track on left.
0.3 ▲ SO Track on left and track on right.

▼ 8.0 SO Track on left.
0.1 ▲ SO Track on right.

▼ 8.1 BR Small track on left, then major graded road on left to Horseshoe Canyon and Green River. Information board for the Maze District and Horseshoe Canyon at the junction. Zero trip meter.
0.0 ▲ Continue toward the ridge of Texas Hill. Immediately small track on right.
GPS: N 38°28.37' W 110°16.79'

▼ 0.0 Continue into Antelope Valley.
6.7 ▲ SO Major graded road on right to Horseshoe Canyon and Green River. Information board for the Maze District and Horseshoe Canyon at the junction. Zero trip meter.

▼ 1.6 SO Faint track on left.
5.1 ▲ SO Faint track on right.

▼ 3.4 SO Cattle guard, then track on left.
3.3 ▲ SO Track on right, then cattle guard.
GPS: N 38°25.49' W 110°17.70'

▼ 4.6 SO Track on left and faint track on right. Main trail runs along a slight ridge with views left into the Maze and Bluejohn Canyon.
2.1 ▲ SO Track on right and faint track on left. Main trail runs along a slight ridge with views right into the Maze and Bluejohn Canyon.

▼ 6.5 SO Faint track on left, then cross over wash.
0.2 ▲ SO Cross over wash, then faint track on right.

▼ 6.7 BL Top of Burr Pass. Track on right is Central #20: Robbers Roost Spring Trail. Zero trip meter and bear left, following sign to Hans Flat Ranger Station.
0.0 ▲ Continue toward Utah 24.
GPS: N 38°22.65' W 110°18.28'

▼ 0.0 Continue toward ranger station.
13.2 ▲ SO Top of Burr Pass. Track on left is Central #20: Robbers Roost Spring Trail. Zero trip meter.

▼ 2.5 BR Track on left.

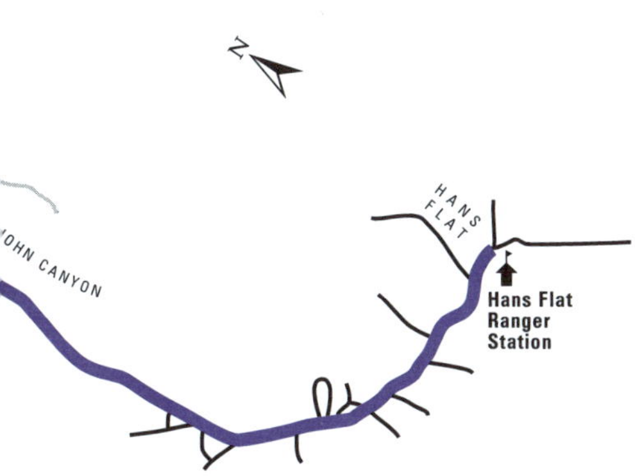

10.7 ▲ SO Second entrance to track on right.
GPS: N 38°20.44' W 110°17.65'

▼ 2.6 SO Second entrance to track on left.
10.6 ▲ SO Track on right.

▼ 5.5 SO Track on right.
7.7 ▲ SO Track on left.
GPS: N 38°17.81' W 110°17.29'

▼ 6.3 SO Track on right.
6.9 ▲ SO Track on left.

▼ 6.5 SO Track on right.
6.7 ▲ SO Track on left.
GPS: N 38°16.95' W 110°16.95'

▼ 7.0 SO Cattle guard.
6.2 ▲ SO Cattle guard.

▼ 7.4 SO Cross through wash.
5.8 ▲ SO Cross through wash.

▼ 7.6 SO Cross over wash.
5.6 ▲ SO Cross over wash.

▼ 7.9 SO Track on right.
5.3 ▲ SO Track on left.
GPS: N 38°15.97' W 110°16.05'

▼ 8.6 SO Track on left.
4.6 ▲ SO Track on right.

▼ 8.9 SO Track on right.
4.3 ▲ SO Track on left.

▼ 9.5 SO Faint track on right.
3.7 ▲ SO Faint track on left.

▼ 10.7 SO Track on right.
2.5 ▲ SO Track on left.
GPS: N 38°15.11' W 110°13.39'

▼ 12.6 SO Track on left to limited use area. Enter Hans Flat.
0.6 ▲ SO Track on right to limited use area. Leave Hans Flat.
GPS: N 38°15.32' W 110°11.41'

▼ 12.8 SO Track on right.
0.4 ▲ SO Track on left.

▼ 13.2 Trail ends at Hans Flat Ranger Station in the Maze District of Canyonlands National Park.
0.0 ▲ Trail commences at the Hans Flat Ranger Station in the Maze District of Canyonlands National Park. Zero trip meter at the ranger station and proceed west along the graded dirt road.
GPS: N 38°15.31' W 110°10.73'

CENTRAL REGION TRAIL #20

Robbers Roost Spring Trail

STARTING POINT Burr Pass on Central #19: Hans Flat Road
FINISHING POINT Overlook into Robbers Roost Canyon
TOTAL MILEAGE 9.3 miles
UNPAVED MILEAGE 9.3 miles
DRIVING TIME 1 hour (one-way)
ELEVATION RANGE 4,900–5,600 feet
USUALLY OPEN Year-round
DIFFICULTY RATING 2
SCENIC RATING 8
REMOTENESS RATING +1

Special Attractions

- Area was historic hideout for Butch Cassidy and other outlaws.
- Viewpoint over both North and Middle Forks of Robbers Roost Canyon.
- Robbers Roost Spring and Cottrell cabin ruins.

History

The Robbers Roost area was a hideout for cattle rustlers long before Butch Cassidy gave the area its notoriety. A maze of deep canyons, Robbers Roost allowed outlaws to move through undetected and go to ground when the law closed in. Robbers Roost Spring, located in the South Fork of Robbers Roost Canyon, was used by Butch Cassidy and the Wild Bunch as one of their hiding places.

Slightly upstream from the spring are the stone remains of the Cottrell cabin, which was built in 1890 by Joe Bernard, the foreman of the 3B Ranch, as a line cabin for the hands to use when rounding up cattle. Jack Cottrell became the foreman of the 3B Ranch soon after and moved his family to the cabin. After he moved out in the mid-1890s, the cabin continued to be used as a line cabin and,

BUTCH CASSIDY AND THE WILD BUNCH

Butch Cassidy

Shadowed in notoriety, the Wild Bunch was a gang of outlaws whose exploits are legendary. Butch Cassidy (Robert Leroy Parker) served as the gang's head, and under his leadership the Wild Bunch was responsible for the robberies of several banks and trains throughout the West. Although the gang existed before his arrival, it was Cassidy who tempered the outlaws' wild behavior and prompted them to extensively plan each hold-up. Their horses were trained to remain perfectly still in the midst of shouting, gunshots, and other disturbances. This way, when members of the Wild Bunch robbed a bank, they could sprint to their horses under a hail of gunfire without the animals becoming spooked. Other members of the gang would be stationed at various spots along the getaway route with fresh teams of horses. This enabled the robbers to keep ahead of the posses chasing them. It also allowed them to ride great distances to safety, earning the group the nickname, Long-riders.

The Wild Bunch also had a network of hideouts that extended from Wyoming to Mexico. Their most famous one, called Robbers Roost, was located in the canyons of central Utah. Behind Cassidy rode such colorful characters as Kid Curry (Harvey Logan), the McCarty Brothers, the Tall Texan (Ben Kilpatrick), the Sundance Kid (Harry Longabaugh), Elza Lay (William Ellsworth), and Matt Warner (Willard Christianson).

One of the outlaws' most infamous robberies took place on April 21, 1897, in Castle Gate, Utah. Along with Elza Lay and Joe Walker, Butch Cassidy robbed the Pleasant Valley Coal Company payroll to the tune of $7,000. No one was shot during the course of the robbery. The Wild Bunch continued to haunt western railways until 1901, after which Cassidy and the Sundance Kid fled to South America. They were killed in Bolivia in 1908.

Although most of the members of the Wild Bunch would end up dead or in prison, Matt Warner would eventually join the side of law and order. After killing two men he turned himself in and served three years and four months in a Utah State Prison. After his release he became the justice of the peace and night marshal at Green River, Utah. Today, witnessing a piece of history is easy; Matt Warner's signature (spelled Mat Warner) can still be seen on the side of a rock along Central #1: Buckhorn Wash Trail.

A view over the south fork of Robbers Roost Canyon

increasingly, as shelter for outlaws until it burnt to the ground. Only the stone chimney remains today. Supposedly, so the story goes, it burned down when someone tried to smoke out a rat!

Just north of the Cottrell cabin is Silvertip Spring, which was named after a horsethief who often used the Robbers Roost Spring and cabin to hide from the sheriff.

Description

This spur trail runs just over 9 miles and ends at a high viewpoint over the North and Middle Forks of Robbers Roost Canyon, but there is plenty to see before you get there! The smooth, sandy trail runs around the head of the South Fork of Robbers Roost Canyon. After 5.7 miles, a track to the left leads down to the Robbers Roost Spring and the Cottrell cabin. A small cairn marks the turnoff, which leads 0.2 miles to a turnaround under a large cottonwood on the edge of the wash. The spring is slightly to the west of the end of the trail, down in the wash; you will see the wooden troughs that mark the spring.

To reach the remains of the Cottrell cabin, walk east up the remains of an old washed out 4WD trail for approximately 0.2 miles. To the left of the small creek in a small rocky cove is the cabin's chimney.

The main trail past the spring is less used; it can have some small gullies from washouts, but it remains graded for the next 2.3 miles to the oil drilling post. At the drill hole, there is an ambiguously placed WSA sign—it is near enough to the trail that it almost looks like it is blocking the way. The National Park Service at Hans Flat says that the track is accessible to vehicles, but that an inexperienced person placed the signs and some of them were in the wrong position. From here the trail is an ungraded two track as it runs out on the narrow point, giving glimpses into both North and Middle Forks, until it ends above the confluence.

Current Road Information

BLM Henry Mountain Field Station
PO Box 99
Hanksville, UT 84734
(435) 542-3461

Map References

BLM Hanksville
USGS 1:24,000 Whitbeck Knoll, Robbers Roost Flats, Angel Point
1:100,000 Hanksville
Maptech CD-ROM: Moab/Canyonlands
Utah Atlas & Gazetteer, p. 29

Central Trail #20: Robbers Roost Spring Trail

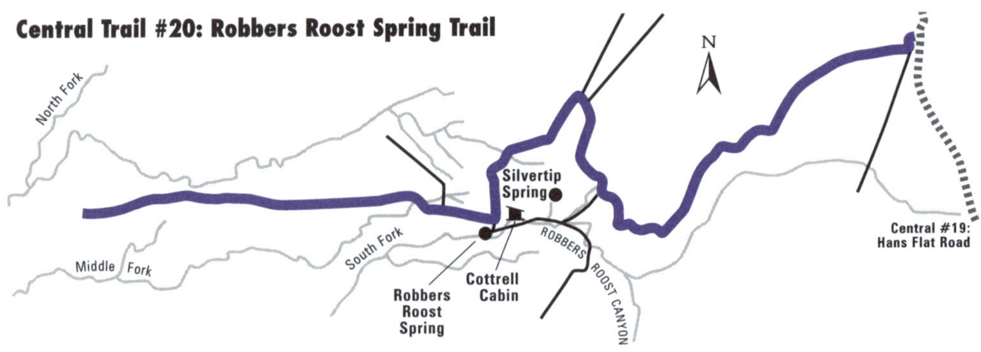

Route Directions

▼ 0.0 At Burr Pass on Central #19: Hans Flat Road, 29.5 miles from Utah 24, turn southwest on the graded track, following the sign for Ekker Ranch, and zero trip meter.
GPS: N 38°22.65' W 110°18.28'

▼ 0.1 TR Track continues straight to Ekker Ranch.
GPS: N 38°22.59' W 110°18.30'

▼ 3.1 SO Turnout on left with overlook of the South Fork of Robbers Roost Canyon.
▼ 3.4 SO Two tracks on left.
▼ 4.3 SO Faint track on right.
▼ 5.6 SO Cross through wash.
▼ 5.7 BR Trail forks at small cairn. The track on left goes 0.2 miles to Robbers Roost Spring and stone chimney ruins. Zero trip meter.
GPS: N 38°21.76' W 110°22.28'

▼ 0.0 Continue toward overlook.
▼ 0.5 BR Faint track on left.
▼ 0.6 SO Cross through wash.
▼ 1.6 SO View left into Middle Fork and view right into North Fork of Robbers Roost Canyon.
▼ 2.3 SO Drill hole on left. Trail is now ungraded.
GPS: N 38°21.99' W 110°24.85'

▼ 2.8 SO Turnout on right with overlook of North Fork of Robbers Roost Canyon.
GPS: N 38°22.17' W 110°25.34'

▼ 3.6 Trail ends at small turning circle and overlook of the confluence of North Fork and Middle Fork of Robbers Roost Canyon.
GPS: N 38°22.04' W 110°26.15'

CENTRAL REGION TRAIL #21

Burr Point Trail

STARTING POINT Utah 95, 0.6 miles south of mile marker 15
FINISHING POINT Burr Point
TOTAL MILEAGE 10 miles
UNPAVED MILEAGE 10 miles
DRIVING TIME 30 minutes (one-way)
ELEVATION RANGE 4,900–5,400 feet
USUALLY OPEN Year-round
DIFFICULTY RATING 1
SCENIC RATING 8
REMOTENESS RATING +0

Special Attractions

- Panoramic view over Dirty Devil River Canyon.
- Access to a network of graded roads and trails to viewpoints.
- Historic Robbers Roost region.

Description

There are many trails in the Robbers Roost area, but most of them peter out before long. This trail is a graded dirt road that goes to an overlook over the Dirty Devil River Canyon. It is an easy trail that's suitable for passenger vehicles in dry weather. Short sections of the trail run in a creek wash. There are side trails that lead down to overlooks at Poison

Spring Canyon and Adobe Swale.

On the return trip, there are excellent views west over the towering volcanic Henry Mountains.

A view into the Dirty Devil River from the near end of the trail

Current Road Information

BLM Henry Mountain Field Station
PO Box 99
Hanksville, UT 84734
(435) 542-3461

Map References

BLM Hanksville
USGS 1:24,000 Baking Skillet Knoll, Burr Point
1:100,000 Hanksville
Maptech CD-ROM: Moab/Canyonlands
Trails Illustrated, #213
Utah Atlas & Gazetteer, p. 29
Utah Travel Council #5
Other: Recreation Map of the Henry Mountains Area

Route Directions

▼ 0.0 On Utah 95, 0.6 miles south of mile marker 15, turn northeast on the graded dirt road at sign for Burr Point.
GPS: N 38°09.53' W 110°37.25'

▼ 0.1 SO Track on right.
▼ 1.7 SO Track on left.
GPS: N 38°09.83' W 110°35.35'

▼ 1.9 SO Track on left.
▼ 2.5 SO Cattle guard.
▼ 2.8 SO Track on right.
▼ 3.1 SO Enter wash.
▼ 3.2 SO Track on right to corral.
GPS: N 38°09.85' W 110°33.69'

▼ 3.3 SO Exit wash.
▼ 3.4 SO Track on right rejoins from corral, then track on left.

Central Trail #21: Burr Point Trail

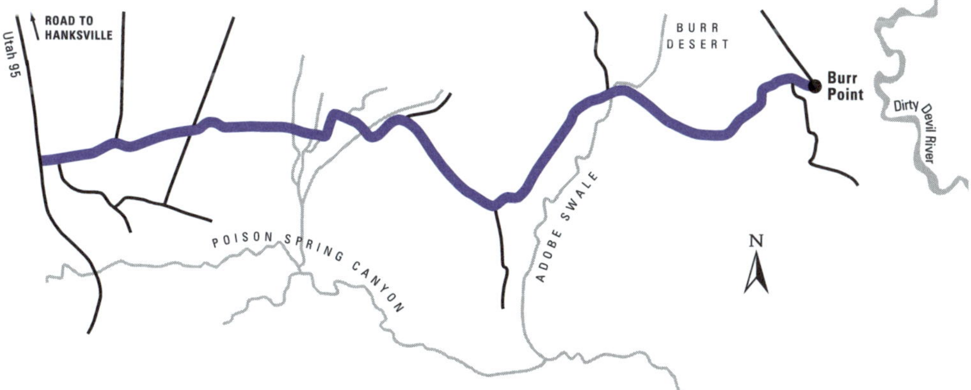

▼ 3.7 SO Cross through wash.
▼ 4.2 BR Graded track on left to dam and tank. Zero trip meter.
GPS: N 38°09.98' W 110°32.78'

▼ 0.0 Continue east to Burr Point.
▼ 0.1 SO Cross through wash.
▼ 0.3 SO Cross through wash.
▼ 0.7 SO Cross through wash, then track on left up wash.
▼ 1.0 SO Cross through wash.
▼ 1.3 BL Track on right to Adobe Swale.
GPS: N 38°09.14' W 110°31.65'

▼ 1.8 SO Adobe Swale Canyon on right.
▼ 3.2 BR Small track on right, then larger graded track on left.
GPS: N 38°10.20' W 110°30.17'

▼ 3.4 BR Track on left.
▼ 3.5 SO Cross small dam wall; dam on left.
GPS: N 38°10.21' W 110°29.88'

▼ 4.6 SO Track on left to drill hole.
▼ 5.6 SO Track on right.
GPS: N 38°10.32' W 110°27.98'

▼ 5.8 Trail ends at a drill hole on Burr Point at overlook of Dirty Devil River. Track on right and track on left at end of trail.
GPS: N 38°10.30' W 110°27.71'

CENTRAL REGION TRAIL #22

Copper Globe Mine Trail

STARTING POINT I-70, exit 114
FINISHING POINT Copper Globe Mine near Central #24: Kimball Draw Trail
TOTAL MILEAGE 6.6 miles
UNPAVED MILEAGE 6.3 miles
DRIVING TIME 1 hour
ELEVATION RANGE 6,800–7,200 feet
USUALLY OPEN Year-round
DIFFICULTY RATING 3
SCENIC RATING 10
REMOTENESS RATING +1

One of the Copper Globe Mine adits

Special Attractions

- Many artifacts remain at the Copper Globe Mine.
- The area is home to a herd of wild mustangs.
- Varied and scenic terrain.
- The Sheepherder's End marker.

History

In the days of the Old West, Justensen Flats used to be a favorite place for local cowboys to chase wild horses. Although these untamed horses used to be a common sight in the West, today it is a rare treat to spot one. The herd around Justensen Flats is one of the largest, so keep your eyes peeled for the horses as you drive along to the Copper Globe Mine.

Toward the end of the trail, you come across the Sheepherder's End marker. This unusual monument relates the story of local sheepherder Henry H. Jensen, who was found dead in the snow here in December 1890. It is said that the gang at Robbers Roost warned Jensen to keep his sheep out of the area, though no one knows for sure who actually killed him. Take a moment to read the marker's story on your way to the remains of the old mine.

The Copper Globe Mine was worked by Jessie Fugate and his son, Conn, between

1900 and 1905. The ore mined at Copper Globe was of a rather poor quality and was not worth hauling out by wagon. So Fugate built a smelter on the site. There is still a pile of wood about 75 feet long near the mine, which was used, along with a large bellows, to fire the ore in the smelter. Although this self-contained mining operation seemed like a good idea at first, the miners soon found they had used the wrong bricks. Built of building brick rather than refractory brick, the smelter melted before the ore inside it and soon collapsed.

While you are there, take a minute to look at the entrances to the mine shafts. There is one in particular that stands out as having an almost perfectly square opening and very smooth walls. Nearby, the remains of a man-made drainage basin, which was used to catch rainwater, sit along the cliff wall to the west. A few old cabins used by the miners round out the scene of this remote copper mine.

Description

Starting out from I-70, the trail runs through a sandy plateau with an abundance of side tracks and campsites. The yellow or buff-colored sands of Justensen Flats are the same color as the cliffs rising above them. As you drive through the thick pinyon and juniper, just past a sign for Copper Globe, you can see the San Rafael Knob about 3 miles southeast of Justensen Flats.

The periodically graded trail is narrow at first, and it is not very difficult even though it is very dusty and can be rather bumpy at times. The only real potential difficulty is passing through some of the sandier sections. There is a bit of shelf road, but none of it is dangerously narrow, and the road widens every now and then to allow for passing.

Overall, the varied terrain and mine remains make for a very scenic drive.

Current Road Information

Emery County Road Department
120 West Highway 29
Castle Dale, UT 84513
(435) 381-2550

BLM Price Field Office
125 South 600 West
Price, UT 84501
(435) 636-3600

Map References

BLM San Rafael Desert
USGS 1:24,000 Copper Globe
1:100,000 San Rafael Desert
Maptech CD-ROM: Central/San Rafael
Trails Illustrated, #712
Utah Atlas & Gazetteer, p. 39
Utah Travel Council #5
Other: Recreation Map of the San Rafael Swell and San Rafael Desert

Route Directions

▼ 0.0 On the south side of I-70 at exit 114 (signed for Moore and as a "View Area"), zero trip meter at intersection of the overpass and the entry/exit ramps.
6.2 ▲ Trail ends at I-70, exit 114. Turn right for Green River, left for Salina.

GPS: N 38°51.28' W 110°54.55'

▼ 0.2 SO Cattle guard.
5.9 ▲ SO Cattle guard.

▼ 0.7 SO Travel through cutting.
5.5 ▲ SO Travel through cutting.

▼ 1.2 SO Travel past Justensen Flats.
5.0 ▲ SO Travel past Justensen Flats.

An old cabin at the Copper Globe Mine

Central Trail #22: Copper Globe Mine Trail

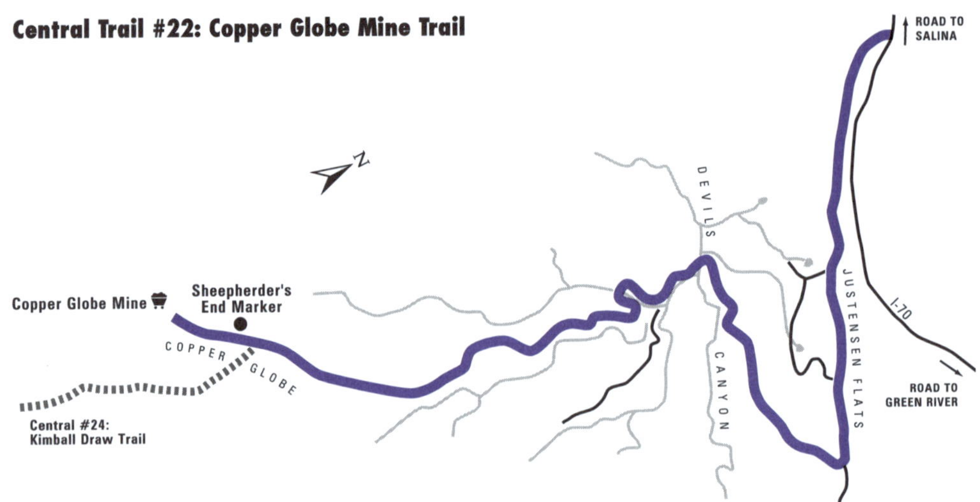

▼ 1.3 SO Road on right signed to Justensen Flats.
4.8 ▲ SO Road on left signed to Justensen Flats.

▼ 1.4 SO Road on left.
4.8 ▲ SO Road on right.

▼ 1.7 SO Track on right.
4.5 ▲ SO Track on left.

▼ 2.2 BR Turn right toward Copper Globe Road and Devils Canyon. San Rafael Knob (elevation 7,921 feet) is straight ahead.
3.9 ▲ BL Follow road to the left.

▼ 3.6 SO Cross through large, sandy wash.
2.6 ▲ SO Cross through large, sandy wash.
GPS: N 38°50.19' W 110°53.84'

▼ 4.0 SO Cross through wash.
2.2 ▲ SO Cross through wash.

▼ 6.2 BR Bear right at fork in road. Left is Central #24: Kimball Draw Trail. Zero trip meter.
0.0 ▲ Continue along trail.
GPS: N 38°48.44' W 110°54.32'

▼ 0.0 Continue along toward Copper Globe Mine.
0.4 ▲ BL Road on right is Central #24: Kimball Draw Trail. Zero trip meter.

▼ 0.1 SO Sheepherder's End marker 20 yards off the road on right.
0.3 ▲ SO Sheepherder's End marker 20 yards off the road on left.

▼ 0.4 Trail ends at Copper Globe Mine historic site.
0.0 ▲ At the Copper Globe Mine, zero trip meter and return along the trail.
GPS: N 38°48.21' W 110°54.57'

CENTRAL REGION TRAIL #23

Reds Canyon Overlook Trail

STARTING POINT Central #24: Kimball Draw Trail
FINISHING POINT Central #24: Kimball Draw Trail
TOTAL MILEAGE 4.5 miles
UNPAVED MILEAGE 4.5 miles
DRIVING TIME 45 minutes
ELEVATION RANGE 5,400–7,200 feet
USUALLY OPEN Year-round
DIFFICULTY RATING 3
SCENIC RATING 8
REMOTENESS RATING +1

Special Attractions

- Panoramic viewpoint over Reds Canyon.
- Access to backcountry campsites on Link Flats.

Description

This short loop trail includes a spur trail to an overlook high above Reds Canyon to the south. It makes an interesting side trip to Central #24: Kimball Draw Trail. The trail crosses Link Flats on an ungraded two-track before swinging around and climbing to the overlook. The trail is not difficult, but there are a couple of narrow gullies that may catch the rear of longer vehicles or those with less clearance. The climb to the overlook is a little loose, but any driver who is confident navigating the Kimball Draw Trail will have no problems on this one. Those driving wider vehicles may find that a couple of sections may be a little brushy.

At the overlook, you can see into Reds Canyon and the San Rafael Swell; vehicle trails are visible in the bottom running along the creek. To the south, you can see over the Hondoo country to the Henry Mountains. Tomsich Butte and a nearby unnamed butte are closer to the southwest, while Family Butte is east.

There are a couple of secluded backcountry campsites tucked into the juniper, some with views over Reds Canyon. Others are easy to find on the grassy Link Flats.

From the turn to the overlook, the trail continues another mile across Link Flats to finish back on the Kimball Draw Trail, 1.6 miles from the start of the loop.

Current Road Information

Emery County Road Department
120 West Highway 29
Castle Dale, UT 84513
(435) 381-2550

BLM Price Field Office
125 South 600 West
Price, UT 84501
(435) 636-3600

Map References

BLM San Rafael Desert (incomplete)
USGS 1:24,000 Copper Globe (incomplete)
1:100,000 San Rafael Desert, (incomplete)
Maptech CD-ROM: Central/San Rafael
Trails Illustrated, #712
Utah Atlas & Gazetteer, p. 38
Other: Recreation Map of the San Rafael Swell and San Rafael Desert

Route Directions

▼ 0.0	On Central #24: Kimball Draw Trail, 15.3 miles from I-70, zero trip meter and turn south on ungraded dirt trail at sign for Link Flats.
1.9 ▲	Trail ends at Central #24: Kimball Draw Trail; turn left for I-70, right for Central #22: Copper Globe Mine Trail.
	GPS: N 38°47.19' W 110°57.38'

A view of the Reds Canyon Trail from Reds Canyon Overlook

Central Trail #23: Reds Canyon Overlook Trail

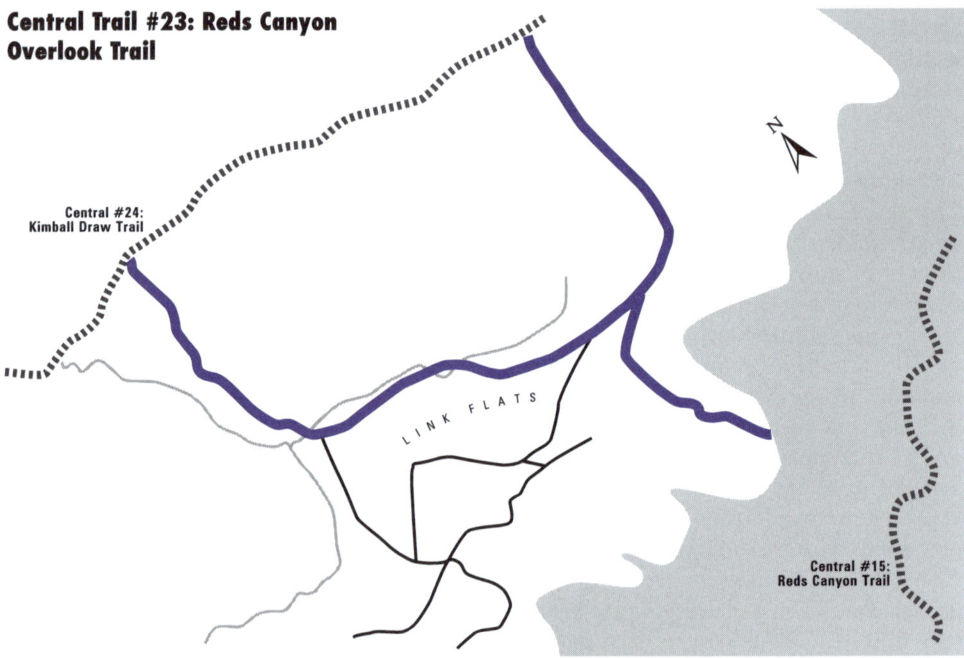

▼ 0.2 SO Cross through small sandy wash.
1.7 ▲ SO Cross through small sandy wash.

▼ 0.3 SO Cross through small sandy wash.
1.6 ▲ SO Cross through small sandy wash.

▼ 0.4 SO Cross through small sandy wash.
1.5 ▲ SO Cross through small sandy wash.

▼ 0.5 SO Cross through sandy wash.
1.4 ▲ SO Cross through sandy wash.

▼ 0.8 BL Track on right goes partway to alternative overlook. Trail is washed out after 0.8 miles.
1.1 ▲ BR Track on left goes partway to alternative overlook. Trail is washed out after 0.8 miles.

GPS: N 38°46.46′ W 110°57.12′

▼ 1.9 TR T-intersection. Take sharp right for spur trail to overlook. Take left to loop back to Kimball Draw Trail. Zero trip meter.
0.0 ▲ Continue the loop back to Kimball Draw Trail.

GPS: N 38°46.24′ W 110°55.86′

Spur Trail to Overlook

▼ 0.0 Continue toward overlook. A large washout immediately past the turn may catch the rear of some vehicles.
▼ 0.5 SO Short rocky climb to overlook.
▼ 0.8 UT Trail reaches overlook on promontory over Reds Canyon. Return to main trail intersection, zero trip meter, and continue straight to finish loop to Kimball Draw Trail.

GPS: N 38°45.72′ W 110°55.78′

Continuation of Loop

▼ 0.0 Continue straight around loop. Track immediately on right goes 0.2 miles to campsite and alternate viewpoint over Reds Canyon.
1.0 ▲ SO Spur trail to overlook is straight ahead. Right continues loop to Kimball Draw Trail. Zero trip meter.

GPS: N 38°46.24′ W 110°55.86′

▼ 0.1 SO Old machinery on right.
0.9 ▲ SO Old machinery on left.

GPS: N 38°46.30′ W 110°55.79′

▼ 0.5 SO Faint track on left.

0.5 ▲ SO Faint track on right.

▼ 0.7 SO Faint track on left, then track on right.

0.3 ▲ BR Bear right at track on left, and then immediately bear left at track on right.

▼ 1.0 Trail ends at Central #24: Kimball Draw Trail; turn left for I-70, right for Central #22: Copper Globe Mine Trail.

0.0 ▲ On Central #24: Kimball Draw Trail, 2.6 miles from junction with Central #22: Copper Globe Mine Trail, zero trip meter and turn south on ungraded, unmarked dirt trail.

GPS: N 38°47.04' W 110°55.66'

CENTRAL REGION TRAIL #24

Kimball Draw Trail

STARTING POINT I-70, exit 105

FINISHING POINT Central #22: Copper Globe Mine Trail

TOTAL MILEAGE 19.5 miles

UNPAVED MILEAGE 19.5 miles

DRIVING TIME 2 hours

ELEVATION RANGE 5,400–7,100 feet

USUALLY OPEN Year-round

DIFFICULTY RATING 4

SCENIC RATING 7

REMOTENESS RATING +1

Special Attractions

- Remote route that travels along two canyons.
- Rockhounding for selenite in Kimball Draw.
- Access to a network of 4WD trails.

Description

This trail loops around in the San Rafael Swell to the south of I-70. It follows the path of two canyons: the gentle Kimball Draw and the narrow, twisting Cat Canyon. The most challenging part of the trail is the very deep, loose sand near the western end of the trail just south of I-70. This section can be several miles long and makes the trail suitable only for 4WD vehicles. It may be necessary to lower tire pressures to avoid getting stuck.

From I-70, exit 105, the trail takes CR 923 south for a few miles, running along Salt Creek, where the worst of the sand is, before turning east to follow Kimball Draw.

Once in Kimball Draw, the gravelly trail surface is firmer and smooth. The trail follows the wash, sometimes traveling along it for long stretches. One bonus for rock hounds is a section of the canyon wall where there are prolific selenite (gypsum) crystals. On sunny days they are easy to spot, as they reflect the sun's rays and can be seen from quite a distance. There are plenty of small crystals on the surface, and larger specimens can be found with a bit of hunting.

The trail climbs gradually out of Kimball Draw, crosses a ridge top with great views west over to Fishlake National Forest, and drops down along some switchbacks into the narrower and deeper Cat Canyon. The descent is along a wide section of trail with a good surface. Once inside Cat Canyon, the trail is tighter and twists within the confines

Looking into Cat Canyon

One of the very sandy sections along the trail

of the walls. The exit out of the canyon has some loose sandy sections, but these are shorter and generally not as difficult as the county road section.

Once out of Cat Canyon, the trail intersects with Central #23: Reds Canyon Overlook Trail, a loop trail that returns to this trail 1.6 miles farther, then it crosses the northern end of Link Flats before following the Cat Canyon wash once again. Sections in the wash could be brushy; drivers of wider vehicles risk scratching their paint. From here, the trail is rockier as it descends to cross over Cat Canyon wash before joining Central #22: Copper Globe Mine Trail near the Sheepherder's End marker, where the trail ends.

Like most trails in the region, this trail is likely to be impassable following heavy rainfall and may wash out after heavy runoff. Snow may temporarily close parts of the trail in winter.

Current Road Information

Emery County Road Department
120 West Highway 29
Castle Dale, UT 84513
(435) 381-2550

BLM Price Field Office
125 South 600 West
Price, UT 84501
(435) 636-3600

Map References

BLM San Rafael Desert, Salina
USGS 1:24,000 Copper Globe, Big Bend Draw
1:100,000 San Rafael Desert, Salina
Maptech CD-ROM: Central/San Rafael
Trails Illustrated, #712
Utah Atlas & Gazetteer, p. 38
Utah Travel Council #5
Other: Recreation Map of the San Rafael Swell and San Rafael Desert

Route Directions

▼ 0.0		From I-70, exit 105, turn southwest on CR 923 and zero trip meter at cattle guard.
5.0 ▲		Trail ends at I-70, exit 105. Turn right for Green River, left for Salina.
		GPS: N 38°50.50' W 111°03.78'
▼ 0.1	TR	Track on left.
4.9 ▲	TL	Track on right.
▼ 0.4	BR	Track on left. Follow the smaller, sandy trail right. From this point the trail is extremely sandy.
4.6 ▲	SO	Track on right. Join larger graded county road, CR 923.
		GPS: N 38°50.16' W 111°03.85'
▼ 0.7	SO	Track on left.
4.3 ▲	SO	Track on right.
▼ 0.9	SO	Cross through sandy wash.
4.1 ▲	SO	Cross through sandy wash.
▼ 1.1	SO	Track on left.
3.9 ▲	SO	Track on right.
▼ 3.2	SO	Cross over wash.
1.8 ▲	SO	Cross over wash.
▼ 3.7	SO	Cross through wash.
1.3 ▲	SO	Cross through wash.
▼ 4.2	SO	Cross through Salt Creek.
0.8 ▲	SO	Cross through Salt Creek.
		GPS: N 38°47.90' W 111°06.01'
▼ 4.5	SO	Cross through small wash.
0.5 ▲	SO	Cross through small wash.
▼ 4.6	SO	Cross through small wash.

0.4 ▲	SO	Cross through small wash.

▼ 4.7	SO	Cross through small wash.
0.3 ▲	SO	Cross through small wash.

▼ 4.8	SO	Cross through wash.
0.2 ▲	SO	Cross through wash.

▼ 5.0	TL	T-intersection. Track on right to Muddy River. Turn left, following sign for Kimball Draw, and zero trip meter.
0.0 ▲		Continue toward I-70. From this point the trail is extremely sandy.
		GPS: N 38°47.29' W 111°05.84'

▼ 0.0		Continue into Kimball Draw.
4.8 ▲	BR	Track ahead to Muddy River. Zero trip meter at intersection.

▼ 0.5	SO	Two faint tracks on left. Enter wash. Trail in or alongside wash, with numerous crossings, for next 5.8 miles.
4.3 ▲	SO	Exit wash. Two faint tracks on right.

▼ 0.6	SO	Cattle trough on left.
4.2 ▲	SO	Cattle trough on right.

▼ 1.4	SO	Track on right.
3.4 ▲	SO	Track on left.
		GPS: N 38°47.08' W 111°04.57'

▼ 4.0	SO	Spring in hollow on left.
0.8 ▲	SO	Spring in hollow on right.
		GPS: N 38°47.80' W 111°02.09'

▼ 4.2	SO	Selenite crystals can be found on both sides of the trail in the canyon walls.
0.6 ▲	SO	Selenite crystals can be found on both sides of the trail in the canyon walls.

▼ 4.8	BL	Well-used track on right. Zero trip meter.
0.0 ▲		Continue along Kimball Draw.
		GPS: N 38°47.85' W 111°01.50'

▼ 0.0		Continue along Kimball Draw.
5.5 ▲	SO	Well-used track on left. Zero trip meter.

▼ 0.4	SO	Faint track on left.
5.1 ▲	SO	Faint track on right.

▼ 1.0	SO	Timber footings and pipes of oil drilling hole on left.
4.5 ▲	SO	Timber footings and pipes of oil drilling hole on right.
		GPS: N 38°47.63' W 111°00.61'

▼ 1.5	SO	Leaving Kimball Draw across ridge top.
4.0 ▲	SO	Trail descends into Kimball Draw and runs in or alongside wash, with numerous crossings for next 5.8 miles.

▼ 2.4	SO	Top of ridge. Views west to Fishlake

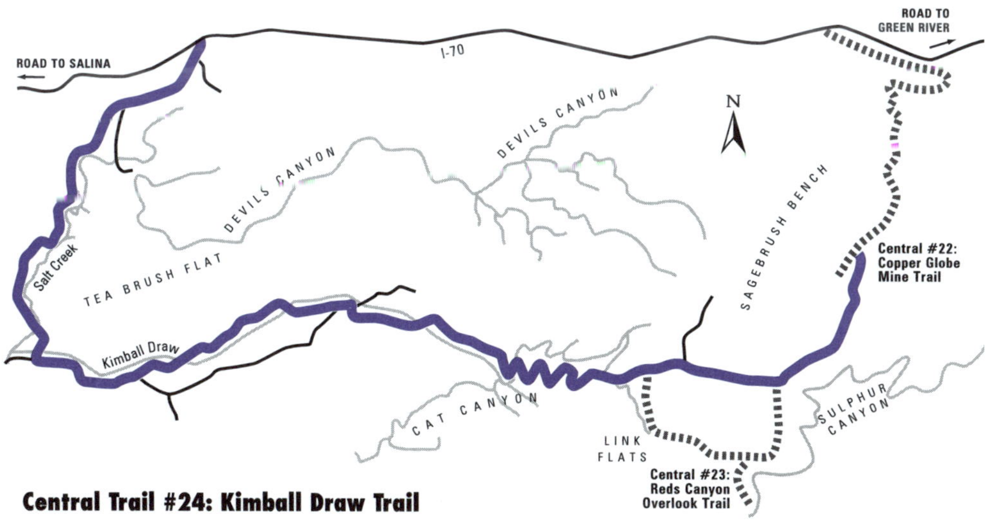

Central Trail #24: Kimball Draw Trail

National Forest. Trail descends into Cat Canyon.

3.1 ▲ SO Top of ridge and end of climb out of Cat Canyon. Views west to Fishlake National Forest.

GPS: N 38°47.31' W 110°59.30'

▼ 2.8 SO Trail follows along the bottom of Cat Canyon in wash.

2.7 ▲ SO Trail climbs out of Cat Canyon.

GPS: N 38°47.23' W 110°59.11'

▼ 3.4 SO Cross through old fence line.

2.1 ▲ SO Cross through old fence line.

▼ 4.5 SO Cattle trough on left.

1.0 ▲ SO Cattle trough on right.

▼ 4.9 SO Track on left.

0.6 ▲ SO Track on right.

▼ 5.4 SO Exit Cat Canyon wash.

0.1 ▲ SO Enter Cat Canyon wash.

▼ 5.5 SO Track on right at sign for Link Flats is western end of Central #23: Reds Canyon Overlook Trail. Zero trip meter.

0.0 ▲ Continue into Cat Canyon.

GPS: N 38°47.19' W 110°57.39'

▼ 0.0 Continue across the northern end of Link Flats.

1.6 ▲ SO Track on left at sign for Link Flats is western end of Central #23: Reds Canyon Overlook Trail. Zero trip meter.

▼ 0.4 SO Cross through wash.

1.2 ▲ SO Cross through wash.

▼ 0.5 SO Cross through wash.

1.1 ▲ SO Cross through wash.

▼ 0.6 SO Faint track on left. Short brushy section along wash.

1.0 ▲ SO Faint track on right.

▼ 1.3 SO Trail leaves wash.

0.3 ▲ SO Trail enters wash. Short brushy section along wash.

▼ 1.6 SO Track on right is eastern end of Central #23: Reds Canyon Overlook Trail. Zero trip meter.

0.0 ▲ Continue along main trail.

GPS: N 38°47.03' W 110°55.67'

▼ 0.0 Continue along main trail.

2.6 ▲ SO Track on left is eastern end of Central #23: Reds Canyon Overlook Trail.

▼ 0.4 BR Swing right on flat rock in front of Cat Canyon.

2.2 ▲ BL Swing left on flat rock in front of Cat Canyon.

GPS: N 38°47.18' W 110°55.23'

▼ 0.6 TL T-intersection. Smaller track on right.

2.0 ▲ TR Turn right on main trail; smaller track straight ahead.

GPS: N 38°47.14' W 110°55.15'

▼ 0.8 SO Cross through Cat Canyon wash. Old dam on left.

1.8 ▲ SO Cross through Cat Canyon wash. Old dam on right.

▼ 1.2 SO Track on left.

1.4 ▲ SO Track on right.

▼ 1.7 SO Cross through the sandy Cat Canyon wash.

0.9 ▲ SO Cross through the sandy Cat Canyon wash.

GPS: N 38°47.70' W 110°54.46'

▼ 2.0 SO Cross through wash.

0.6 ▲ SO Cross through wash.

▼ 2.6 Small track on right, then trail ends at Central #22: Copper Globe Mine Trail near the Sheepherder's End marker. Turn left for Copper Globe Mine, right for I-70.

0.0 ▲ On Central #22: Copper Globe Mine Trail, near the Sheepherder's End marker, zero trip meter and turn south following the sign for Muddy River.

GPS: N 38°48.44' W 110°54.32'

CENTRAL REGION TRAIL #25

Book Cliffs Loop

STARTING POINT I-70, exit 225
FINISHING POINT I-70, exit 225
TOTAL MILEAGE 76.3 miles
UNPAVED MILEAGE 65.9 miles
DRIVING TIME 4 hours
ELEVATION RANGE 4,700–8,400 feet
USUALLY OPEN May to November
DIFFICULTY RATING 1
SCENIC RATING 7
REMOTENESS RATING +2

The inscription by Antoine Robidoux

Special Attractions

- Panoramic views from high elevations.
- An interesting, remote trail through one of America's foremost hydrocarbon fields.

History

In the early 1800s, there were only a few trails leading into the Uinta Basin. Once fur traders discovered this area of eastern Utah, they quickly began trapping in the region. One of the routes followed the Colorado River into eastern Utah and then turned toward the Roan Plateau via Westwater Creek.

It was along this route that Antoine Robidoux, who established Utah's first non-Indian settlement and business, came into the area. He left proof of his passing in the form of a French inscription written on a rock. The translation reads, "Antoine Robidoux passed here November 13, 1837, to establish a house of trade on the Green or Uinta River." However, some scholars disagree as to whether this indicates the Uinta or the White River as there are trading posts (or the remains of buildings thought to have been trading posts) at both places.

From the mid-1900s to the present, Grand and Uintah Counties have both relied heavily on their reserves of natural gas. In 1925, natural gas was discovered in the Ashley Valley Field and provided both Vernal and

A view of the San Arroyo mining camp

Ashley Valley with the valuable fuel. Reserves began to dwindle in the early 1940s, and the Public Service Commission decided to stop piping gas to Uintah County. However, in 1960, the Mountain Fuel Supply Company found other gas reserves in western Uintah County and five years later helped build a pipeline to Bonanza. Today, natural gas production in Utah continues to reach new highs, and it contributes approximately 2 percent of the national average.

Description

This is a very long and remote trail with no facilities along it. Whether you complete the loop or take one of its connecting trails, it is highly recommended that you fill up your tank with gasoline before starting.

The Book Cliffs Loop begins at I-70, exit 225, and proceeds for 8.5 miles along the old US 6, which is a paved but deteriorated road. Moving through grasslands and sagebrush, and after passing the state line into Colorado, the trail then turns northwest onto a wide, country gravel road and heads through Grande Valley toward the Book Cliffs. The elevation at the start of the trail is about 4,700 feet, and along the way you will climb about 3,700 feet higher to the top of the Roan Plateau before coming back down into the valley. The beginning of the trail crosses several well-maintained side roads used by fuel companies for extensive oil and gas exploration in the area.

Leaving the flat ranchlands, the trail begins to run through the canyons, which are filled with saltbush, pinyon, and juniper. Then the trail follows a broad shelf road and gains altitude quickly along a 3.5-mile climb, passing the main regional base for the San Arroyo natural gas operations on the way.

From the high vantage point on top of the plateau, where pinyon pines dominate the immediate landscape, there are great views of the surrounding country. A few miles farther and about halfway along, the trail intersects with Northern #29: Dragon Ghost Town Trail near some radio towers. Information

ANTOINE ROBIDOUX

Antoine Robidoux was born on September 24, 1794, in Florissant, Missouri and grew up in St. Louis. Moving to Santa Fe, he established himself as a prominent fur trader. In 1828, he married Carmel Benevides, the adopted daughter of a Mexican governor. What is now the American Southwest was then still part of Mexico and Robidoux became a citizen of that nation in order to avoid stiff fines and penalties for illegal trading.

Antoine Robidoux

In 1832, Robidoux purchased the Reed Trading Post, renamed it Fort Robidoux (sometimes called Fort Uinta), and expanded his business by bringing in trappers to hunt beavers in the tributaries of the Green and Uintah Rivers. Fort Robidoux became the first permanent non-Indian settlement and business in Utah. In addition to trading with settlers, Robidoux also dabbled in trading horses, illegal guns, and liquor with the local Ute Indians. Never a terribly scrupulous businessman, Robidoux is also rumored to have sold Ute women and children for prostitution and slavery; one account claims he even used the children for target practice.

However immoral Robidoux's business practices may have been, his trading enterprises flourished and he was able to build another trading post in the Uinta Basin. However his success was not without its price. In 1844, Ute Indians attacked and burned both of Robidoux's Utah forts. The reason for the attacks is unclear, but historians speculate that Robidoux's cheating and mistreatment of the Indians angered the Ute. Robidoux retired to St. Louis in 1857 and died there a blind, decrepit man on August 29, 1860.

about this trail can be found in *4WD Trails: Northern Utah*. Broad, panoramic views continue to unfold in all directions as you drive from here, and 7 miles later another intersection leads to Northern #28: Rainbow and Watson Ghost Towns Trail, which can be found in *4WD Trails: Northern Utah*.

The last leg of the Book Cliffs Loop runs down through Hay Canyon along a broad shelf road with plenty of room to allow passing. The dusty surface can sometimes become slippery, but usually it is an easy, 1-rated road. From the intersection before Hay Canyon, the trail descends sharply, dropping over 1,000 feet in 2 miles along steep canyon walls dotted with pine trees. Toward the end of the trail, a side trail leads about 75 yards to a corral, where you can see the rock with the inscription by fur trader and explorer Antoine Robidoux. However, the inscription is on private property, so don't go into the corral or cross the fence line to get a closer look.

Current Road Information

BLM Moab Field Office
82 East Dogwood
Moab, UT 84532
(435) 259-2100

Map References

BLM Westwater
USGS 1:24,000 Harley Dome, Bitter Creek Well, Bar X Wash, Bryson Canyon, San Arroyo Ridge, Jim Canyon, PR Spring, Cedar Camp Canyon, Preacher Canyon, Dry Canyon
1:100,000 Westwater
Maptech CD-ROM: High Uinta/Flaming Gorge
Utah Atlas & Gazetteer, pp. 41, 49
Utah Travel Council #5 (incomplete)

Route Directions

▼ 0.0 On I-70, take exit 225 (marked "Westwater") toward the Book Cliffs. Zero trip meter at the intersection of the entry/exit ramps and the underpass on the north side of the freeway.
8.5 ▲ Trail ends at I-70, exit 225; turn right for Crescent Junction, left for Colorado.
GPS: N 39°10.50' W 109°07.66'

▼ 0.2 TR Turn north onto Old Highway 6 (Harley Dome to State Line Road), which parallels I-70 for a while.
8.3 ▲ TL Turn left at intersection.

▼ 2.4 SO Intersection with other end of the Book Cliffs Loop.
6.1 ▲ SO Track on right is the Book Cliffs Loop.
GPS: N 39°12.24' W 109°06.85'

▼ 3.1 SO Cross bridge.
5.4 ▲ SO Cross bridge.

▼ 4.4 SO Cross bridge.
4.1 ▲ SO Cross bridge.

▼ 5.6 SO Cross bridge.
2.9 ▲ SO Cross bridge.

▼ 5.7 SO State line marker; cross Utah/Colorado border.
2.8 ▲ SO State line marker; cross Utah/Colorado border.
GPS: N 39°12.39' W 109°03.05'

▼ 8.5 TL Turn north on gravel road and zero trip meter.
0.0 ▲ Continue southwest.
GPS: N 39°14.13' W 109°00.89'

▼ 0.0 Continue north.
9.8 ▲ TR Turn southwest on Old Highway 6 and zero trip meter.

▼ 1.0 SO Track on right.
8.7 ▲ SO Track on left.

▼ 4.1 SO Cross through fence line at Colorado/Utah border. Road on right.
5.7 ▲ SO Road on left. Cross through fence line at Colorado/Utah border.
GPS: N 39°17.20' W 109°03.02'

▼ 4.8 SO Cross through wash.
5.0 ▲ SO Cross through wash.

▼ 5.7 SO Road on left.
4.0 ▲ SO Road on right.

▼ 8.7 SO Track on right.
1.0 ▲ SO Track on left.

▼ 9.6 SO Road on left.
0.1 ▲ SO Road on right.

▼ 9.8 BR Fork in road. Zero trip meter.
0.0 ▲ Continue along main road.
GPS: N 39°19.88' W 109°08.43'

▼ 0.0 Continue along track.
5.7 ▲ BL Road enters on right. Zero trip meter.

▼ 0.1 SO Track on right.
5.6 ▲ SO Track on left.

▼ 0.2 SO Track on left.
5.5 ▲ SO Track on right.

▼ 0.3 SO Track on right.
5.3 ▲ SO Track on left.

▼ 0.5 SO Road on right.
5.2 ▲ SO Road on left.

▼ 0.9 SO Cross through Bitter Creek Wash.
4.7 ▲ SO Cross through Bitter Creek Wash.

▼ 1.4 SO Track on left.
4.3 ▲ SO Track on right.

▼ 1.9 SO Track on left.
3.8 ▲ SO Track on right.

▼ 2.3 SO Track on left.
3.3 ▲ SO Track on right.

▼ 2.8 SO Road on left.
2.9 ▲ SO Road on right.
GPS: N 39°21.97' W 109°08.18'

▼ 3.1 SO Track on left.
2.6 ▲ SO Track on right.

▼ 3.5 SO Track on right.
2.1 ▲ SO Track on left.

▼ 4.3 SO Track on right.
1.4 ▲ SO Track on left.
GPS: N 39°23.04' W 109°07.67'

▼ 5.0 SO Track on right.
0.6 ▲ SO Track on left.

▼ 5.4 SO Track on left.
0.2 ▲ SO Track on right.

▼ 5.7 BL Fork in road. San Arroyo Gas Plant truck loading station on right. Zero trip meter.
0.0 ▲ Continue along main trail.
GPS: N 39°24.08' W 109°07.48'

▼ 0.0 Proceed uphill.
7.4 ▲ BR Track enters on left. Zero trip meter.

▼ 0.3 SO The main San Arroyo Gas Plant on left.
7.1 ▲ SO The main San Arroyo Gas Plant on right.

▼ 1.5 SO Track on right to mining works.
5.9 ▲ SO Track on left to mining works.

▼ 2.6 UT Intersection. U-turn right.
4.7 ▲ UT U-turn left.

▼ 3.3 BL Track on right to gas well.
4.0 ▲ BR Track on left to gas well.

▼ 3.5 SO Track on right. Proceed downhill.
3.9 ▲ SO Track on left.
GPS: N 39°24.14' W 109°08.89'

▼ 4.3 BR Switchback past oil well facility on left.
3.0 ▲ BL Switchback past oil well facility on right.

▼ 4.4 SO Road on left.
3.0 ▲ SO Road on right.

▼ 4.6 BR Track on left.
2.8 ▲ SO Track on right.

▼ 5.3 SO Track on left.
2.0 ▲ SO Track on right.
GPS: N 39°25.06' W 109°09.32'

▼ 7.2 SO Cattle guard.
0.2 ▲ SO Cattle guard.

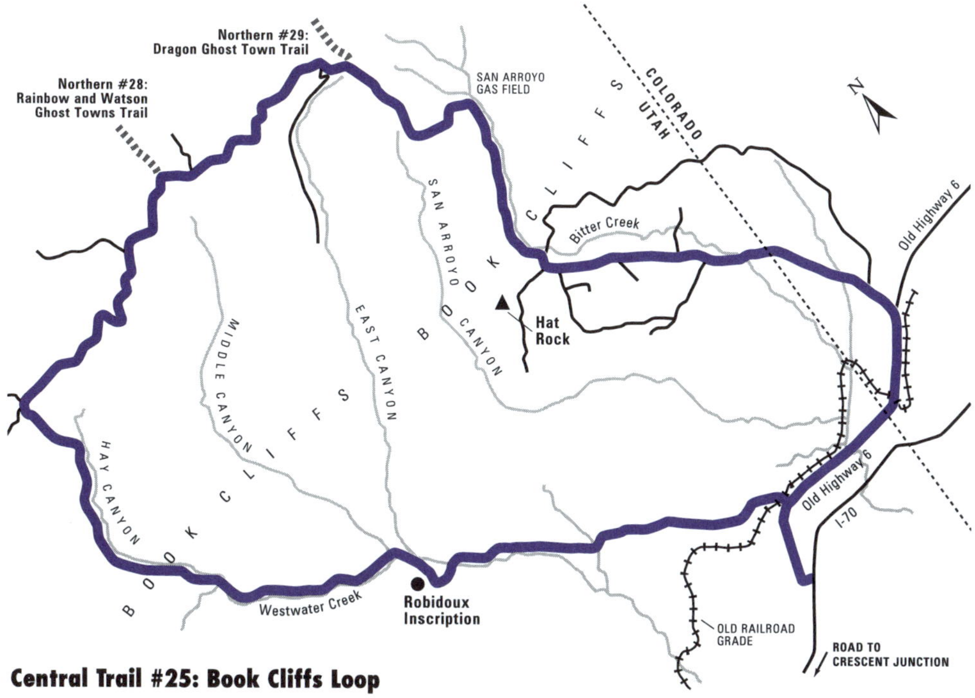

Central Trail #25: Book Cliffs Loop

▼ 7.4 SO Intersection. Road on right is Northern #29: Dragon Ghost Town Trail *(4WD Trails: Northern Utah)*, signed to Atchee Ridge and McCook Ridge. Road on left to radio tower. Zero trip meter in the middle of intersection.

0.0 ▲ Proceed straight across toward San Arroyo and Grand Junction.

GPS: N 39°26.59' W 109°09.84'

▼ 0.0 Proceed straight across toward PR Spring and Ouray.

7.1 ▲ SO Road on right to radio tower. Road on left is Northern #29: Dragon Ghost Town Trail *(4WD Trails: Northern Utah)*, signed to Atchee Ridge and McCook Ridge. Zero trip meter in the middle of intersection.

▼ 0.5 SO Intersection. Road on left to East Canyon. Proceed straight along Seep Ridge Road.

6.6 ▲ SO Road on right to East Canyon.

GPS: N 39°26.87' W 109°10.27'

▼ 1.4 SO Track on right.

5.6 ▲ SO Track on left.

▼ 2.7 SO Track on right.

4.4 ▲ SO Track on left.

▼ 3.0 SO Track on right.

4.0 ▲ SO Track on left.

▼ 3.6 SO Gas well on left.

3.5 ▲ SO Gas well on right.

▼ 4.4 SO Tracks on left and right.

2.7 ▲ SO Tracks on right and left.

GPS: N 39°26.77' W 109°13.91'

▼ 5.0 BR Road and radio tower on left.

2.0 ▲ BL Road and radio tower on right.

▼ 5.5 SO Cattle guard. Corral and track on right.

1.6 ▲ SO Corral and track on left. Cattle guard.

▼ 6.1 SO Road on right to South Canyon and Sweetwater Canyon.

1.0 ▲ SO Road on left to South Canyon and Sweetwater Canyon.

▼ 6.5 SO Track on right to Black Horse Canyon; it ends in 6 miles.
0.5 ▲ SO Track on left to Black Horse Canyon; it ends in 6 miles.

GPS: N 39°26.91′ W 109°15.90′

▼ 7.1 TL Intersection. Turn left, following sign to Winter Ridge Junction, and zero trip meter. Straight is Northern #28: Rainbow and Watson Ghost Towns Trail *(4WD Trails: Northern Utah)*, which also leads to Seep Ridge Road and Ouray.
0.0 ▲ Continue along trail.

GPS: N 39°27.14′ W 109°16.43′

▼ 0.0 Continue toward Winter Ridge Junction.
8.9 ▲ TR Intersection. Turn right to McCook Ridge and zero trip meter. Left is Northern #28: Rainbow and Watson Ghost Towns Trail *(4WD Trails: Northern Utah)*.

▼ 1.0 SO Track on left.
7.9 ▲ SO Track on right.

▼ 2.6 SO Cross cattle guard.
6.2 ▲ SO Cross cattle guard.

▼ 3.2 SO Eroded track on right.
5.6 ▲ SO Track on left.

▼ 5.5 SO Track on right.
3.4 ▲ SO Track on left.

▼ 5.8 SO Gas well on right.
3.1 ▲ SO Gas well on left.

▼ 5.9 SO Track on right.
2.9 ▲ SO Track on left.

▼ 6.7 SO Track on left.
2.1 ▲ SO Track on right.

▼ 8.0 SO Cross cattle guard.
0.9 ▲ SO Cross cattle guard.

▼ 8.5 BL Road forks.
0.4 ▲ SO Road on left.

▼ 8.6 SO Road on right.
0.3 ▲ BR Road forks.

▼ 8.8 BL Road on right.
0.1 ▲ SO Road on left.

▼ 8.9 TL Intersection. Straight ahead is Cedar Camp and Steer Ridge. Right to Winter Ridge and Bull Canyon. Zero trip meter.
0.0 ▲ Proceed toward Seep Ridge.

GPS: N 39°24.98′ W 109°23.90′

▼ 0.0 Continue along trail toward Hay Canyon and I-70.
14.4 ▲ TR Intersection. Straight is Winter Ridge and Bull Canyon. Left is Cedar Camp, and Steer Ridge. Zero trip meter.

▼ 2.2 SO Track on left.
12.2 ▲ SO Track on right.

▼ 5.2 SO Track on right.
9.2 ▲ SO Track on left.

▼ 6.0 SO Cross cattle guard.
8.4 ▲ SO Cross cattle guard.

▼ 8.0 SO Cross through large wash.
6.4 ▲ SO Cross through large wash.

▼ 8.5 SO Two tracks on right.
5.9 ▲ SO Two tracks on left.

▼ 9.0 SO Cattle guard.
5.4 ▲ SO Cattle guard.

▼ 9.4 SO Cross through creek. The trail crosses Westwater Creek and its tributaries many times over next 2.0 miles.
5.0 ▲ SO Cross through creek.

▼ 9.6 SO Cross through creek.
4.8 ▲ SO Cross through creek.

▼ 10.8 SO Cross through creek.
3.6 ▲ SO Cross through creek.

▼ 11.4 SO Cross through creek.
3.0 ▲ SO Cross through creek. The trail crosses

Westwater Creek and its tributaries many times over next 2.0 miles.

▼ 12.0 SO Track on left.
2.4 ▲ BL Track on right.

▼ 13.9 TR Intersection. Left goes to Middle Canyon
0.5 ▲ TL Straight goes to Middle Canyon. Continue toward Hay Canyon.

▼ 14.1 SO Cross through creek.
0.3 ▲ SO Cross through creek.

▼ 14.4 SO Cross cattle guard, then intersection; zero trip meter. Left to East Canyon. Right leads to Antoine Robidoux inscription on rock by a corral (private property) against the canyon wall.
0.0 ▲ Continue along trail.

GPS: N 39°16.56' W 109°17.13'

▼ 0.0 Continue along trail.
14.5 ▲ SO Intersection; zero trip meter. Continue straight to Hay Canyon, right to East Canyon. Left to Antoine Robidoux inscription on rock by a corral (private property) against canyon wall.

▼ 0.7 SO Track on right.
13.8 ▲ SO Track on left.

▼ 1.0 SO Cattle guard.
13.4 ▲ SO Cattle guard.

▼ 1.4 SO Cattle guard.
13.0 ▲ SO Cattle guard.

▼ 1.8 SO Cross through creek.
12.7 ▲ SO Cross through creek.

▼ 2.2 SO Cross through wash, then gas plant on right.
12.2 ▲ SO Gas plant on left, then cross through wash.

▼ 4.1 SO Cattle guard, then cross through large wash.
10.3 ▲ SO Cross through large wash, then cattle guard.

▼ 4.4 SO Road on right.
10.1 ▲ SO Road on left.

▼ 6.3 BL Road on right.
8.1 ▲ BR Road on left.

GPS: N 39°14.04' W 109°12.30'

▼ 6.7 BR Road to Bryson Ridge and San Arroyo Canyon on left.
7.8 ▲ BL Bear left toward Hay Canyon.

▼ 10.3 SO Dirt road on left.
4.1 ▲ SO Dirt road on right.

▼ 12.1 TR Intersection with Old Highway 6.
2.3 ▲ TL Turn left onto road.

GPS: N 39°12.24' W 109°06.85'

▼ 14.3 TL Turn left toward I-70.
0.2 ▲ TR Turn right onto Old Highway 6.

GPS: N 39°10.59' W 109°07.89'

▼ 14.5 Trail ends at I-70, exit 225. Turn right for Crescent Junction, left for Colorado.
0.0 ▲ On I-70, take exit 225 (marked "Westwater") toward the Book Cliffs. Zero trip meter at the intersection of the entry/exit ramps and the underpass on the north side of freeway.

GPS: N 39°10.50' W 109°07.66'

CENTRAL REGION TRAIL #26

Sego Ghost Town Trail

STARTING POINT I-70 at Thompson Springs, exit 185
FINISHING POINT Gate at Uintah and Ouray Indian Reservation
TOTAL MILEAGE 15.1 miles
UNPAVED MILEAGE 11 miles
DRIVING TIME 1.25 hours (one-way)
ELEVATION RANGE 5,100–8,400 feet
USUALLY OPEN Year-round (as far as Sego ghost town)
DIFFICULTY RATING 2
SCENIC RATING 9
REMOTENESS RATING +1

Special Attractions

- Rock art panels.
- Sego ghost town and the old railroad grade.
- Connects with Central #28: Sagers Canyon Trail and Central #27: Floy Wash Trail.
- Panoramic views.

History

This trail starts in the small town of Thompson Springs, which sits at the mouth of Thompson Canyon near a natural spring. The land at this favorable location was originally purchased by brothers Harry and Arthur P. Ballard in the 1880s; they then laid out and promoted the town. With its water supplies and the successful coal mining operations at nearby Sego, it was for a time an important railroad stop.

A few miles north of Thompson Springs, both pictographs and petroglyphs of three Indian cultures can be found on the walls of Sego Canyon. The BLM acquired the panels in 1993 and has begun efforts to preserve them. They contain Barrier Canyon style art, which dates from 500 B.C. to A.D. 500; Fremont Indian art, which dates from A.D. 1000 to 1150; and Ute Indian pictographs from the 19th century. The Ute consider the area sacred.

Named for Utah's state flower, the sego lily, Sego was a coal mining town whose boom-and-bust history was repeated many times in Utah. After Harry Ballard discovered coal here in the early 1890s, he bought up the land and started mining operations on a small scale. Soon after, he sold his business to Salt Lake City investors who built a store, a boardinghouse, and other buildings as part of a grand plan for a long run of coal production. Sego grew to nearly 500 residents, and the Denver & Rio Grande Railroad built a subsidiary railroad from the Thompson Springs station to the mines. Although Sego's mines were productive for many years, a series of mining disasters and financial mismanagement eventually doomed the operation. Production ceased in 1947, and the property was sold at auction. Today, several original structures still stand in the ghost town of Sego.

The old boardinghouse at Sego ghost town

Description

The Sego Ghost Town Trail may be short, but it makes up in beauty and historical interest what it lacks in length. This trail makes an easy side trip along I-70 if you want to take in some local scenery and don't have much time.

From I-70, exit 185, Thompson Springs is about three-quarters of a mile north. As you drive through town, you cross a railroad line with a small station and pass by many buildings that have seen better days. One of the more interesting buildings in Thompson is the tiny, pink post office at the railroad

One of the panels of pictographs along the trail

crossing; it looks as if it were built in miniature.

After about 4 miles, you come to a small parking area on the left with some information boards and public toilets. From here you can walk to the panels of Indian rock art that adorn some of the surrounding canyon walls. There is also rock art on the right of the trail beside the cattle guard. As you continue along the trail through the canyon, you cross the main wash many times. About a half mile beyond the petroglyphs, you reach the intersection with Central #27: Floy Wash Trail and, a little farther, Central #28: Sagers Canyon Trail.

As you approach the ruins of Sego, you pass by a railroad cutting and an old cemetery. Sego still has a couple of buildings standing above their foundations, including the stone general store, which remains in pretty good shape. Across from it, the old saloon/boardinghouse is not holding up as well, but you can still make out its basic structure.

The sign indicating the boundary of the Uintah and Ouray Reservation at the end of the trail

About 1.2 miles past the ghost town, the trail drops into the wash, traveling along it for about 2 miles up Sego Canyon. Navigation in the canyon is not an issue, as there are no real side trails.

Toward the end, the trail climbs easy, 1-rated switchbacks out of the canyon. The road is wide and maintained and could easily take passenger cars. At the end of the climb, the road heads west across a saddle with views south of Sego Canyon, and then it ends at a gate into the Uintah and Ouray Indian Reservation. No trespassing is allowed beyond this point.

Overall, the Sego Ghost Town Trail is a varied but easy trail. It offers impressive views of the Book Cliffs and travels through vegetation ranging from saltbush in the canyon to aspen, pinyon, and juniper in the mountains. The trail itself is rather smooth, though some rocky sections and variable levels of water in the washes (depending on the recent weather) could pose minor difficulties.

Current Road Information

BLM Moab Field Office
82 East Dogwood
Moab, UT 84532
(435) 259-2100

Map References

BLM Moab, Westwater
USGS 1:24,000 Thompson Springs, Sego Canyon, Bogart Canyon
1:100,000 Moab, Westwater
Maptech CD-ROM: Moab/Canyonlands; High Uinta/Flaming Gorge
Utah Atlas & Gazetteer, p. 40
Utah Travel Council #3; #5

Route Directions

▼ 0.0		On I-70, take exit 185 and zero trip meter at intersection of the entry/exit ramps and the underpass on north side of highway. Proceed north on SSR 94 toward Thompson Springs. **GPS: N 38°57.80' W 109°43.30'**
▼ 0.1	BR	Intersection.
▼ 0.8	SO	Two stop signs. Cross Thompson Springs railroad tracks.
▼ 0.9	SO	Post office on left. Then bear left where the road forks.
▼ 1.2	BL	Road on right. Follow BLM sign toward Sego Canyon.
▼ 2.1	SO	Road on right.
▼ 4.1	SO	Two washes with short, unmarked track on left between them. Track leads to numerous pictographs and

petroglyphs with BLM information boards.

▼ 4.2 SO Cattle guard. Further rock art panels are down a track on right immediately prior to cattle guard.

▼ 4.3 SO Cross wash. Note old railway bridge on right.

▼ 4.4 SO Cross through wash.

▼ 4.5 SO Cross through wash. Then track on right to old building and railroad cutting; track rejoins at the turnoff to Central #28: Sagers Canyon Trail.

GPS: N 39°01.42′ W 109°42.71′

▼ 4.6 TR Turn right toward Sego Canyon. Left is Central #27: Floy Wash Trail.

GPS: N 39°01.49′ W 109°42.73′

▼ 4.7 SO Cemetery on right.

GPS: N 39°01.41′ W 109°42.59′

▼ 4.8 SO Track on right is Central #28: Sagers Canyon Trail.

GPS: N 39°01.45′ W 109°42.51′

▼ 5.3 SO Cross through wash.

▼ 5.4 SO Cross through wash. Railway bridge on right and old structures on left.

▼ 5.5 SO Cross through wash. Railway bridge on left.

▼ 5.6 SO Buildings on right and left are remains of Sego. Stone building on right was the company/general store. Wooden building on left was the old boardinghouse. Zero trip meter between buildings.

GPS: N 39°02.03′ W 109°42.16′

▼ 0.0 Continue along main trail.

▼ 0.4 SO Cross through wash. Stone foundation on left.

▼ 0.5 SO Track on left ends in about 100 yards from where you can see old houses and foundations in the overgrowth if you look over the edge of the hill toward the main road.

GPS: N 39°02.40′ W 109°42.09′

▼ 0.6 SO Cross through wash.

▼ 0.7 SO Cross through wash.

▼ 1.2 SO Cattle guard.

▼ 3.3 SO Cross through large wash.

▼ 7.7 SO Travel along a ridgeline with views.

GPS: N 39°07.86′ W 109°42.64′

▼ 9.5 Sego hiking and horse trail on left (open May to November). Then trail ends at gate to the Uintah and Ouray Indian Reservation.

GPS: N 39°08.98′ W 109°43.00′

Central Trail #26: Sego Ghost Town Trail

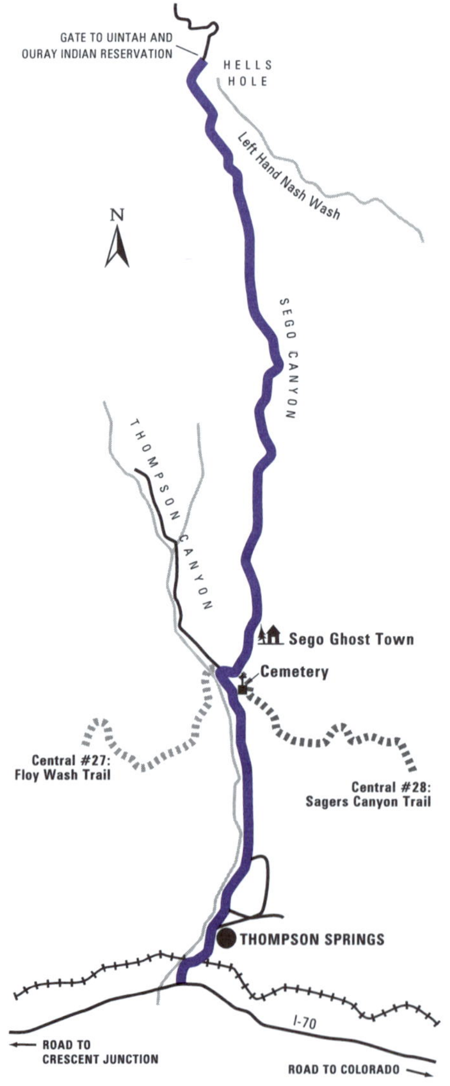

Floy Wash Trail

STARTING POINT Central #26: Sego Ghost Town Trail
FINISHING POINT I-70, exit 173 (11 miles east of Green River)
TOTAL MILEAGE 23.3 miles
UNPAVED MILEAGE 23 miles
DRIVING TIME 1.75 hours
ELEVATION RANGE 4,600–6,000 feet
USUALLY OPEN Year-round
DIFFICULTY RATING 2
SCENIC RATING 8
REMOTENESS RATING +0

Special Attractions

- Spectacular views from the edge of the Book Cliffs.
- Forms a loop trail off of I-70 when combined with Central #26: Sego Ghost Town Trail.

History

During the construction of the Denver & Rio Grande Western Railroad through eastern Utah, Floy Station (also called Little Grande Station) served as a construction camp for the workers. The town is located just west of Crescent Junction on I-70, which follows the same route as the railroad.

Over the years, people have attempted to mine various minerals around Floy. A small gold discovery was made along the Floy Wash in 1929, though it did not amount to much. Manganese mining proved to be more successful; the Colorado Fuel and Iron Company ran a manganese mill and mining camp at Floy Station for many years.

Description

The Floy Wash Trail departs Central #26: Sego Ghost Town Trail at the 4.6-mile mark through sandy soil and thick juniper. The wide, single-lane, 2-rated road is periodically graded. You loop around the heads of deep canyons, which cut through the edge of the Book Cliffs and offer distant views through the canyons, across Crescent Flat, and into the San Rafael Desert far below. Initially, the road follows the upper rim of the Book Cliffs, which rise over 1,000 feet above the flat country to the south.

For the last 10 to 12 miles, the trail follows a wide, well-maintained two-lane road, though there are some deep sandy sections

A view along Blaze Canyon through the Book Cliffs to the flats below

A sandy crossing of Floy Wash

that are potential hazards if the road is wet.

Near the end, the trail emerges from a somewhat narrow canyon into wide ranchland. After driving through the broad flatland, the canyon once again narrows before opening up into a vast expanse of flat grassland that stretches for miles.

Current Road Information

BLM Moab Field Office
82 East Dogwood
Moab, UT 84532
(435) 259-2100

Map References

BLM Westwater, Moab
USGS 1:24,000 Sego Canyon, Crescent Junction, Floy Canyon South, Hutch Mesa
1:100,000 Westwater, Moab
Maptech CD-ROM: High Uinta/Flaming Gorge; Moab/Canyonlands
Utah Atlas & Gazetteer, p. 40
Utah Travel Council #3; #5

Route Directions

▼ 0.0 On Central #26: Sego Ghost Town Trail, 4.6 miles from I-70, zero trip meter and take left trail. Note that straight goes to Thompson Canyon and right goes to Sego.

10.6 ▲ Trail ends at Central #26: Sego Ghost Town Trail; go straight for Sego, right for I-70.

GPS: N 39°01.49' W 109°42.73'

▼ 0.1 SO Cross through wash.
10.5 ▲ SO Cross through wash.

▼ 0.4 SO Cross through wash.
10.1 ▲ SO Cross through wash.

▼ 0.6 SO Cross through gate and leave it as you found it.
10.0 ▲ SO Cross through gate and leave it as you found it.

GPS: N 39°01.15' W 109°42.90'

▼ 2.1 SO Track on left.
8.4 ▲ SO Track on right.

GPS: N 39°00.30' W 109°43.97'

▼ 2.6 SO Track on left.
8.0 ▲ SO Track on right.

▼ 2.7 SO Cross through gate and leave it as you found it.
7.9 ▲ SO Cross through gate and leave it as you found it.

GPS: N 39°00.57' W 109°44.37'

▼ 3.1 SO Cross through wash.
7.5 ▲ SO Cross through wash.

▼ 3.3 SO Track on right.
7.3 ▲ SO Track on left.

▼ 3.3 SO Cross through wash.
7.2 ▲ SO Cross through wash.

▼ 3.4 SO Old cabin on right. Cross through gate.
7.1 ▲ SO Cross through gate. Old cabin on left.

▼ 3.5 SO Cross through wash.
7.1 ▲ SO Cross through wash.

▼ 3.7 SO Cross through wash.
6.9 ▲ SO Cross through wash.

▼ 3.8 SO Cross through gate.
6.7 ▲ SO Cross through gate.

▼ 4.2 SO Cross through wash.
6.4 ▲ SO Cross through wash.

▼ 5.1 SO Cross through wash.
5.5 ▲ SO Cross through wash.

▼ 5.4 SO Cross through gate and leave it as you found it.
5.2 ▲ SO Cross through gate and leave it as you found it.

GPS: N 38°59.83′ W 109°45.66′

▼ 6.5 SO Cross through wash.
4.1 ▲ SO Cross through wash.

▼ 7.6 SO Cross through wash.
3.0 ▲ SO Cross through wash.

▼ 8.7 SO Cross through wash.
1.9 ▲ SO Cross through wash.

▼ 9.3 SO Cross through wash.
1.3 ▲ SO Cross through wash.

▼ 9.9 SO Cross through wash.
0.7 ▲ SO Cross through wash.

▼ 10.2 SO Track on right.
0.3 ▲ SO Track on left.

▼ 10.6 TR Intersection. Zero trip meter.
0.0 ▲ Continue along trail.

GPS: N 39°00.29′ W 109°48.26′

▼ 0.0 Continue along trail.
3.8 ▲ TL Intersection. Zero trip meter.

▼ 0.7 SO Cross through wash.
3.0 ▲ SO Cross through wash.

▼ 1.1 SO Cross through washes.
2.7 ▲ SO Cross through washes.

▼ 1.3 SO Cattle guard.
2.4 ▲ SO Cattle guard.

▼ 2.0 SO Track on left.
1.8 ▲ SO Track on right.

▼ 3.5 SO Cross through wash.
0.3 ▲ SO Cross through wash.

▼ 3.8 TL Intersection. Zero trip meter.
0.0 ▲ Continue along trail.

GPS: N 39°00.92′ W 109°50.67′

▼ 0.0 Continue along trail.
5.3 ▲ BR Turn onto track on right. Zero trip meter.

▼ 0.2 SO Cross through wash.
5.1 ▲ SO Cross through wash.

▼ 0.3 SO Corral on right.
4.9 ▲ SO Corral on left.

▼ 0.4 SO Cross through Floy Wash several times over next mile.
4.8 ▲ SO Cross through wash.

Central Trail #27: Floy Wash Trail

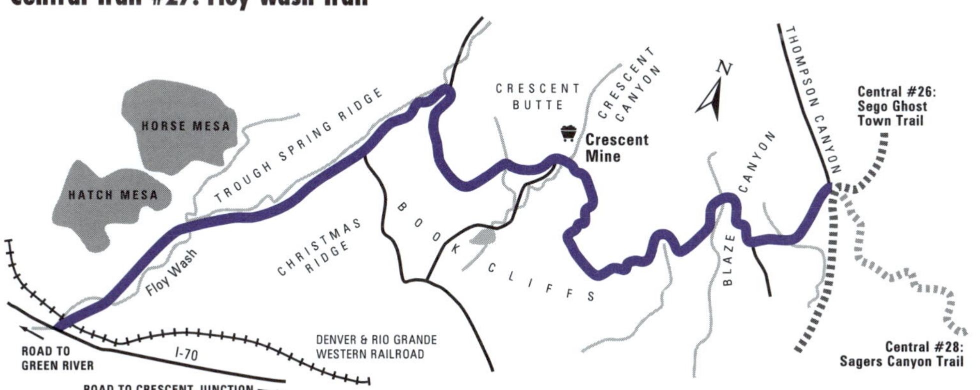

▼ 0.6 SO Cross through wash.
4.7 ▲ SO Cross through wash.

▼ 0.7 SO Cross through wash.
4.6 ▲ SO Cross through wash.

▼ 1.4 SO Cross through wash.
3.9 ▲ SO Cross through Floy Wash several times over next mile.

▼ 2.0 BR Road forks.
3.3 ▲ SO Road on right.

GPS: N 38°59.63' W 109°51.87'

▼ 4.2 SO Cattle guard.
1.1 ▲ SO Cattle guard.

GPS: N 38°58.15' W 109°53.34'

▼ 5.3 BL Cross through wash with very sandy road surface. Then left at fork in road. Zero trip meter.
0.0 ▲ Continue along trail.

GPS: N 38°57.71' W 109°54.41'

▼ 0.0 Continue along trail.
3.6 ▲ BR Road on left. Cross through wash with very sandy road surface. Zero trip meter.

▼ 0.3 SO Cross through washes.
3.3 ▲ SO Cross through washes.

▼ 1.6 SO Cattle guard.
2.0 ▲ SO Cattle guard.

▼ 2.4 SO Cross through wash.
1.2 ▲ SO Cross through wash.

▼ 2.5 SO Track on right.
1.1 ▲ SO Track on left.

▼ 3.0 SO Cross railroad tracks. Then track on left; bear right.
0.6 ▲ SO Track on right, then bear left across railroad tracks.

GPS: N 38°55.50' W 109°56.14'

▼ 3.3 TL Cross through fence line. Then intersection. Turn onto paved frontage road.
0.3 ▲ TR Road on left. Turn onto unpaved road and follow sign to Floy Canyon.

GPS: N 38°55.34' W 109°56.38'

▼ 3.5 SO Cattle guard.
0.1 ▲ SO Cattle guard.

▼ 3.6 Trail ends at I-70, exit 173; turn right for Green River, left for Crescent Junction.
0.0 ▲ On I-70, take exit 173 and zero trip meter at intersection of exit/entry ramps and highway overpass on north side. Proceed north before turning west on frontage road.

GPS: N 38°55.31' W 109°56.09'

CENTRAL REGION TRAIL #28

Sagers Canyon Trail

STARTING POINT Central #26: Sego Ghost Town Trail
FINISHING POINT I-70, exit 190
TOTAL MILEAGE 14.9 miles
UNPAVED MILEAGE 14 miles
DRIVING TIME 1.25 hours
ELEVATION RANGE 4,800–6,000 feet
USUALLY OPEN Year-round
DIFFICULTY RATING 2
SCENIC RATING 7
REMOTENESS RATING +1

Special Attractions

- Interesting, remote trail.
- Combined with Central #26: Sego Ghost Town Trail, it forms a loop trail off I-70.

History

Like Floy Station, Sagers Station was a railroad camp along the Denver & Rio Grande Western Railroad's line across eastern Utah. The station was located about seven miles east of Thompson Springs but has since disappeared. There is, however, a local legend about a Japanese cook who was murdered for a cache of money he was thought to have buried somewhere in the area. The money

A view of the trail as it winds around to cross Sagers Canyon

was never found, and local legend has it that it may still lie buried somewhere in the vicinity of Sagers Station or Sagers Canyon.

Description

From Central #26: Sego Ghost Town Trail at the 4.8-mile mark, the Sagers Canyon Trail runs along an occasionally graded road. If it has rained recently, you may need to carefully negotiate some rough mud holes. Also, the first part of the trail contains a number of washes—only the most conspicuous have been marked in the route directions.

After 7.2 miles, you begin a steep descent and enjoy some spectacular views as the trail switchbacks to the canyon floor. Driving along the bottom of the narrow canyons, the trail again crosses a number of washes. Carry on through the sagebrush and juniper until you reach the end of the trail at I-70, exit 190. Sagers Station was located about a mile east of where you cross under the railway line.

Current Road Information

BLM Moab Field Office
82 East Dogwood
Moab, UT 84532
(435) 259-2100

Map References

BLM Westwater, Moab
USGS 1:24,000 Sego Canyon, Calf Canyon, Sagers Flat
1:100,000 Westwater, Moab
Maptech CD-ROM: High Uinta/Flaming Gorge; Moab/Canyonlands
Utah Atlas & Gazetteer, p. 40
Utah Travel Council #3; #5

Route Directions

▼ 0.0		On Central #26: Sego Ghost Town Trail, 4.8 miles from I-70, zero trip meter and turn right on side road. Take the left fork and cross through wash.
9.8 ▲		Trail ends at Central #26: Sego Ghost Town Trail; turn right for Sego, left for I-70.
		GPS: N 39°01.45' W 109°42.51'
▼ 0.1	SO	Cross through old fence line.
9.7 ▲	SO	Cross through old fence line.
▼ 0.2	SO	Cross through wash, then cross through gate.
9.5 ▲	SO	Cross through gate, then cross through wash.

Central Trail #28: Sagers Canyon Trail

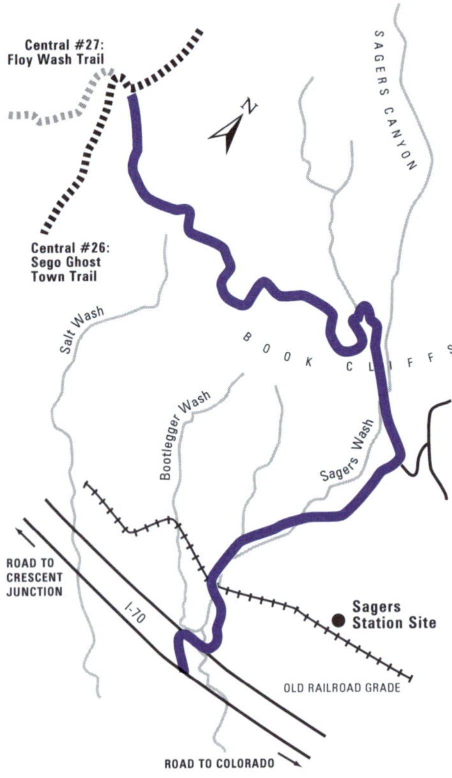

▼ 0.6 SO Cross through wash.
9.1 ▲ SO Cross through wash.

▼ 0.7 SO Cross through wash.
9.0 ▲ SO Cross through wash.

▼ 1.1 SO Track on right.
8.7 ▲ SO Track on left.

▼ 2.7 SO Cross through wash.
7.0 ▲ SO Cross through wash.

▼ 2.8 SO Cross through gate.
6.9 ▲ SO Cross through gate.
GPS: N 39°00.68' W 109°40.22'

▼ 3.1 SO Cross through wash.
6.6 ▲ SO Cross through wash.

▼ 4.7 SO Cross through Bootlegger Wash.
5.1 ▲ SO Cross through Bootlegger Wash.

▼ 5.8 SO Cross through fence line.
3.9 ▲ SO Cross through fence line.
GPS: N 39°00.76' W 109°38.04'

▼ 7.2 SO Steep descent into canyon.
2.5 ▲ SO Steep descent into canyon.

▼ 8.1 SO Track on left.
1.7 ▲ SO Track on right.

▼ 9.8 TR T-Intersection. Zero trip meter.
0.0 ▲ Continue along trail.
GPS: N 38°59.97' W 109°36.05'

▼ 0.0 Continue along trail.
5.1 ▲ BL Track on left. Zero trip meter.

▼ 2.2 SO Cross through Sagers Wash several times over next mile.
2.9 ▲ SO Cross through wash.
GPS: N 38°58.39' W 109°37.04'

▼ 2.5 SO Cross through wash.
2.6 ▲ SO Cross through wash.

▼ 2.9 SO Cross through wash.
2.2 ▲ SO Cross through wash.

▼ 3.1 SO Cross through wash and under railroad line.
2.0 ▲ SO Cross under railroad line and then cross through Sagers Wash several times over next mile.
GPS: N 38°57.67' W 109°37.27'

▼ 3.2 SO Track on right. Then track on left.
1.9 ▲ SO Track on right. Then track on left.

▼ 3.5 SO Track on left.
1.6 ▲ BL Track on right.

▼ 3.9 SO Track on right.
1.2 ▲ SO Track on left.
GPS: N 38°57.12' W 109°36.79'

▼ 4.2 TR Intersection with paved frontage road.
0.9 ▲ TL Turn onto dirt road. BLM sign reads, "Sagers Canyon 6."
GPS: N 38°56.95' W 109°36.70'

▼ 4.3 SO Cross bridge over wash.
0.8 ▲ SO Cross bridge over wash.

▼ 4.6 UT U-turn left.
0.5 ▲ UT U-turn right onto frontage road.
GPS: N 38°56.93' W 109°37.25'

▼ 5.1 Trail ends at I-70, exit 190; turn right for Thompson Springs, left for Colorado.
0.0 ▲ On I-70, take exit 190 and zero trip meter at intersection of the overpass and the entry/exit ramps on north side. This exit is 5.7 miles east of Thompson Springs.
GPS: N 38°56.62' W 109°36.85'

CENTRAL REGION TRAIL #29

Gooseberry-Fremont Road

STARTING POINT Utah 72, 4.8 miles northeast of Fremont
FINISHING POINT I-70, exit 61
TOTAL MILEAGE 40.2 miles
UNPAVED MILEAGE 23.2 miles
DRIVING TIME 2.5 hours
ELEVATION RANGE 7,500–10,500 feet
USUALLY OPEN June to October
DIFFICULTY RATING 1
SCENIC RATING 7
REMOTENESS RATING +0

Special Attractions

- Long, easy trail for scenic touring.
- Access to a network of 4WD, ATV, and hiking trails.
- Fishing and camping opportunities, both developed and primitive.

Description

This long trail through Fishlake National Forest is a pleasant drive, and in dry weather, it is traversable by passenger vehicles. The first 12.6 miles are paved, as are the last 4.4 miles, and the rest of the trail is a good graded gravel road. It is common to see wildlife on this trail, including mule deer at all times of day. There are also large herds of elk and a herd of moose in Fishlake Basin. Other animals to watch out for include coyotes, ground squirrels, and the less-appealing skunks and rattlesnakes.

The trail first passes the large Mill Meadow Reservoir and then follows alongside the Fremont River. Camping is restricted along this stretch. RVs and vehicles can use the paved pull-ins to park overnight. Walk-in tent camping is permitted in some of the river meadows.

At Johnson Valley Reservoir in Fishlake Basin, the road follows around the northeast shore, giving good views over the lake. Camping is permitted in developed campgrounds only, and the operation of ATVs is prohibited. Here the trail becomes a smaller graded gravel road and climbs gradually to the plateau alongside Sevenmile Creek. Dispersed camping is permitted on this part of the route after the first 1.5 miles. Once on the plateau, the trail runs mainly through open meadows interspersed with stands of aspen and pine. There are some pleasant

Stands of aspen along the trail

The bridge across Sevenmile Creek

camping areas, but they are fairly exposed.

About 6 miles from Johnson Valley Reservoir, you can see Lost Creek Reservoir to the west and Mount Terrill (11,547 feet) to the east. The Mount Terrill Guard Station is hidden in the trees, down a short track, just before the turnoff for Lost Creek Reservoir. The forest service is hoping to make the guard station available for overnight accommodation sometime in 2000. The trail then winds down, offering wide views to the east. It passes by the trailheads for many ATV trails and some interesting 4WD roads—mainly dead-end trails or short loops. There is a wider variety of campsites on this northern end of the trail.

The trail passes the Gooseberry Guard Station, Gooseberry Youth Camp, and the Gooseberry National Forest Campground (with facilities) before leaving Fishlake National Forest. There are several seasonal closure gates on this end of the trail. The forest service uses them mainly to control vehicle access during spring runoff, when the trail can be easily damaged. Exact dates vary, but the trail is normally accessible in part by May and completely by June.

The trail ends at I-70, exit 61, 7 miles east of Salina.

Current Road Information

BLM Richfield Field Office
150 East 900 North
Richfield, UT 84701
(435) 896-1500

Fishlake National Forest
Loa Ranger District
138 South Main
Loa, UT 84747
(435) 836-2811

Map References

BLM Loa, Salina
USFS Fishlake National Forest: Loa Ranger District
USGS 1:24,000 Lyman, Forsyth Reservoir, Fish Lake, Mt. Terrill, Gooseberry Creek, Steves Mt.
1:100,000 Loa, Salina
Maptech CD-ROM: Escalante/Dixie National Forest; Central/San Rafael
Trails Illustrated, #707
Utah Atlas & Gazetteer, pp. 27, 37
Utah Travel Council #4

Route Directions

▼ 0.0 On Utah 72, 4.8 miles northeast of Fremont, zero trip meter and turn west onto paved CR 3268, following signs to Mill Meadow Reservoir.
12.6 ▲ Trail ends at Utah 72. Turn right for Fremont.

GPS: N 38°29.37' W 111°32.46'

▼ 1.3 SO Scenic overlook on left.
11.3 ▲ SO Scenic overlook on right.

▼ 1.4 SO Entrance to Mill Meadow Dam on left. Route follows east shore of Mill Meadow Dam.
11.2 ▲ SO Entrance to Mill Meadow Dam on right.

▼ 1.5 SO Cattle guard.
11.1 ▲ SO Cattle guard.

▼ 1.6 SO Enter Fishlake National Forest; road becomes FR 036. Many access tracks lead left to lakeshore. Camping restricted to designated areas.

11.0 ▲ SO Leaving Fishlake National Forest; road becomes CR 3268.

GPS: N 38°30.02' W 111°33.75'

▼ 2.8 SO Track on right.

9.8 ▲ SO Track on left.

▼ 3.2 SO Road leaves Mill Meadow Dam.

9.4 ▲ SO Mill Meadow Dam on right. Many access tracks lead right to lakeshore.

▼ 3.5 SO FR 046, Mytoge Mountain Road, on left.

9.1 ▲ SO FR 046, Mytoge Mountain Road, on right.

▼ 5.1 SO Pole Canyon Trail (#117) on left.

7.5 ▲ SO Pole Canyon Trail (#117) on right.

GPS: N 38°32.60' W 111°35.05'

▼ 5.8 SO Ivie Canyon Trail (#366) on left; trail on right is #143.

6.8 ▲ SO Ivie Canyon Trail (#366) on right; trail on left is #143.

▼ 6.5 SO Track on left.

6.1 ▲ SO Track on right.

▼ 6.6 SO Cattle guard.

6.0 ▲ SO Cattle guard.

▼ 7.4 SO Splatter Canyon Trail (#118) on left.

5.2 ▲ SO Splatter Canyon Trail (#118) on right.

▼ 8.7 SO Track on left.

3.9 ▲ SO Track on right.

▼ 9.2 SO Cattle guard.

3.4 ▲ SO Cattle guard.

▼ 9.7 SO Track on left.

2.9 ▲ SO Track on right.

▼ 10.1 SO Cross over Fremont River on bridge.

2.5 ▲ SO Cross over Fremont River on bridge.

▼ 10.4 SO Two tracks on right, then tracks left and right.

2.2 ▲ SO Tracks on left and right, then two tracks on left.

▼ 10.5 SO Gravel road on right, FR 015, to U. M. Creek and Sheep Valley.

2.1 ▲ SO Gravel road on left, FR 015, to U. M. Creek and Sheep Valley.

GPS: N 38°36.43' W 111°37.06'

▼ 11.0 SO Track on left. Main trail enters Fishlake Basin; camping in developed campgrounds only.

1.6 ▲ SO Track on right.

▼ 11.3 SO Johnson Valley Reservoir on left.

1.3 ▲ SO Leaving Johnson Valley Reservoir.

▼ 11.6 SO Road on left to boat ramp.

1.0 ▲ SO Road on right to boat ramp.

▼ 12.6 TR Cross over Sevenmile Creek on bridge, then turn north onto graded gravel road, FR 640. Zero trip meter.

0.0 ▲ Continue on paved road past Johnson Valley Reservoir.

GPS: N 38°37.27' W 111°38.81'

▼ 0.0 Continue north.

6.8 ▲ TL Johnson Valley road is directly ahead. Turn left onto paved road, FR 036, toward Fremont. Zero trip meter.

▼ 0.1 SO Seasonal closure gate.

6.7 ▲ SO Seasonal closure gate.

▼ 0.9 SO Cattle guard.

5.9 ▲ SO Cattle guard.

▼ 1.0 SO Cross over Sevenmile Creek on narrow wooden bridge.

5.8 ▲ SO Cross over Sevenmile Creek on narrow wooden bridge.

▼ 1.3 SO Track on right. Entering dispersed camping area. Many tracks on right lead to campsites over next mile.

5.5 ▲ SO Track on left, entering restricted camping area.

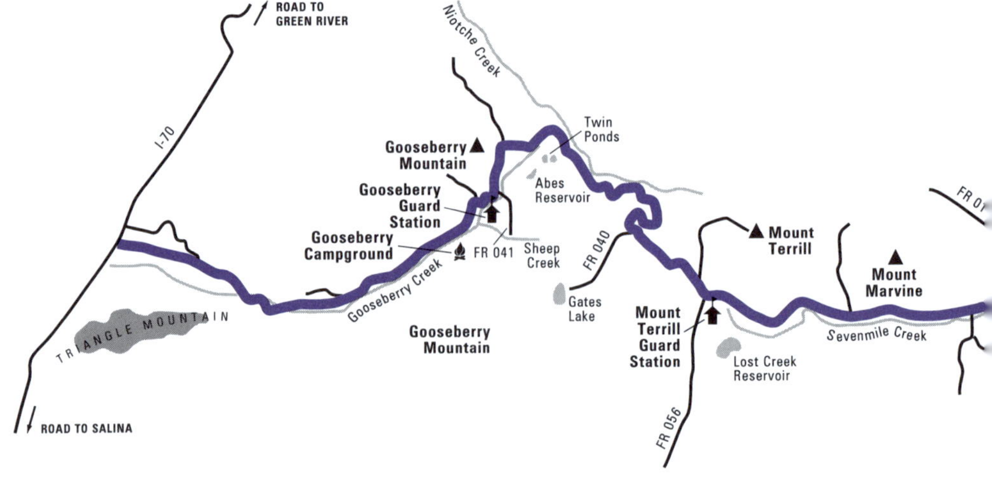

Central Trail #29: Gooseberry-Fremont Road

▼ 2.3 SO Cattle guard. Route is now CR 2554.
4.5 ▲ SO Cattle guard. Route is now CR 3268. Many tracks on left lead to campsites over next mile.

▼ 3.1 SO Cattle guard.
3.7 ▲ SO Cattle guard.

▼ 3.5 SO Track on right is FR 942.
3.3 ▲ SO Track on left is FR 942.

▼ 3.9 SO Cattle guard.
2.9 ▲ SO Cattle guard.

▼ 4.1 SO Track on right to corral.
2.7 ▲ SO Track on left to corral.

▼ 4.5 SO Small track on right.
2.3 ▲ SO Small track on left.

▼ 5.1 SO Cattle guard.
1.7 ▲ SO Cattle guard.

▼ 5.5 SO Track on right, then campsite on left.
1.3 ▲ SO Campsite on right, then track on left.

▼ 5.8 SO Track on left to Mount Terrill Guard Station. Hilgard Mountain on right.
1.0 ▲ SO Track on right to Mount Terrill Guard Station. Hilgard Mountain on left.

GPS: N 38°42.41' W 111°40.83'

▼ 6.4 SO Track on left, track on right, then cattle guard. Lost Creek Reservoir on left.
0.4 ▲ SO Cattle guard, track on left, then track on right. Lost Creek Reservoir on right.

▼ 6.8 SO Track on left is FR 056 to Lost Creek Reservoir. Zero trip meter at intersection.
0.0 ▲ Continue south.

GPS: N 38°42.81' W 111°40.80'

▼ 0.0 Continue north.
10.6 ▲ SO Track on right is FR 056 to Lost Creek Reservoir. Zero trip meter at intersection.

▼ 0.4 SO Track on left.
10.2 ▲ SO Track on right.

▼ 0.5 SO Track on right to Mount Terrill (11,547 feet).
10.1 ▲ SO Track on left to Mount Terrill (11,547 feet).

GPS: N 38°43.23' W 111°40.68'

▼ 0.6 SO Track on left is FR 1242.
10.0 ▲ SO Track on right is FR 1242.

▼ 0.9 SO Cattle guard.

9.7 ▲ SO Cattle guard.

▼ 1.0 SO Track on left.
9.6 ▲ SO Track on right.

▼ 2.4 SO Track on left is FR 040 to Gates Lake.
8.2 ▲ SO Track on right is FR 040 to Gates Lake.
GPS: N 38°44.73′ W 111°40.05′

▼ 2.5 SO Track on right.
8.1 ▲ SO Track on left.

▼ 2.7 BL FR 1240 on right, then track on right.
7.9 ▲ BR Track on left, then FR 1240 on left.

▼ 2.8 SO Niotche–Lost Creek Divide. Two tracks on left.
7.8 ▲ SO Niotche–Lost Creek Divide. Two tracks on right.
GPS: N 38°45.00′ W 111°39.79′

▼ 4.2 SO Track on right to campsite, then track on left.
6.4 ▲ SO Track on right, then track on left to campsite.

▼ 4.8 SO Track on left.
5.8 ▲ SO Track on right.

▼ 4.9 SO Track on right to Niotche Creek.
5.7 ▲ SO Track on left to Niotche Creek.
GPS: N 38°45.14′ W 111°38.90′

▼ 5.7 SO Large campsite on left, then Salina Reservoir on left.
4.9 ▲ SO Salina Reservoir on right, then large campsite on right.
GPS: N 38°45.67′ W 111°39.13′

▼ 5.8 SO Track on left.
4.8 ▲ SO Track on right.

▼ 6.4 SO Track on left to Harves River.
4.2 ▲ SO Track on right to Harves River.
GPS: N 38°46.13′ W 111°39.10′

▼ 6.8 BR Campsite on left, then track on left. Remain on gravel road.
3.8 ▲ BL Track on right, then campsite on right. Remain on gravel road.
GPS: N 38°46.38′ W 111°38.79′

▼ 6.9 SO Track on left.
3.7 ▲ SO Track on right.

▼ 7.5 SO Track on left to Cold Spring. Campsite at intersection.
3.1 ▲ SO Track on right to Cold Spring. Campsite at intersection.
GPS: N 38°46.94′ W 111°38.47′

▼ 7.7 SO Campsite on right.
2.9 ▲ SO Campsite on left.

▼ 7.9 SO Track on left to Twin Ponds, then corral on right.
2.7 ▲ SO Corral on left, then track on right to Twin Ponds.
GPS: N 38°47.18′ W 111°38.22′

▼ 8.0 SO Cattle guard, then Beaver Dams Road on right to Niotche Creek.
2.6 ▲ SO Beaver Dams Road on left to Niotche Creek, then cattle guard.
GPS: N 38°47.25′ W 111°38.13′

▼ 9.3 SO Campsites on right and left. Gooseberry Mountain is directly ahead.
1.3 ▲ SO Campsites on right and left. Gooseberry Mountain is on left.

▼ 9.4 SO Gravel road on right is FR 038 to Antone Hollow.
1.2 ▲ SO Gravel road on left is FR 038 to Antone Hollow.
GPS: N 38°48.15' W 111°39.01'

▼ 10.2 SO Track on right.
0.4 ▲ SO Track on left.

▼ 10.5 SO Track on left is FR 041 to Sheep Creek.
0.1 ▲ SO Track on right is FR 041 to Sheep Creek.

▼ 10.6 SO Track on right is Oak Ridge Road (FR 032) to Squaw Hollow. Zero trip meter.
0.0 ▲ Continue east.
GPS: N 38°47.95' W 111°40.27'

▼ 0.0 Continue west.
10.2 ▲ SO Track on left is Oak Ridge Road (FR 032) to Squaw Hollow. Zero trip meter.

▼ 1.0 SO Track on left to Gooseberry Guard Station and Gooseberry Youth Camp. Track on right.
9.2 ▲ SO Track on right to Gooseberry Guard Station and Gooseberry Youth Camp. Track on left.
GPS: N 38°48.18' W 111°40.95'

▼ 1.1 SO Seasonal closure gate.
9.1 ▲ SO Seasonal closure gate.
GPS: N 38°48.22' W 111°41.10'

▼ 1.2 SO Gooseberry Campground on left.
9.0 ▲ SO Gooseberry Campground on right.

▼ 2.2 SO Seasonal closure gate.
8.0 ▲ SO Seasonal closure gate.

▼ 3.4 SO Track on right at German Flat.
6.8 ▲ SO Track on left at German Flat.

▼ 3.9 SO Track on right.
6.3 ▲ SO Track on left.

▼ 4.2 SO Cross over creek on bridge, seasonal closure gate, then track on left.
6.0 ▲ SO Track on right, seasonal closure gate, then cross over creek on bridge.

▼ 4.7 SO Corral on left.
5.5 ▲ SO Corral on right.

▼ 5.1 SO Cross over Gates Creek, then track on left.
5.1 ▲ SO Track on right, then cross over Gates Creek.

▼ 5.4 SO Track on right.
4.8 ▲ SO Track on left.

▼ 5.5 SO Track on right.
4.7 ▲ SO Track on left.

▼ 5.8 SO Cattle guard, then corral on left. Road is now paved.
4.4 ▲ SO Corral on right, then cattle guard. Road is now graded gravel.
GPS: N 38°51.23' W 111°44.61'

▼ 5.9 SO Track on left.
4.3 ▲ SO Track on right.

▼ 6.2 SO Track on left to Salina.
4.0 ▲ SO Track on right to Salina.
GPS: N 38°51.60' W 111°44.65'

▼ 6.3 SO Cattle guard.
3.9 ▲ SO Cattle guard.

▼ 7.8 SO Track on left.
2.4 ▲ SO Track on right.

▼ 8.3 SO Cattle guard.
1.9 ▲ SO Cattle guard.

▼ 8.6 SO Track on right.
1.6 ▲ SO Track on left.

▼ 10.1 SO Cross frontage road, then cattle guard.
0.1 ▲ SO Cattle guard, then cross frontage road.

▼ 10.2 Trail ends at I-70, exit 61; turn west for Salina, east for Green River.
0.0 ▲ On I-70 at exit 61, 7 miles east of Salina, turn south on paved FR 640 and zero trip meter.
GPS: N 38°54.97' W 111°44.35'

Richfield Pioneer Road

STARTING POINT US 50, 6.3 miles north of Salina
FINISHING POINT Richfield, at I-70 underpass
TOTAL MILEAGE 34.9 miles
UNPAVED MILEAGE 34.9 miles
DRIVING TIME 3.5 hours
ELEVATION RANGE 5,300–9,700 feet
USUALLY OPEN Late June to October
DIFFICULTY RATING 2
SCENIC RATING 9
REMOTENESS RATING +0

Special Attractions

- Long, easy route for scenic touring.
- Access to a network of 4WD, ATV, and hiking trails.
- Spectacular views from the Pahvant Range.

History

The town of Richfield was established in the 1860s as a Mormon settlement. Unlike most Mormon pioneer settlements, Richfield was not settled at the direct request of Brigham Young, but by a band of pioneers acting on their own initiative and led by Albert Lewis, formerly of Manti. Attracted by the fertile valleys, reliable water source, and nearby forest, the pioneers arrived in January 1864, and by February of that year the first house was built. The new settlement was originally named Warm Springs; it was later changed to Omni (in honor of a Mormon prophet) and finally became Richfield for the richness of the farmlands.

Traditionally, the Pahvant Range and neighboring areas were used by Ute Indians, and they resented the growing intrusion on their land. When access to Ute hunting grounds became restricted, a series of small armed conflicts escalated into what became known as the Black Hawk War, though this was more a series of skirmishes than a full-scale war. A fort was built at Richfield in 1865 for defense, but in April 1867, the Mormon Church leaders in Salt Lake City ordered the town evacuated. A peace treaty ending the war was signed in 1868, but fighting continued sporadically for several years. However, by 1871, most settlers had returned to Richfield. The Utes had done very little damage to property.

The Richfield Pioneer Road crosses the Pahvant Range, which runs from Scipio Valley to the northeast to Clear Creek to the southwest. Pahvant is a Paiute word thought to mean "water people." Several peaks in the range exceed 10,000 feet, including White Pine Peak, Jacks Peak, and Mount Catherine.

The road was originally built by the pioneers to serve as a timber-access road. The Pahvant Range was a rich source of timber for building, fencing, and firewood. As the

A view of the trail as it crosses a ridgeline

Looking over Mahogany Ridge to Beehive Peak

lower and more accessible sources of timber were used, the road across the plateau was developed to provide access to deeper sources of timber. The Mormon settlers also established cooperatively owned herds of cattle and sheep, which grazed the meadows of the Pahvant Range. There was no management of the grazing, and the range became seriously overgrazed, causing erosion and flooding in the valley towns. Locals petitioned the government to correct the problem, and in 1899, President William McKinley established a forest reserve, which eventually became part of Fishlake National Forest.

Description

This beautiful touring route is traversable by most high-clearance vehicles in dry weather. It offers a wide variety of features and views, mainly on the eastern side of the range. It is part of the 230-mile-long Paiute ATV Trail (PATVT), a loop trail that circles Richfield. Many parts of this trail are accessible to 4WD vehicles. The route leaves from US 50, 6.3 miles north of Salina, and enters Fishlake National Forest 3 miles later. It winds up to the top of the Pahvant Plateau by way of Willow Creek. There are some lovely shady campsites along the lower sections of the creek. It is an easy grade as the trail climbs up onto the Pahvant Range. The last part of climb provides spectacular views to the east over Scipio Lake, the distinctive pyramid of Beehive Peak, and the deep canyon of Willow Creek.

After 6 miles the trail reaches the ridge top, and from the ridge, many roads and trails run down into the valleys on both sides, including Central #31: Coffee Peak Trail. The trail crosses mainly open meadows, interspersed with aspens and hardwood mahogany. As the trail descends toward Richfield, it reenters stands of sagebrush and scattered pinyon and juniper.

In wet weather, particularly during the spring runoff and the summer monsoon season, the trail can be very slippery. Much of the surface is clay, which is also highly prone to rutting. The trail is graded and maintained, but it can still be rough going.

Current Road Information

BLM Fillmore Field Office
PO Box 778
Fillmore, UT 84631
(435) 743-6811

Fishlake National Forest
Fillmore Ranger District
390 South Main
Fillmore, UT 84631
(435) 743-5721

Map References

BLM Richfield
USFS Fishlake National Forest: Fillmore Ranger District
USGS 1:24,000 Beehive Peak, Mt. Catherine, White Pine Peak, Richfield
1:100,000 Richfield
Maptech CD-ROM: King Canyon/Fillmore
Trails Illustrated, #708
Utah Atlas & Gazetteer, pp. 36, 37
Utah Travel Council #4

Route Directions

▼ 0.0 On US 50, 6.3 miles northwest of Salina, turn west onto unmarked gravel road across a cattle guard and zero trip meter.

3.5 ▲ Trail ends at US 50. Turn right for Salina, left for I-15.

GPS: N 38°58.90' W 111°59.48'

▼ 0.7 SO Track on right.

2.8 ▲ SO Track on left.

▼ 0.8 SO Track on left.

2.7 ▲ SO Track on right.

▼ 1.4 SO Track on left.

2.1 ▲ SO Track on right.

▼ 1.6 SO Track on right, then track on left is Paiute ATV Trail #01 (PATVT#01).

1.9 ▲ SO Track on right is PATVT#01, then track on left.

GPS: N 38°59.18' W 112°01.25'

▼ 2.5 SO Cattle guard.

1.0 ▲ SO Cattle guard.

▼ 2.6 SO Track on left.

0.9 ▲ SO Track on right.

▼ 2.7 SO Track on right.

0.8 ▲ SO Track on left.

▼ 3.5 SO Track on left, then cattle guard. Entering Fishlake National Forest. Trail is now FR 102. Zero trip meter.

0.0 ▲ Trail crosses a small section of private land.

GPS: N 38°58.89' W 112°03.33'

▼ 0.0 Continue into Fishlake National Forest.

6.1 ▲ SO Cattle guard; zero trip meter. Leaving Fishlake National Forest, followed by track on right.

▼ 0.6 SO Campsites on right and left.

5.5 ▲ SO Campsites on right and left.

▼ 0.7 SO Cross through Willow Creek, followed by seasonal closure gate. Trail follows Willow Creek, with many campsites along creek for next 2.1 miles.

5.4 ▲ SO Seasonal closure gate, then cross through Willow Creek. Trail leaves creek.

▼ 2.8 BL PATVT#01 goes right, ATV use only.

3.3 ▲ BR PATVT#01 goes left, ATV use only. Main trail follows Willow Creek, with many campsites along creek for next 2.1 miles.

GPS: N 38°58.68' W 112°06.01'

▼ 4.8 BR Red Canyon Hiking Trail (#015) on left to Aurora.

1.3 ▲ BL Red Canyon Hiking Trail (#015) on right to Aurora.

GPS: N 38°57.64' W 112°05.48'

▼ 5.1 SO Track on right to campsite.

1.0 ▲ SO Track on left to campsite.

▼ 5.3 SO Track on left to exposed camping area with great view.

0.8 ▲ SO Track on right to exposed camping area with great view.

▼ 5.5 SO Track on left to corral, then cattle guard.

0.6 ▲ SO Track on right to corral, then cattle guard.

▼ 6.1 SO Track on right is Central #31: Coffee Peak Trail (FR 096). Main trail is now FR 096. Travel information board at intersection.

0.0 ▲ Descend into Willow Creek Canyon.

GPS: N 38°57.54' W 112°06.69'

▼ 0.0 Continue along ridge top.

1.4 ▲ SO Track on left is Central #31: Coffee Peak Trail (FR 096). Travel information board at intersection. Main trail is now FR 102.

▼ 0.9 SO Valley on right is North Fork Chalk Creek.

0.5 ▲ SO Valley on left is North Fork Chalk Creek.

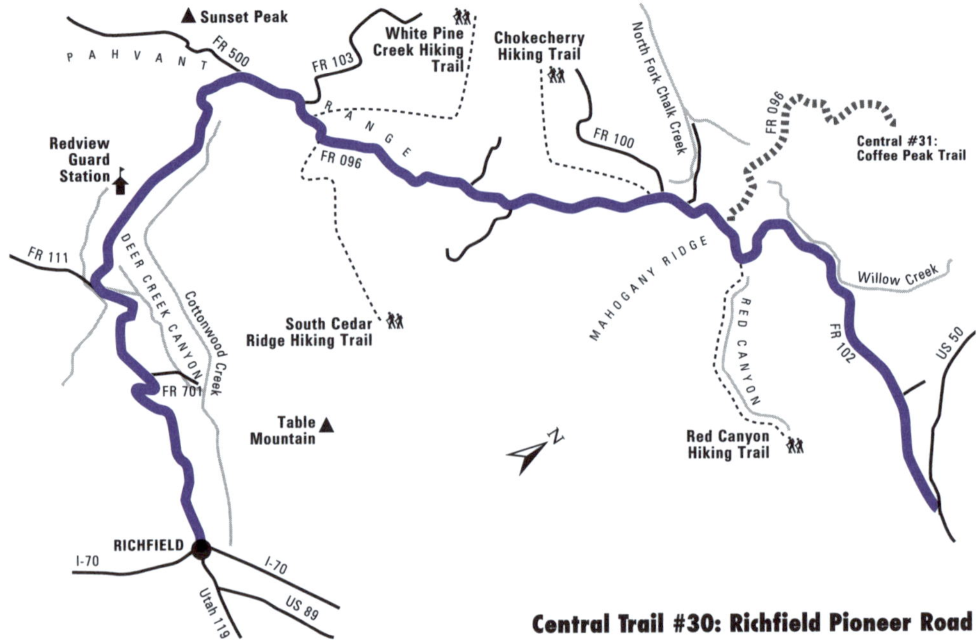

Central Trail #30: Richfield Pioneer Road

▼ 1.2 BL Track on right.
0.2 ▲ SO Track on left.

▼ 1.4 BL Track on right is FR 100 to Fillmore. Zero trip meter.
0.0 ▲ Continue on FR 096.
GPS: N 38°56.70' W 112°07.80'

▼ 0.0 Continue on FR 096.
9.1 ▲ SO Track on left is FR 100 to Fillmore. Zero trip meter.

▼ 0.3 SO Chokecherry hiking trail (#024) on right, then track on right (FR 392).
8.8 ▲ SO Track on left (FR 392), then Chokecherry hiking trail (#024) on left.
GPS: N 38°56.36' W 112°07.86'

▼ 1.0 SO Faint track on right to campsite.
8.1 ▲ SO Faint track on left to campsite.

▼ 1.1 SO Small track on left to campsite.
8.0 ▲ SO Small track on right to campsite.

▼ 1.8 SO Cattle guard.
7.3 ▲ SO Cattle guard.

▼ 3.2 SO Track on left.
5.9 ▲ SO Track on right.

▼ 3.5 SO Campsite on left.
5.6 ▲ SO Campsite on right.

▼ 4.4 SO Track on left to remains of Solitude Guard Station.
4.7 ▲ SO Track on right to remains of Solitude Guard Station.

▼ 5.0 SO Cattle guard, then small track on right.
4.1 ▲ SO Small track on left, then cattle guard.

▼ 6.6 SO Track on right, then track on left.
2.5 ▲ SO Track on right, then track on left.
GPS: N 38°52.33' W 112°11.42'

▼ 7.7 SO Trail on left is South Cedar Ridge hiking trail (#028).
1.4 ▲ SO Trail on right is South Cedar Ridge hiking trail (#028).
GPS: N 38°51.56' W 112°12.11'

▼ 8.0 SO Cattle guard.
1.1 ▲ SO Cattle guard.

▼ 8.7 SO White Pine Creek hiking trail (#027) on right. Vehicles can drive first 0.5

miles to an old cabin.

0.4 ▲ SO White Pine Creek hiking trail (#027) on left. Vehicles can drive first 0.5 miles to an old cabin.

GPS: N 38°51.38' W 112°13.10'

▼ 9.1 SO Track right is FR 103 to Fillmore. Zero trip meter.

0.0 ▲ Continue on FR 096.

GPS: N 38°51.25' W 112°13.58'

▼ 0.0 Continue on FR 096.

7.4 ▲ SO Track on left is FR 103 to Fillmore. Zero trip meter.

▼ 0.3 SO Cabin on left and track on left.

7.1 ▲ SO Cabin on right and track on right.

▼ 1.1 SO Meadow Creek hiking trail (#032) on right.

6.3 ▲ SO Meadow Creek hiking trail (#032) on left.

GPS: N 38°50.51' W 112°14.26'

▼ 1.6 TL FR 500 on right to Goat Springs. Travel information board at intersection. Sunset Peak is directly ahead.

5.8 ▲ TR FR 500 on left to Goat Springs. Travel information board at intersection. Sunset Peak is on left.

GPS: N 38°50.34' W 112°14.74'

▼ 2.9 SO Track on right is FR 508.

4.5 ▲ SO Track on left is FR 508.

▼ 4.2 SO Track on right to dam.

3.2 ▲ SO Track on left to dam.

▼ 4.5 SO Track on right to campsite.

2.9 ▲ SO Track on left to campsite.

▼ 5.3 SO Cattle guard.

2.1 ▲ SO Cattle guard.

▼ 5.4 SO Redview Guard Station on right.

2.0 ▲ SO Redview Guard Station on left.

GPS: N 38°47.90' W 112°12.90'

▼ 6.2 SO Track on left, then cross through Deer Creek.

1.2 ▲ SO Cross though Deer Creek, then track on right.

▼ 6.8 SO Track on right is FR 506.

0.6 ▲ SO Track on left is FR 506. View ahead to Redview Guard Station.

GPS: N 38°46.97' W 112°11.88'

▼ 7.1 SO Track on left, then track on right.

0.3 ▲ SO Track on left, then track on right.

▼ 7.4 TL T-intersection. Right is FR 111, the southern continuation of PATVT#01. Zero trip meter

0.0 ▲ Continue on FR 096, which is now PATVT#01.

GPS: N 38°46.53' W 112°11.65'

▼ 0.0 Continue on FR 096, which is now Paiute ATV Side Trail #04.

7.4 ▲ TR Ahead is FR 111, the southern continuation of PATVT#01. Zero trip meter.

▼ 0.2 SO Track on right.

7.2 ▲ SO Track on left.

▼ 0.6 SO Track on left.

6.8 ▲ SO Track on right.

▼ 0.7 SO Track on left.

6.7 ▲ SO Track on right.

▼ 1.1 SO Cattle guard.

6.3 ▲ SO Cattle guard.

▼ 2.6 SO Cross through wash.

4.8 ▲ SO Cross through wash.

▼ 2.7 SO Track on left.

4.7 ▲ SO Track on right.

▼ 2.8 SO Track on left.

4.6 ▲ SO Track on right.

▼ 3.0 SO Track on left is FR 701, also track on right.

4.4 ▲ SO Track on right is FR 701, also track on left.

GPS: N 38°46.75' W 112°09.20'

▼ 5.3 SO Tracks on left and right. Many tracks right and left over next 0.9 miles lead to campsites.
2.1 ▲ SO Tracks on left and right.

▼ 6.2 SO Seasonal closure gate.
1.2 ▲ SO Seasonal closure gate. Many tracks right and left over next 0.9 miles lead to campsites.

▼ 6.3 BR Track on left is FR 1747.
1.1 ▲ BL Track on right is FR 1747.
GPS: N 38°46.81' W 112°06.64'

▼ 6.6 SO Leaving Fishlake National Forest.
0.8 ▲ SO Entering Fishlake National Forest.
GPS: N 38°46.69' W 112°06.43'

▼ 7.0 SO Town water tank on left.
0.4 ▲ SO Town water tank on right.

▼ 7.4 Trail ends as it passes underneath I-70. Continue into Richfield. ATVs are permitted on some streets in Richfield; regulation board at end of trail.
0.0 ▲ On US 89 in Richfield, turn west onto 300 North Street. Trail commences as it passes underneath I-70 overpass; zero trip meter. ATV regulation board at start of trail.
GPS: N 38°46.33' W 112°05.93'

CENTRAL REGION TRAIL #31

Coffee Peak Trail

STARTING POINT Central #30: Richfield Pioneer Road (FR 102), 9.6 miles from US 50
FINISHING POINT Coffee Peak
TOTAL MILEAGE 11.2 miles
UNPAVED MILEAGE 11.2 miles
DRIVING TIME 1.5 hours (one-way)
ELEVATION RANGE 8,700–9,800 feet
USUALLY OPEN July to October
DIFFICULTY RATING 3
SCENIC RATING 9
REMOTENESS RATING +0

View of the trail as it passes through a small stand of aspens

Special Attractions

- Spectacular ridge trail with views to the east and west.
- Mountain peaks of Jacks Peak, Willow Creek Peak, and Coffee Peak.
- Access to a number of hiking trails.

Description

This breathtaking spur trail leads off Central #30: Richfield Pioneer Road. For most of its length it runs across the narrow ridge tops, with sheer drops on one or both sides. The views are awesome; you can see Willow Creek Canyon, Beehive Peak, Chalk Creek Canyon, and Scipio Lake. The trail surface is rough but easily traversable in dry weather. The National Forest Service has realigned one section of the route just after the turn to Pioneer Peak. The realigned track is steep and has loose, deep bulldust, which in wet weather turns into a greasy slide downhill.

Returning up this section could be difficult to impossible in adverse weather.

The trail is entirely within a restricted travel area of Fishlake National Forest. Vehicle travel, including ATVs, is restricted to designated trails.

The trail is mainly across open meadows, with stands of aspen and a small stand of bristlecone pine just after the turn for Pioneer Peak. There are some sections of shelf road, but they are wide enough for a single vehicle and there are plenty of passing places. There are some quiet backcountry campsites as well as the more developed sites at Maple Grove and Maple Hollow.

The trail ends for vehicle travel immediately north of Coffee Peak; a hiking trail continues all the way to Scipio. To exit, vehicles must return to Richfield Pioneer Road.

Current Road Information

BLM Fillmore Field Office
PO Box 778
Fillmore, UT 84631
(435) 743-6811

Fishlake National Forest
Fillmore Ranger District
390 South Main
Fillmore, UT 84631
(435) 743-5721

Map References

BLM Richfield, Delta
USFS Fishlake National Forest: Fillmore Ranger District
USGS 1:24,000 Beehive Peak, Mt. Catherine, Coffee Peak, Scipio Lake
1:100,000 Richfield, Delta
Maptech CD-ROM: King Canyon/Fillmore
Trails Illustrated, #708 (incomplete)
Utah Atlas & Gazetteer, p. 37
Utah Travel Council #4 (incomplete)

Route Directions

▼ 0.0 On Central #30: Richfield Pioneer Road (FR 102), 9.6 miles from US 50, turn north on FR 096, following sign for Coffee Peak Trail. Cross cattle guard and zero trip meter. (Note that FR 096 also continues south along the ridge).

GPS: N 38°57.54' W 112°06.69'

▼ 0.1 SO Views left over North Fork Chalk Creek.
▼ 0.3 SO Views right over Willow Creek Canyon.
▼ 0.7 SO Campsite on right with view over Willow Creek Canyon.
▼ 1.7 SO Track on left.

GPS: N 38°58.35' W 112°07.65'

▼ 2.4 SO Willow Creek Canyon on right. FR 102 is visible below.
▼ 3.1 SO Cattle guard.

Central Trail #31: Coffee Peak Trail

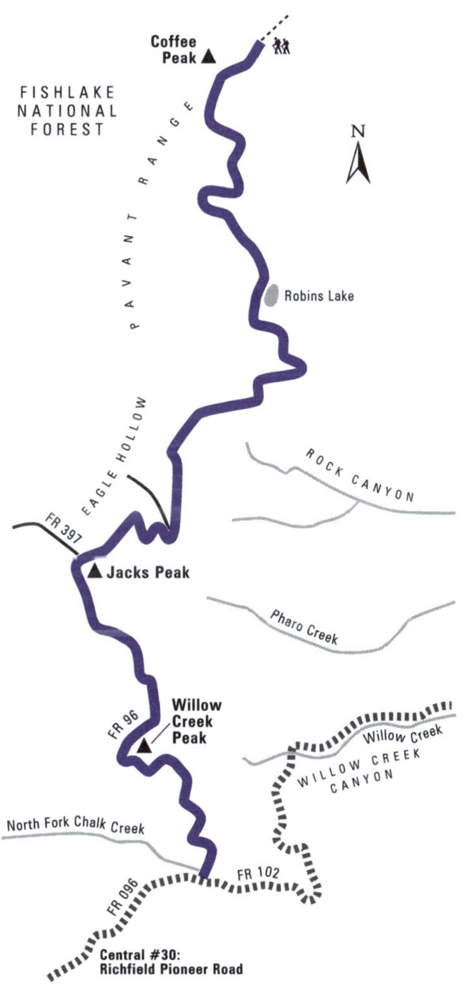

GPS: N 38°59.23' W 112°07.83'

▼ 4.1 SO Track on left is FR 397 to Pioneer Peak. Jacks Peak (10,072 feet) is on right; summit is marked by cairn. Zero trip meter.

GPS: N 38°59.71' W 112°08.48'

▼ 0.0 Continue on FR 096. Cross cattle guard and pass through some scattered bristlecone pines.

▼ 0.8 SO Track on left. Main graded trail descends steeply. Surface is deep bull-dust.

▼ 1.0 SO Track on left rejoins, followed by cattle guard and second track on left to Eagle Hollow.

GPS: N 39°00.01' W 112°07.67'

▼ 1.5 SO Track on right is viewpoint.

▼ 2.1 BR Track on left is undesignated route FR 867 (closed to vehicle travel).

GPS: N 39°00.96' W 112°07.64'

▼ 2.5 SO Trail #013 on right. Hiking and horse access only.

GPS: N 39°01.07' W 112°07.31'

▼ 3.1 SO Scipio Lake is visible in valley on right.

▼ 4.0 SO Track on left, followed by track on right. Main trail crosses the head of Robins Valley. Dry lake on right.

▼ 4.1 SO Cattle guard, followed by track on right to sheltered campsite in grassy depression.

▼ 4.2 SO Track on left to campsite. Hiking Trail #012 on right to Maple Grove Campground.

GPS: N 39°02.08' W 112°07.38'

▼ 6.3 SO Hiking Trail #010 on the left to Maple Hollow Campground.

GPS: N 39°03.18' W 112°08.14'

▼ 7.1 Trail ends just north of Coffee Peak. Hiking Trail #005 continues north. Some limited camping at end of vehicle trail.

GPS: N 39°03.84' W 112°07.76'

CENTRAL REGION TRAIL #32

Cove Mountain and Magleby Pass Trail

STARTING POINT Utah 62 at Koosharem
FINISHING POINT Center Street in Glenwood
TOTAL MILEAGE 33.7 miles
UNPAVED MILEAGE 33.7 miles
DRIVING TIME 2 hours
ELEVATION RANGE 5,300–10,400 feet
USUALLY OPEN June to October
DIFFICULTY RATING 1
SCENIC RATING 6
REMOTENESS RATING +0

Special Attractions

- Access to a number of ATV and hiking trails.
- Easy, scenic drive through a variety of forest scenery.
- Access to a number of backcountry campsites.

History

The town of Koosharem was settled in 1877. The name comes from an Indian word meaning "clover blossom;" Indians considered this plant's edible tubers a staple food. Farther up the trail, the Koosharem Guard Station, built in 1911, is the oldest National Forest Service guard station in Utah. The forest service has plans to use it as an interpretive site for the area.

Cove Mountain takes its name from Cove Fort, which is due west, just south of the Pahvant Range near the intersection of I-15 and I-70. The fort has influenced the names of many features around this general area. Located in an extremely protected site, Cove Fort was built in 1867 as a refuge for Mormon travelers during the Black Hawk War, which was a series of skirmishes between Ute Indians and Mormon settlers.

In 1872, a sawmill was established on Cove Mountain by Joseph Young, a prominent local Mormon. However, three years later, for unknown reasons, it was moved to Clear Creek Canyon. More recently, a TV booster station was located on Cove Mountain, but its presence was never authorized by the forest service. In 1957, the forest service was successful in its case to have it removed as "unlicensed equipment," and it was moved farther down the mountain onto private land.

Glenwood, at the north end of the trail, was settled in 1864. Mormon settlers were sent by Brigham Young to establish the community. The settlement was originally named Glens Cove, after an early pioneer, John Wilson Glenn, and the name metamorphosed into "Glencoe" before becoming Glenwood. A stone fort was built there in 1866 to protect the settlers during the Black Hawk War.

The fish hatchery at the trail's northern endpoint was completed in 1921, and at the time it was Utah's third largest trout hatchery. Today, it is double the size of the original hatchery and handles over 135,000 pounds of fish.

Description

This gentle trail links the small towns of Koosharem and Glenwood via a graded dirt forest road. The trail rises up to over 10,000 feet in elevation and mainly passes through the mature pine and spruce forests on Cove Mountain. The Paiute ATV Trail (PATVT) intersects with this route for the first few miles and follows along the route in some sections.

The trail commences in Koosharem and gradually climbs up the sagebrush-covered benches onto Cove Mountain Plateau. After 5.6 miles, you reach the popular camping area of Milos Kitchen. Located in a flat area in a small valley alongside Greenwich Creek, the campground has a pit toilet but no other facilities.

After passing the turnoff for Koosharem Guard Station, the trail enters the forest. Large sections of the forest are currently being harvested for timber, so public access is restricted in some areas. Logging trucks are likely to be active on the road. The trail winds through the mature forest to Magleby Pass. Hiking trails lead off from the pass to Monument Peak and Signal Peak. Since the pass is among the trees, it does not have particularly widespread views. From here, the trail continues through the forest, giving glimpses east over Plateau Valley and Grass Valley. As the trail descends past Cove Mountain, it leaves the forest and reenters the sagebrush, crossing Hunters Flat and heading toward Glenwood. There are some excellent views to the north during the descent. The trail finishes at the Glenwood Trout Hatchery.

Big Lake

A view of the trail at Hunters Flat

Current Road Information

BLM Richfield Field Office
150 East 900 North
Richfield, UT 84701
(435) 896-1500

Fishlake National Forest
Richfield Ranger District
115 East 900 North
Richfield, UT 84701
(435) 896-9233

Map References

BLM Salina
USFS Fishlake National Forest: Richfield Ranger District
USGS 1:24,000 Sigourd, Water Creek Canyon, Koosharem
1:100,000 Salina
Maptech CD-ROM: Central/San Rafael
Trails Illustrated, #708
Utah Atlas & Gazetteer, pp. 27, 28
Utah Travel Council #4 (incomplete)

Route Directions

▼ 0.0 On Utah 62 in Koosharem, turn west on FR 076 (Koosharem Road) and zero trip meter. Cross over Koosharem Canal on bridge and continue west to the edge of town.
6.5 ▲ Cross over Koosharem Canal on bridge, then trail ends in Koosharem at Utah 62.

GPS: N 38°30.63' W 111°52.84'

▼ 0.3 SO Intersection. Road is also Paiute ATV Trail #01 (PATVT#01).
6.2 ▲ SO Intersection. Continue straight into town.

▼ 0.4 BR Track on left.
6.1 ▲ SO Track on right.

▼ 0.6 SO Multiple tracks on right and left. Proceed northwest on main track.
5.9 ▲ SO Multiple tracks on left and right. Proceed southeast on main track.

▼ 1.1 SO Tracks on right and left.
5.4 ▲ SO Tracks on left and right.

▼ 1.6 SO Entering Fishlake National Forest. Track on left.
4.9 ▲ SO Leaving Fishlake National Forest. Track on right.

GPS: N 38°31.40' W 111°54.22'

▼ 2.2 BL Track on right is continuation of PATVT#01. Many unmarked trails on right and left, mainly to campsites, around junction.
4.3 ▲ SO Track on left. PATVT#01 joins main trail here. Many unmarked trails on left and right, mainly to campsites, around junction.

▼ 4.1 BR Two tracks on left.
2.4 ▲ BL Two tracks on right.

GPS: N 38°31.53' W 111°56.21'

▼ 5.6 SO Milos Kitchen camping area on left. Paiute ATV Side Trail #33 (PATVST#33/Pine Canyon Trail) crosses trail; right to Hunters Flat, left to Pine Canyon.
0.9 ▲ SO Milos Kitchen camping area on right. PATVST#33 (Pine Canyon Trail) crosses trail; left to Hunters Flat, right to Pine Canyon.

GPS: N 38°31.94' W 111°57.11'

▼ 5.9 SO PATVT#01 enters on right and joins main trail.

0.6 ▲ SO PATVT#01 leaves main trail on left.

▼ 6.0 BL Track on right is Killian–Pine Canyon Trail #4076; hiking and horses only.
0.5 ▲ BR Track on left is Killian–Pine Canyon Trail #4076; hiking and horses only.
GPS: N 38°32.24' W 111°57.34'

▼ 6.2 SO Cattle guard.
0.3 ▲ SO Cattle guard.

▼ 6.3 SO Track on right.
0.2 ▲ SO Track on left.

▼ 6.5 SO Go straight; trail becomes FR 068 and PATVST#68. Zero trip meter. Track on left is FR 068 and PATVT#01.
0.0 ▲ Continue on FR 076 toward Koosharem.
GPS: N 38°32.23' W 111°57.64'

▼ 0.0 Continue on FR 068 toward Koosharem Guard Station.
8.7 ▲ SO Go straight; trail becomes FR 076 and PATVT#01. Zero trip meter. Track on right is FR 068 and PATVT#01.

▼ 0.1 SO Track on right.
8.6 ▲ SO Track on left.

▼ 0.5 SO Track on right.
8.2 ▲ SO Track on left.

▼ 0.8 SO Track on left is FR 165.
7.9 ▲ SO Track on right is FR 165.

▼ 1.7 SO Track on left is FR 163 (PATVST#44) to Koosharem Guard Station. Cross cattle guard.
7.0 ▲ SO Cross cattle guard, then track on right is FR 163 (PATVST#44) to Koosharem Guard Station.
GPS: N 38°33.48' W 111°58.67'

▼ 1.8 SO Track on right is Koosharem Canyon ATV Trail.
6.9 ▲ SO Track on left is Koosharem Canyon ATV Trail.

▼ 2.4 SO Small track on left.
6.3 ▲ SO Small track on right.

▼ 2.7 SO Track on right.
6.0 ▲ SO Track on left.

▼ 3.4 SO Track on right, cattle guard, then track on left.
5.3 ▲ SO Track on right, cattle guard, then track on left.

▼ 3.5 SO Seasonal closure gate.
5.2 ▲ SO Seasonal closure gate.

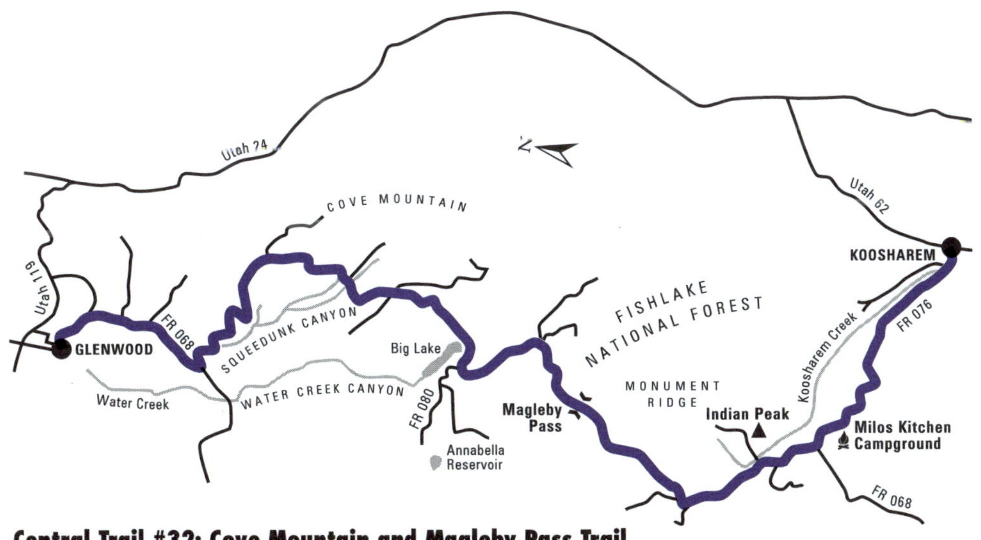

Central Trail #32: Cove Mountain and Magleby Pass Trail

GPS: N 38°33.97' W 111°57.04'

▼ 4.3 SO Track on left.
4.4 ▲ SO Track on right.

▼ 6.7 SO Track on right is timber sale area—closed to public. Many such closed areas on right and left for next 2 miles.
2.0 ▲ SO Track on left is the end of current timber sale area.

▼ 8.5 SO Track on right.
0.2 ▲ SO Track on left.

▼ 8.7 SO Magleby Pass. Parking area and hiking trail on left. Two hiking trails on left are both #110 to Monument Peak and Signal Peak. Zero trip meter.
0.0 ▲ Continue southwest toward Koosharem.

GPS: N 38°36.76' W 111°58.03'

▼ 0.0 Continue northeast toward Glenwood.
4.6 ▲ SO Magleby Pass. Parking area and hiking trail on right. Two hiking trails on right are both #110 to Monument Peak and Signal Peak. Zero trip meter. Many tracks on right and left in next 2 miles lead to timber sale areas, which are closed to public.

▼ 2.4 SO Track on left is timber sale area.
2.2 ▲ SO Track on right is timber sale area.

▼ 2.7 SO Cattle guard.
1.9 ▲ SO Cattle guard.

▼ 4.6 TL Track on right is FR 176, followed by T-intersection. Turn left at T-intersection toward Glenwood. Zero trip meter.
0.0 ▲ Continue toward Koosharem.

GPS: N 38°38.28' W 111°57.63'

▼ 0.0 Continue toward Glenwood.
9.1 ▲ TR Turn at signpost for Koosharem, and zero trip meter. Then continue straight past a track on left (FR 176).

▼ 0.7 BR Track on left is FR 080 to Annabella Reservoir.
8.4 ▲ BL Track on right is FR 080 to Annabella Reservoir.

GPS: N 38°38.78' W 111°57.74'

▼ 1.1 SO Track on right. Trail skirts south end of Big Lake.
8.0 ▲ SO Track on left. Trail skirts south end of Big Lake.

▼ 1.2 SO Two tracks on right.
7.9 ▲ SO Two tracks on left.

▼ 1.4 SO Track on left is FR 154, which skirts northwest shore of Big Lake.
7.7 ▲ SO Track on right is FR 154, which skirts northwest shore of Big Lake.

▼ 1.5 SO Track on right is FR 155.
7.6 ▲ SO Second entrance to FR 155.

▼ 1.6 SO Second entrance to FR 155, then cattle guard.
7.5 ▲ SO Cattle guard, then track on left is FR 155.

▼ 1.8 SO Track on right.
7.3 ▲ SO Track on left.

▼ 2.0 SO Track on left to large camping area.
7.1 ▲ SO Track on right to large camping area.

▼ 2.5 SO Track on right.
6.6 ▲ SO Track on left.

▼ 3.5 SO Track on left to campsite.
5.6 ▲ SO Track on right to campsite.

▼ 3.6 SO ATV staging area on right, track on right, then cattle guard.
5.5 ▲ SO Cattle guard, track on left, then ATV staging area on left.

GPS: N 38°40.23' W 111°56.48'

▼ 4.2 SO Track on left.
4.9 ▲ SO Track on right.

▼ 4.7 BL Track on left is Killian Hollow Trail.
4.4 ▲ BR Track on right is Killian Hollow Trail.

GPS: N 38°40.94' W 111°56.46'

▼ 4.9 SO Track on left.
4.2 ▲ SO Track on right.

▼ 5.0 SO Cattle guard.
4.1 ▲ SO Cattle guard.

▼ 5.3 SO Davis Hollow. Track on right and track on left (FR 1142).
3.8 ▲ SO Davis Hollow. Track on left and track on right (FR 1142).
GPS: N 38°41.21' W 111°56.18'

▼ 5.8 SO Track on left.
3.3 ▲ SO Track on right.

▼ 6.3 BL Two tracks on right at small dam.
2.8 ▲ BR Two tracks on left at small dam.

▼ 6.6 SO Track on left.
2.5 ▲ SO Track on right.

▼ 6.7 BL Track on right.
2.4 ▲ BR Track on left.

▼ 7.2 BL Track on right.
1.9 ▲ BR Track on left.

▼ 7.3 BL Two tracks on right.
1.8 ▲ BR Two tracks on left.

▼ 7.4 SO Cattle guard.
1.7 ▲ SO Cattle guard.

▼ 7.5 SO Track on right.
1.6 ▲ SO Track on left.
GPS: N 38°42.61' W 111°56.51'

▼ 8.0 SO Bell Rock Ridge. Track on right.
1.1 ▲ SO Bell Rock Ridge. Track on left.

▼ 8.2 SO Cattle guard.
0.9 ▲ SO Cattle guard.

▼ 9.1 SO Leaving Fishlake National Forest over cattle guard. Zero trip meter.
0.0 ▲ Continue toward Koosharem.
GPS: N 38°42.85' W 111°57.67'

▼ 0.0 Continue toward Glenwood.
4.8 ▲ SO Entering Fishlake National Forest over cattle guard. Road becomes FR 068. Zero trip meter.

▼ 2.0 TR Road ahead to Annabella.
2.8 ▲ TL T-intersection. Road on right to Annabella.
GPS: N 38°43.29' W 111°58.96'

▼ 2.9 SO Track on right, then cattle guard.
1.9 ▲ SO Cattle guard, then track on left.

▼ 3.3 SO Track on right. Many small ATV tracks on right and left from here to end of trail.
1.5 ▲ SO Track on left.

▼ 4.8 Trail ends at Glenwood Fish Hatchery. Continue straight on paved road to Glenwood.
0.0 ▲ At Glenwood Fish Hatchery, 0.7 miles southeast of Glenwood, on Center Street, zero trip meter, and continue southeast toward Cove Mountain on graded dirt road. Many small ATV trails on right and left for first 1.5 miles.
GPS: N 38°45.47' W 111°48.61'

CENTRAL REGION TRAIL #33

Pahvant Range Trail

STARTING POINT Elsinore
FINISHING POINT Kanosh
TOTAL MILEAGE 31.2 miles
UNPAVED MILEAGE 30.1 miles
DRIVING TIME 3 hours
ELEVATION RANGE 5,000–9,000 feet
USUALLY OPEN June to October
DIFFICULTY RATING 4
SCENIC RATING 7
REMOTENESS RATING +0

Special Attractions

- Albinus and Kanosh Canyons.
- Access to a network of 4WD and ATV trails.
- Excellent for viewing wildlife and fall foliage.

Looking back down Albinus Canyon toward Elsinore

History

Mount Joseph, midway along this trail, is named after Joseph A. Young, the first president of the Mormon Church in Sevier County. The town of Joseph, 6 miles southwest of Elsinore, is also named after him.

The town of Kanosh takes its name from Chief Kanosh, the peacemaker. Kanosh—whose name means "willow bowl" (Kanoush)—first came here with his mother and three brothers, and by 1850, he was the chief of a band of 500 Indians living in the Pahvant Valley. One of his brothers was the famous Chief Walker, who was active in the Black Hawk War. Kanosh was as peaceful as his brother was fierce, and after the Mormon settlement of the region, he devoted himself to keeping the peace between the Indians and white settlers.

Utah has many tales of lost Spanish treasure and mines. One such tale centers around the communities of Fillmore and Kanosh. In 1852, the Mormon leader Brigham Young paid a visit to Fillmore. A young Indian told him of a legendary Spanish silver mine in western Millard County. Brigham Young commissioned John Brown to lead a party to investigate and to "take possession of the mine." The party departed Salt Lake City in June 1852, stopped at Fillmore for wagon repairs, and then proceeded to Corn Creek to talk to Chief Kanosh. Kanosh was unaware of the supposed Spanish mine, but he had heard rumor of another one on the Beaver River. Brown's party hired an Indian guide, and they went to search the Beaver River, but no mine was ever found.

The expedition then explored up Corn Creek before leaving the wagons behind and traveling farther over the Pahvant Range and south into the Tushar Mountains. At Pine Creek, later renamed Bullion Creek, they panned for gold and quickly decided that "there was no gold and never has been any." Forty years later, the boomtown of Kimberly was founded on the same spot, becoming one of the most successful gold camps in Utah!

Corn Creek was named by early pioneers who arrived to find corn growing there. The corn was planted by the Pahvant Utes, who returned to Corn Creek annually to sow their staple crop. In the early 1980s, Corn Creek was badly damaged by flooding, but it was restored by the Division of Wildlife Resources and the National Forest Service.

Description

This moderate-length trail traverses the Pahvant Range between the towns of Elsinore and Kanosh, and it alternately crosses through Fishlake National Forest and private lands. It leaves Elsinore up Albinus Canyon, a gentle gradient on a predominantly graded gravel road. Once on top of the range, the trail swings around to the southwest and the trail standard becomes harder. The trail surface up on the range can be very greasy and impassable when wet, as some large ruts made by previous travelers testify. Navigation can be a bit tricky as well; although most of the forest roads are signed, there are many unmarked tracks.

After 7 miles, you turn south on FR 111. On the Fishlake National Forest map, this route is shown as traversing private property, though it is a historical right of way. Posted warnings ask you not to trespass off the roadway, and please respect the rights and wishes of local property owners: Do not deviate from the right of way or hunt, fish, or camp on private land. There are many other trails that lead off from the main trail through private property. Access rights to the forest beyond vary; please check with the National Forest Service or the property owners before traveling on other trails.

Just after the turnoff for FR 111 is the intersection with FR 107. While the Fishlake National Forest map shows this route as being open to 4WD vehicles, once the trail passes some private property, it is used almost exclusively by ATVs traveling the Paiute ATV Trail (PATVT). This very scenic route runs parallel to FR 111 and can be driven as an alternate to that section of this trail; it offers extensive views down some of the canyons on the west side of the Pahvant Range. However, it has some extremely narrow sections of muddy shelf road that may be impassable to large vehicles.

The trail described here crosses through private property and passes across the southern flank of Mount Joseph. It travels across a mix of open meadow and large stands of aspen before leaving the private property and traveling along Chokecherry Canyon. Where it rejoins the Paiute ATV Trail, the trail becomes narrower and rougher. It undulates down over a rough, loose rock surface to join the graded road along Second Creek. This descent is the hardest portion of the trail in dry weather, since it is steep with loose rocky sections and a number of washouts. However, it should cause no problems to most high-clearance SUVs.

Once on the graded road, the trail follows Second Creek and then Corn Creek as it runs down Kanosh Canyon. This exceptionally pretty canyon is also extremely prone to flash floods, as the many signs posted by the forest service warn. For this reason, camping is not recommended in the canyon except at the very scenic National Forest Service campground on Corn Creek, though this is still in the flash flood zone.

Wild turkeys were successfully introduced into Utah in the 1950s, and there is a thriving population around Corn Creek. They are often seen around the campground. Best times to see them are just after sunrise, when they fly down to feed from the roost, and around sunset. Corn Creek is also a popular trout fishing spot.

Flash flood warning sign along Corn Creek

Current Road Information

BLM Fillmore Field Office
PO Box 778
Fillmore, UT 84631
(435) 743-6811

Fishlake National Forest
Beaver Ranger District
575 South Main
Beaver, UT 84713
(435) 438-2436

Map References

BLM Richfield
USFS Fishlake National Forest: Beaver Ranger District
USGS 1:24,000 Elsinore, Joseph Peak, Sunset Peak, Kanosh
1:100,000 Richfield
Maptech CD-ROM: King Canyon/Fillmore
Trails Illustrated, #708
Utah Atlas & Gazetteer, p. 36
Utah Travel Council #4

Route Directions

▼ 0.0		In Elsinore, cross underneath I-70 and turn southwest on small paved road. Zero trip meter at cattle guard.
7.2 ▲		Trail ends in Elsinore, where the trail passes underneath I-70. Continue on to join I-70.
		GPS: N 38°40.95' W 112°09.39'
▼ 0.2	SO	Cattle guard, then cross over canal. Track on right. Road is now graded dirt.
7.0 ▲	BR	Track on left; cross over canal, then cattle guard. Road is now paved.
▼ 0.5	SO	Tracks on right and left. Trail swings around into Albinus Canyon.
6.7 ▲	SO	Trail leaves Albinus Canyon. Tracks on left and right.
▼ 1.7	SO	Track on right. Enter Fishlake National Forest. Trail is now FR 105.
5.5 ▲	SO	Track on left. Leave Fishlake National Forest.
▼ 1.8	SO	Track on left.
5.4 ▲	SO	Track on right.
▼ 2.0	SO	Seasonal closure gate.
5.2 ▲	SO	Seasonal closure gate.
		GPS: N 38°41.31' W 112°11.17'
▼ 3.6	SO	Tracks on right and left.
3.6 ▲	SO	Tracks on left and right.
▼ 3.8	BL	Track on right.
3.4 ▲	BR	Track on left.
▼ 4.0	SO	Two tracks on right, track on left.
3.2 ▲	SO	Track on right, two tracks on left.
		GPS: N 38°42.65' W 112°11.11'
▼ 4.1	SO	Track on left. Views on right into Flat Canyon.
3.1 ▲	SO	Track on right. Views on left into Flat Canyon.
▼ 4.2	SO	Tracks on right and left.
3.0 ▲	SO	Tracks on left and right.
▼ 4.3	SO	Track on left.
2.9 ▲	SO	Track on right.
▼ 4.5	SO	Track on left.
2.7 ▲	SO	Track on right.
▼ 4.9	SO	Seasonal closure gate.
2.3 ▲	SO	Seasonal closure gate.
		GPS: N 38°43.21' W 112°11.81'
▼ 5.3	SO	Track on right.
1.9 ▲	SO	Track on left.
▼ 5.4	SO	Track on right.
1.8 ▲	SO	Track on left.
▼ 5.9	SO	Track on left.
1.3 ▲	SO	Track on right.
▼ 6.2	BR	Track on left.
1.0 ▲	SO	Track on right.
▼ 6.8	SO	Cattle guard, then track on left.
0.4 ▲	SO	Track on right, then cattle guard.
▼ 7.0	TL	T-intersection; turn left on FR 111 (PATVT#01), then pass second track on left after junction.
0.2 ▲	TR	Two tracks on right; turn right on second track, FR 105 (unmarked). Paiute ATV Trail continues straight ahead.
▼ 7.2	BL	Continue on FR 111. Track on right is FR 107 (alternate route). Campsite on right. Zero trip meter.
0.0 ▲		Continue toward Albinus Canyon.
		GPS: N 38°43.39' W 112°13.96'
▼ 0.0		Continue along FR 111.
4.7 ▲	SO	Track on left is FR 107 (alternate route). Campsite on left. Zero trip meter.
▼ 0.4	SO	Track on right, then leave Fishlake National Forest. Entering private property for next 3.5 miles.
4.3 ▲	SO	Entering Fishlake National Forest, leaving private property. Track on left.

▼ 0.5 SO Cattle guard.
4.2 ▲ SO Cattle guard.

▼ 0.7 SO Track on right.
4.0 ▲ SO Track on left.

▼ 1.0 SO Cattle guard.
3.7 ▲ SO Cattle guard.

▼ 1.1 SO Track on left.
3.6 ▲ SO Track on right.

▼ 2.3 SO Log cabin on right (private).
2.4 ▲ SO Log cabin on left (private).
GPS: N 38°42.08' W 112°15.81'

▼ 2.9 SO Dam on left.
1.8 ▲ SO Dam on right.

▼ 3.2 SO Cattle guard, followed by track on left.
1.5 ▲ SO Track on right, followed by cattle guard.

▼ 3.7 BL Road closed on right.
1.0 ▲ SO Road closed on left.

▼ 3.9 SO Cattle guard; entering Fishlake National Forest.
0.8 ▲ SO Cattle guard; leaving Fishlake National Forest. Enter private property for next 3.5 miles.
GPS: N 38°41.16' W 112°16.91'

▼ 4.4 SO Track on left.
0.3 ▲ SO Track on right.
GPS: N 38°40.79' W 112°17.09'

▼ 4.7 TR Leave national forest over cattle guard; entering private property for next 4.4 miles. Zero trip meter.
0.0 ▲ Continue northeast.
GPS: N 38°40.76' W 112°17.40'

▼ 0.0 Continue southwest.
7.4 ▲ TL Enter national forest over cattle guard; leaving private property. Zero trip meter.

▼ 0.3 SO Private road on right.
7.1 ▲ SO Private road on left.

▼ 1.5 SO Private road on left.
6.9 ▲ SO Private road on right.
GPS: N 38°40.36' W 112°18.41'

▼ 1.7 SO Track on right.
5.7 ▲ SO Track on left.

▼ 2.3 SO Track on right is PATVST#97.
5.1 ▲ SO Track on left is PATVST#97.
GPS: N 38°40.18' W 112°19.07'

Central Trail #33: Pahvant Range Trail

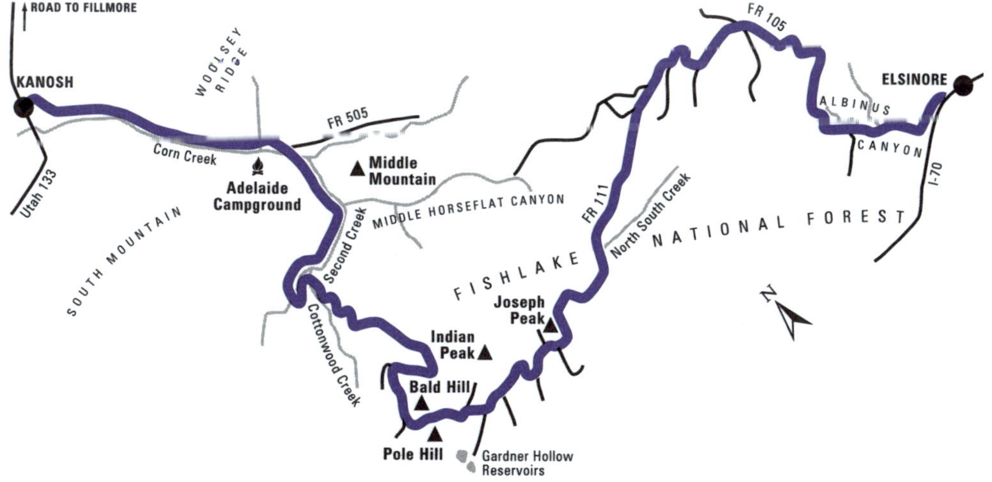

Trail descending the spur road to Cottonwood Creek

▼ 2.8 SO Track on right.
4.6 ▲ SO Track on left.

▼ 3.2 SO Crossroads. PATVT#01 goes left.
4.2 ▲ SO Crossroads. PATVT#01 goes right.
GPS: N 38°40.08' W 112°19.83'

▼ 3.6 BR Track on left is PATVT#01.
3.8 ▲ SO Track on right is PATVT#01.
GPS: N 38°40.01' W 112°20.17'

▼ 4.4 SO Leaving private property; entering Fishlake National Forest.
3.0 ▲ SO Entering private property for next 4.4 miles; leaving Fishlake National Forest.

▼ 4.6 SO Track on right, then track on left.
2.8 ▲ SO Track on right, then track on left.

▼ 4.7 SO Entering private property over cattle guard.
2.7 ▲ SO Leaving private property over cattle guard.

▼ 5.1 BR Track on left is private.
2.3 ▲ SO Track on right is private.

▼ 5.2 SO Entering Fishlake National Forest over cattle guard.
2.2 ▲ SO Leaving Fishlake National Forest over cattle guard.
GPS: N 38°40.39' W 112°21.63'

▼ 5.6 SO Track on right.
1.8 ▲ SO Track on left.

▼ 6.0 SO Track on right, then track on left.
1.4 ▲ SO Track on right, then track on left.

▼ 6.2 TR T-intersection. Turn right; trail follows PATVT#01.
1.2 ▲ TL Turn left.
GPS: N 38°41.28' W 112°21.51'

▼ 7.0 BL Track on right.
0.4 ▲ TR Track on left.

▼ 7.4 TL Turn left, trail follows PATVST#06. PATVT#01 goes right. Zero trip meter.
0.0 ▲ Continue toward Elsinore on wider trail.
GPS: N 38°41.16' W 112°20.68'

▼ 0.0 Continue toward Kanosh on narrower trail.
3.3 ▲ TR Turn right; PATVT#01 goes left. Zero trip meter.

▼ 2.7 SO Track on left is Cottonwood hiking trail #044.
0.6 ▲ SO Track on right is Cottonwood hiking trail #044.

▼ 3.1 SO Ford through small creek, then cattle guard.
0.2 ▲ SO Cattle guard, then ford through small creek.

▼ 3.3 TR Ford through Cottonwood Creek, then turn right on FR 106; trail follows PATVST#06. PATVT#01 goes left. Zero trip meter.
0.0 ▲ Climb away from creek on smaller trail.
GPS: N 38°43.01' W 112°22.46'

▼ 0.0 Follow along with Cottonwood Creek on right.

8.6 ▲ TL Turn left onto unmarked smaller trail and ford Cottonwood Creek; trail follows PATVST#06. Ahead is PATVT#01. Zero trip meter.

▼ 0.1 SO Campsite on right.
8.5 ▲ SO Campsite on left.

▼ 1.0 SO Track on left is FR 490 to First Creek Spring.
7.6 ▲ SO Track on right is FR 490 to First Creek Spring.

▼ 1.6 SO Track on right.
7.0 ▲ SO Track on left.

▼ 2.1 SO Track on right is Horseflat Canyon Trail.
6.5 ▲ SO Track on left is Horseflat Canyon Trail.

▼ 2.6 SO Cattle guard.
6.0 ▲ SO Cattle guard.

▼ 2.7 SO Seasonal closure gate. Trail becomes narrow graded gravel road leading down Kanosh Canyon.
5.9 ▲ SO Seasonal closure gate.

▼ 3.1 SO Cross over Corn Creek on bridge, then track on right is FR 505.
5.5 ▲ SO Track on left is FR 505, then cross over Corn Creek on bridge.

▼ 3.8 SO Adelaide National Forest Campground on left.
4.8 ▲ SO Adelaide National Forest Campground on right.

GPS: N 38°45.24' W 112°21.93'

▼ 4.0 SO Track on right is Leavitts Trail—vehicle use for first part only.
4.6 ▲ SO Track on left is Leavitts Trail—vehicle use for first part only.

GPS: N 38°45.24' W 112°22.04'

▼ 6.0 SO Seasonal closure gate and information board. Leaving Fishlake National Forest over cattle guard.
2.6 ▲ SO Seasonal closure gate and information board. Entering Fishlake National Forest over cattle guard.

▼ 7.6 SO Road on left.
1.0 ▲ SO Road on right.

▼ 7.7 SO Road is now paved.
0.9 ▲ SO Road is now graded gravel.

▼ 8.6 Trail ends in Kanosh at the corner of Main Street and 300 South. Turn right for Utah 133 and Fillmore.
0.0 ▲ In Kanosh at corner of Main Street and 300 South, turn east following sign for FR 106. Road is paved. Zero trip meter.

GPS: N 38°47.69' W 112°26.17'

CENTRAL REGION TRAIL #34

Kimberly and Big John Trail

STARTING POINT I-70, exit 17
FINISHING POINT Utah 153
TOTAL MILEAGE 29.4 miles
UNPAVED MILEAGE 29.4 miles
DRIVING TIME 4 hours
ELEVATION RANGE 6,000–11,400 feet
USUALLY OPEN July to October
DIFFICULTY RATING 4
SCENIC RATING 10
REMOTENESS RATING +0

Special Attractions

- Panoramic mountain scenery and views.
- Moderately challenging, high-mountain driving.
- Old mining remains of Kimberly and the Silver King Mine.

History

The ghost town of Kimberly, originally named Snyder City, is at the northern end of the Tushar Mountains. It was named after Peter Kimberly from Chicago, who bought the major gold mill in town in 1899, renamed it the Annie Laurie Mill, and turned the town into one of Utah's most successful gold camps. Workers earned three dollars a day in the mines, which ran seven days a week, and the town had two hotels, the Southern and Skougaard's, several saloons, a bakery, two newspapers, a dancehall, and an impregnable jail, which is now on display at Lagoon Amusement Park's Pioneer Village north of Salt Lake City. Due to the steep canyon location, the town was split into two areas: Lower Kimberly, which contained the mill, stores, and commercial buildings, and Upper Kimberly, the residential district, home to over 500 people.

At its height, the town earned its Wild West reputation. Butch Cassidy and his Wild Bunch were known to spend time here. Although they never touched the mine's payroll, that didn't mean the mine never lost any gold. As one story goes, the stagecoach from Kimberly was taking gold bars to the railroad at Sevier when the coach overturned and spilled the bars down a steep cliffside. Though most of the gold was recovered, the mining company never revealed its losses, and rumor has it there may still be some out there in the undergrowth.

Mine near the trail

In 1905, Peter Kimberly died and the Annie Laurie was sold to an English company that knew little about mining and less about miners. Workers, previously paid in cash, were now given paper vouchers to redeem at the company store. Many workers just up and left. The new company then ran into debt after building a new mill. The bank foreclosed in 1908, the remaining workers abandoned the mine, and Kimberly faded quickly. It didn't take many years of disuse for the mines to fall into disrepair; water flooded the shafts and caved in others.

There was a brief revival in the 1930s when a new vein was worked by 50 families, but after a few years the vein ran out and the town was once again silent.

Farther along the trail is the Silver King Mine, which was struck by Brigham Daniel Darger of Spanish Fork, Utah, in 1894. The Silver King actually mined gold, which was hauled by mule to the five arrastras on Deer Creek. There the ore was ground down before being shipped out for processing. The National Forest Service has built a quarter-mile interpretive trail that explains the mining features around the Silver King. At the start of the trail is the two-story cabin where Brigham lived with his wife, who was 14 years his junior.

Description

This fantastic trail is somewhat reminiscent of a high-altitude Colorado 4WD trail. The Kimberly and Big John Trail takes you high above the surrounding forests on narrow shelf roads, past small alpine lakes and the remains of mining ghost towns, and finishes by dropping through alpine meadows and pine forests to Big John Flat. The well-used trail is suitable for most high-clearance SUVs, and it is mainly ungraded. There are some minor rocky sections and some long sections on the north side of the saddle that could be difficult in wet weather.

The trail starts at I-70, exit 17, 22 miles south of Richfield. Take FR 113 south; it winds along Mill Creek and climbs into the Tushar Mountains. Much of the trail follows along the same route as the Paiute ATV Trail

A view of the trail winding down to Mud Lake

(PATVT), and you'll find ATV staging areas and clear trail markers. There are some pleasant and extremely popular campsites at the first crossing of Mill Creek, where another trail heads up Sevier Canyon. You reach the remains of Lower Kimberly after about 7 miles; the old Annie Laurie Mill is visible on the far side of the valley, and a track leads down to more mining works.

You reach Upper Kimberly about a mile after Lower Kimberly; there are several mining remains and a log cabin standing at a trail junction. If you explore the area on foot, you can find other old cabins and forgotten relics. Just past this is a more modern artifact, a Snowtel Data Site, which measures precipitation to forecast water supplies.

The trail continues to climb along a wide shelf road to Winkler Point, which has panoramic views north. Winkler Point was named after Ernest Winkler, a former supervisor of Fishlake National Forest. The extensive remains of the Silver King Mine are 1.7 miles farther. The National Forest Service has built a short interpretive trail around the points of interest at the mine.

After Marysvale Road, the trail climbs to its highest point. The shelf road around Beaver Creek is long and rough. It is an adequate width for a full-size vehicle, with sufficient passing places, but drivers should be prepared to reverse up to a passing place if an oncoming vehicle is encountered. At the upper end of the shelf road, the trail comes out of the trees and runs across the bare slopes and scree around Mount Belknap. This is the narrowest part of the shelf road and the most spectacular. Far below are the upper reaches of Beaver Creek and Big Meadow. The elevation at the saddle, the highest part of the trail, between Mount Belknap and Delano Peak is over 11,400 feet, and the area contains a krummholz or elfenwood forest: the stunted trees are shaped by the prevailing winter winds and only have branches on the downwind side. There is a magnificent viewpoint here with a sweeping panorama of Mount Baldy, Mount Belknap, Gold Mountain, and Copper Belt Peak to the north and Shelly Baldy Peak, Mount Delano, and Mount Holly to the south.

From the saddle, the trail switchbacks down to Mud Lake. From here, the trail is an easy gradient as it runs south to Big John Flat. This is an extremely popular camping area, with several pit toilets and many primitive campsites. However, the forest service restricts vehicle travel across the flat itself to reduce environmental impact, so if you are vehicle camping, pick one of the many other camps or hike across the flat to your campsite.

The trail is graded and smoother after Big

ATVs climbing the shelf road around Mount Belknap

John Flat, and passenger vehicles can even access Big John Flat from the south in dry weather. The trail finishes on the paved Utah 153, 2.4 miles west of Elk Meadows Ski area.

Current Road Information

BLM Fillmore Field Office
PO Box 778
Fillmore, UT 84631
(435) 743-6811

Fishlake National Forest
Beaver Ranger District
575 South Main
Beaver, UT 84713
(435) 438-2436

Map References

BLM Richfield, Beaver (incomplete)
USFS Fishlake National Forest: Beaver Ranger District
USGS 1:24,000 Marysvale Canyon, Trail Mt., Mt. Belknap, Mt. Brigham, Shelly Baldy Peak
1:100,000 Richfield, Beaver, (incomplete)
Maptech CD-ROM: King Canyon/ Fillmore
Utah Atlas & Gazetteer, p. 26
Utah Travel Council #4

Route Directions

▼ 0.0 On I-70 at exit 17, turn southwest on the graded gravel FR 113, which is on the north side of the freeway, and zero trip meter. This is also Paiute ATV Side Trail #13 (PATVST#13).
8.0 ▲ Trail ends at I-70, exit 171; go east for Richfield, west for I-15.
GPS: N 38°34.26' W 112°21.06'

▼ 0.3 SO Cattle guard.
7.7 ▲ SO Cattle guard.

▼ 0.8 SO Track on left to ATV staging area.
7.2 ▲ SO Track on right to ATV staging area.

▼ 1.1 SO Track on right.
6.9 ▲ SO Track on left.

▼ 1.3 SO Cattle guard, then track on right to corral; also track on left.
6.7 ▲ SO Track on left to corral, then cattle guard; also track on right.

▼ 1.6 SO Track on right. Trail runs along Mill Creek.
6.4 ▲ SO Track on left.

▼ 2.0 SO Cross through small creek on concrete ford.
6.0 ▲ SO Cross through small creek on concrete ford.

▼ 2.4 SO Pass underneath I-70, then cattle guard.
5.6 ▲ SO Cattle guard, then pass underneath I-70.

▼ 2.5 SO Track on right is FR 115 (PATVST#5).
5.5 ▲ SO Track on left is FR 115 (PATVST#5).
GPS: N 38°32.83' W 112°22.90'

▼ 2.8 SO Track on right is FR 116 to Sevier Canyon. Continue straight on main trail and cross through Mill Creek. Many campsites in this area.
5.2 ▲ SO Cross through Mill Creek, then track on left is FR 116 to Sevier Canyon. Many campsites in this area.
GPS: N 38°32.68' W 112°23.11'

▼ 3.7 SO Cattle guard, entering Middle Canyon.
4.3 ▲ SO Cattle guard, leaving Middle Canyon.

▼ 4.5 BL Track on right, then cross over Mill Creek.
3.5 ▲ SO Cross over Mill Creek, then track on left.
GPS: N 38°31.26' W 112°23.57'

▼ 5.1 SO Track on left.
2.9 ▲ SO Track on right.

▼ 6.1 SO Track on left.
1.9 ▲ SO Track on right.

▼ 6.2 SO Track on left.
1.8 ▲ SO Track on right.

▼ 6.7 SO Track on right to denuded old mine area. Track on left.
1.3 ▲ SO Track on left to denuded old mine area. Track on right.

▼ 7.0 SO Annie Laurie Mill is visible on far side of valley.
1.0 ▲ SO Annie Laurie Mill is visible on far side of valley.
GPS: N 38°29.73' W 112°23.52'

▼ 7.1 SO Track on left.
0.9 ▲ SO Track on right.

▼ 7.2 SO Track on right to Lower Kimberly.
0.8 ▲ SO Track on left to Lower Kimberly.
GPS: N 38°29.50' W 112°23.41'

▼ 7.5 SO Track on left to old mining works and stone foundations.
0.5 ▲ SO Track on right to old mining works and stone foundations.

▼ 7.8 SO Mining ruins on right.
0.2 ▲ SO Mining ruins on left.
GPS: N 38°29.18' W 112°23.73'

▼ 8.0 BL Track on right at old cabin. This is the area of Upper Kimberly. Zero trip meter.
0.0 ▲ Continue northeast.
GPS: N 38°29.12' W 112°23.80'

▼ 0.0 Continue east.
3.4 ▲ BR Track on left at old cabin. This is the area of Upper Kimberly. Zero trip meter.

▼ 0.1 SO Track on right to remains of old cabin, then tracks right and left to campsites.
3.3 ▲ SO Tracks right and left to campsites, then track on left to remains of old cabin.
GPS: N 38°29.12' W 112°23.67'

▼ 0.3 SO Track on left to Snowtel Data Site.
3.1 ▲ SO Track on right to Snowtel Data Site.

▼ 0.6 BL Track on right, then small creek crossing.
2.8 ▲ SO Small creek crossing, then track on left.

▼ 0.9 SO Track on right. Start of shelf road.
2.5 ▲ BR Track on left. Shelf road ends.

▼ 1.7 BR Winkler Point. Views to the north. End of shelf road.
1.7 ▲ BL Winkler Point. Views to the north. Start of shelf road.
GPS: N 38°29.59' W 112°22.85'

▼ 2.5 SO Track on right.
0.9 ▲ SO Track on left.

Central Trail #34: Kimberly and Big John Trail

▼ 3.0 SO Track on left is FR 475. PATVT#01 enters here and follows main trail.
0.4 ▲ SO Track on left is FR 475 (continuation of PATVT#01).

GPS: N 38°29.08' W 112°21.96'

▼ 3.3 SO ATV trail on right.
0.1 ▲ SO ATV trail on left.

▼ 3.4 SO Track on right is parking area for Silver King Mine interpretive trail. Zero trip meter.
0.0 ▲ Continue to climb.

GPS: N 38°28.90' W 112°22.20'

▼ 0.0 Continue descent into Spring Gulch.
2.6 ▲ SO Track on left is parking area for Silver King Mine interpretive trail. Zero trip meter.

▼ 0.5 BL Track on right.
2.1 ▲ SO Track on left.

▼ 0.9 SO Track on left.
1.7 ▲ SO Track on right.

▼ 1.1 SO Track on right.
1.5 ▲ SO Track on left.

▼ 1.3 SO Track on left is Deer Creek Trail (FR 474/PATVST#84) to US 89. Cross over Deer Creek; start of shelf road.
1.3 ▲ SO End of shelf road; cross over Deer Creek. Track on right is Deer Creek Trail (FR 474/PATVST#84) to US 89.

GPS: N 38°28.03' W 112°21.82'

▼ 2.3 SO Track on left; end of shelf road.
0.3 ▲ SO Track on right; start of shelf road.

GPS: N 38°28.24' W 112°20.73'

▼ 2.6 TR T-intersection. Turn right on FR 123 (PATVT#01) toward Big John Flat, and zero trip meter. Track on left is FR 113 (PATVST#02) to Marysvale. Seasonal closure gate; entering vehicle restricted area (remain on designated roads). Start of shelf road; Beaver Creek is below.
0.0 ▲ Continue northeast.

GPS: N 38°28.02' W 112°20.92'

▼ 0.0 Continue southwest.
8.7 ▲ TL Seasonal closure gate; leaving vehicle restricted area. Shelf road ends. Turn left on FR 113; right is FR 113 (PATVST#02) to Marysvale. Zero trip meter. Beaver Creek is below.

▼ 2.8 SO Track on left. Gold Mountain on right.
5.9 ▲ SO Track on right. Gold Mountain on left.

GPS: N 38°26.20' W 112°22.54'

▼ 3.6 SO Track on right.
5.1 ▲ SO Track on left.

GPS: N 38°25.80' W 112°23.12'

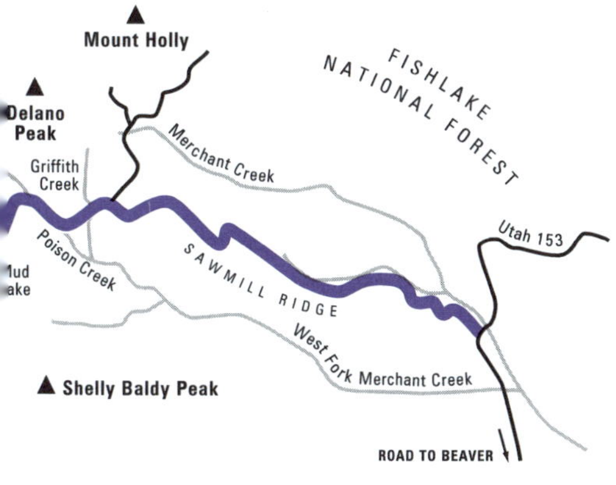

▼ 3.8 SO Track on left.
4.9 ▲ SO Track on right.
GPS: N 38°25.65′ W 112°23.18′

▼ 4.5 SO Track on right, then second track on right.
4.2 ▲ SO Track on left, then second track on left.

▼ 4.8 SO Track on right, then trail crosses scree slope under summit of Mount Belknap.
3.9 ▲ BR Trail crosses scree slope under summit of Mount Belknap, then track on left.

▼ 6.2 BR Miners Park Trail #074 on left—hiking and pack use only.
2.5 ▲ BL Miners Park Trail #074 on right—hiking and pack use only.
GPS: N 38°24.24′ W 112°23.72′

▼ 6.3 SO Track on right.
2.4 ▲ SO Track on left.

▼ 6.8 SO Passing through elfenwood forest. Track on right to panoramic viewpoint.
1.9 ▲ SO Passing through elfenwood forest. Track on left to panoramic viewpoint.
GPS: N 38°23.75′ W 112°24.16′

▼ 7.1 SO Cross saddle between Mount Belknap and Mount Delano.
1.6 ▲ SO Cross saddle between Mount Belknap and Mount Delano.
GPS: N 38°23.52′ W 112°23.98′

▼ 7.7 SO High point of trail.
1.0 ▲ SO High point of trail.
GPS: N 38°23.13′ W 112°23.83′

▼ 8.2 SO Track on left to telecommunications tower.
0.5 ▲ SO Track on right to telecommunications tower.
GPS: N 38°22.98′ W 112°23.78′

▼ 8.7 SO Mud Lake on right. Zero trip meter. Trail on right is Fishlake Trail #172—hiking and pack use only.
0.0 ▲ Continue north.
GPS: N 38°22.77′ W 112°24.01′

▼ 0.0 Continue south.
6.7 ▲ SO Mud Lake on left. Zero trip meter. Trail on left is Fishlake Trail #172—hiking and pack use only.

▼ 0.4 SO Cross through small creek.
6.3 ▲ SO Cross through small creek.

▼ 1.0 SO Track on right.
5.7 ▲ SO Track on left.
GPS: N 38°22.31′ W 112°23.51′

▼ 1.1 SO Seasonal closure gate, then cross through Poison Creek.
5.6 ▲ SO Cross through Poison Creek, then seasonal closure gate.

▼ 2.0 BL Cross through Griffith Creek, then tracks right and left to campsites.
4.7 ▲ BR Tracks right and left to campsites, then cross through Griffith Creek.
GPS: N 38°21.70′ W 112°23.60′

▼ 2.2 SO Skyline National Recreation Trail (hikers, horses, and bicycles only). Trail on left to Big Flat, on right to Blue Lake. Small hut, pit toilet, and forest information board at trailhead.
4.5 ▲ SO Skyline National Recreation Trail (hikers, horses, and bicycles only). Trail on right to Big Flat, on left to Blue Lake. Small hut, pit toilet, and forest information board at trailhead.
GPS: N 38°21.60′ W 112°23.57′

▼ 2.7 SO Track on right.
4.0 ▲ SO Track on left.

▼ 2.8 SO Pit toilet on right and many campsites on right and left.
3.9 ▲ SO Pit toilet on left and many campsites on left and right.

▼ 3.3 SO Seasonal closure gate and cattle guard. Big John Flat, with many scattered campsites, on right. End of vehicle restricted area. Trail standard improves to graded road.
3.4 ▲ SO Big John Flat, with many scattered campsites, on left. Road becomes ungraded smaller trail. Start of vehicle restricted area (on designated roads only). Seasonal closure gate and cattle guard.

GPS: N 38°20.69' W 112°23.93'

▼ 3.5 SO Track on right. PATVT#01 on right; no ATVs allowed on main trail from this point.
3.2 ▲ SO Track on left. PATVT#01 on left; ATVs allowed on main trail from this point.

GPS: N 38°20.61' W 112°24.01'

▼ 4.4 SO Track on left to Hamilton Flat.
2.3 ▲ SO Track on right to Hamilton Flat.

▼ 5.5 SO Track on left is PATVST#26.
1.2 ▲ SO Track on right is PATVST#26.

GPS: N 38°19.16' W 112°24.48'

▼ 6.0 SO Seasonal closure gate.
0.7 ▲ SO Seasonal closure gate.

▼ 6.1 SO PATVT#01 (ATV use only) crosses main trail.
0.6 ▲ SO PATVT#01 (ATV use only) crosses main trail.

GPS: N 38°18.84' W 112°24.89'

▼ 6.5 SO Track on left is FR 128 to Sawmill Fork.
0.2 ▲ SO Track on right is FR 128 to Sawmill Fork.

▼ 6.7 Trail ends at paved Utah 153. Turn left for Elk Meadows ski resort and Junction (through-route in summer only), turn right for Beaver.
0.0 ▲ On paved Utah 153, 2.4 miles west of Elk Meadows ski resort and 16 miles east of Beaver, turn north onto FR 123 and zero trip meter.

GPS: N 38°18.33' W 112°25.10'

Selected Further Reading

Massey, Peter, and Jeanne Wilson. *4WD Adventures: Colorado.* Castle Rock, Colo.: Swagman Publishing Inc., 1999.

—. *4WD Trails: North-Central Colorado.* Castle Rock, Colo.: Swagman Publishing Inc., 1999.

—. *4WD Trails: South-Central Colorado.* Castle Rock, Colo.: Swagman Publishing Inc., 1999.

—. *4WD Trails: Southwest Colorado.* Castle Rock, Colo.: Swagman Publishing Inc., 1999.

—. *4WD Trails: Northern Utah.* Castle Rock, Colo.: Swagman Publishing Inc., 2001.

—. *4WD Trails: Southwest Utah.* Castle Rock, Colo.: Swagman Publishing Inc., 2001.

—. *4WD Trails: Southeast Utah.* Castle Rock, Colo.: Swagman Publishing Inc., 2001.

Alexander, Thomas G. *Utah, the Right Place.* Salt Lake City: Gibbs M. Smith, Inc., 1996.

Allen, Steve. *Canyoneering the San Rafael Swell.* Salt Lake City, Utah: University of Utah Press, 1992.

American Park Network, Utah's National Parks. San Francisco: American Park Network, 1998.

Athearn, Robert. *The Denver and Rio Grande Western Railroad.* Lincoln, Nebr.: University of Nebraska Press, 1962.

Arizona. Salt Lake City: Gibbs M. Smith, Inc., 1983.

Baars, Donald L. *The Colorado Plateau, A Geologic History.* Albequerque, N.Mex.: University of New Mexico Press, 1972.

Baker, Pearl. *The Wild Bunch at Robbers Roost.* Lincoln, Nebr.: University of Nebraska Press. 1989.

Bennett, Cynthia Larsen. *Roadside History of Utah.* Missoula, Mont.: Mountain Press Publishing Company, 1999.

Benson, Joe. *Scenic Driving Utah.* Helena, Mont.: Falcon Publishing, Inc., 1996.

Best Western: Utah Fun Tours. N.p, n.d.

Boren, Kerry Ross, and Lisa Lee Boren. *The Gold of Carre-Shinob.* Salt Lake City: Bonneville Books, 1998.

Canyon Legacy: *A Journal of the Dan O'Laurie Museum—Moab,* Utah. No. 8, 9, 10, 18, 22.

Carr, Stephen L. *The Historical Guide to Utah Ghost Towns.* Salt Lake City: Western Epics, 1972.

Carr, Stephen L., and Robert W. Edwards. *Utah Ghost Rails.* Salt Lake City: Western Epics, 1989.

Castle Country Chapter of the League of Utah Writers and Guest Writers of Carbon and Emery Counties. *Legends of Carbon and Emery Counties.* N.p., 1996.

Chronic, Halka. *Roadside Geology of Utah.* Missoula, Mont.: Mountain Press Publishing Co., 1990.

Clark, Carol. *Explorers of the West.* Salt Lake City: Great Mountain West Supply, 1997.

DeCourten, Frank. *Dinosaurs of Utah.* Salt Lake City: University of Utah Press, 1998.

Egan, Ferol. *Frémont: Explorer for a Restless Nation.* Reno, Neva.: University of Nevada Press, 1985.

Fife, Carolyn Perry, and Wallace Dean Fife, eds. *Travelers' Choice: A Guide to the Best of Utah's National Parks, Monuments, and Recreation Areas.* Salt Lake City: D and C Publishing, 1998.

Harris, Edward D. *John Charles Frémont and the Great Western Reconnaissance.* New York: Chelsea House Publishers, 1990.

Heck, Larry E. *The Adventures of Pass Patrol. Vol. 1, In Search of the Outlaw Trail.* Aurora, Colo.: Outback Publications, Inc., 1996.

—. *The Adventures of Pass Patrol. Vol. 2, 4-Wheel Drive Trails and Outlaw Hideouts of Utah.* Aurora, Colo.: Outback Publications, Inc., 1999.

Hemingway, Donald W. *Utah and the Mormons.* Salt Lake City: Great Mountain West Supply, 1994.

Hinton, Wayne K. *Utah: Unusual Beginning to Unique Present.* New York: Windsor Publications, Inc., 1988.

Huegel, Tony. *Utah Byways: Backcountry Drives for the Whole Family.* Idaho Falls, Idaho: Post Company, 1996.

Kelly, Charles. *The Outlaw Trail: A History of Butch Cassidy and His Wild Bunch.* Lincoln, Nebr.: University of Nebraska Press, 1996.

Kelsey, Michael R. *Canyon Hiking Guide to the Colorado Plateau,* 4th ed. Provo, Utah: Kelsey Publishing, 1999.

Korns, J. Roderic, and Dale L. Morgan, eds. *West from Fort Bridger: The Pioneering of Immigrant Trails across Utah, 1846-1850.* Logan, Utah: Utah State University Press, 1994.

May, Dean L. *Utah: A People's History.* Salt Lake City: University of Utah Press, 1987.

McClenahan, Owen. *Utah's Scenic San Rafael Swell.* Castle Dale, Utah: McClenahan, 1993.

McGrath, Roger D. *Gunfighters, Highwaymen and Vigilantes.* Los Angeles: University of California Press, 1984.

Notarianni, Philip F., ed. *Carbon County: Eastern Utah's Industrialized Island,* 1st ed. Salt Lake City: Utah State Historical Society, 1981.

The Outlaw Trail Journal, 1992-1999.

Patterson, Richard. *Historical Atlas of the Outlaw West.* Boulder, Colo.: Johnson Publishing Co., 1997

Peterson, Charles S. *Utah: A Bicentennial History.* New York: W. W. Norton and Co., Inc., 1977.

Pettit, Jan. *Utes: The Mountain People.* Boulder, Colo.: Johnson Books, 1990.

Poll, Richard D., ed. *Utah's History.* Logan, Utah: Utah State University Press, 1989.

Powell, Allan Kent. *The Utah Guide.* Golden, Colo.: Fulcrum Publishing, 1995.

—. *The Utah History Encyclopedia.* Salt Lake City: University of Utah Press, 1994.

Rutter, Michael. *Utah: Off the Beaten Path.* Guilford, Conn.: The Globe Pequot Press, 1999.

Thompson, George A. *Some Dreams Die: Utah's Ghost Towns and Lost Treasures.* Salt Lake City: Dream Garden Press, 1999.

Thrapp, Dan L. *Encyclopedia of Frontier Biography.* 3 vols. London: University of Nebraska Press, 1988.

Utah Historical Quarterly. Spring 2000, vol. 68, no. 2.

Utah State Historical Society. Utah History Suite CD-ROM. Provo, Utah: Historical Views, 1998-99.

Van Cott, John W. *Utah Place Names.* Salt Lake City: University of Utah Press, 1990.

Weibel, Michael R. *Utah Travel Smart.* Santa Fe, N.Mex.: John Muir Publications, 1999.

—. *Utah: Travel Smart.* Santa Fe, N.Mex.: John Muir Publications, 1999.

Wharton, Gayen, and Tom Wharton. *It Happened in Utah.* Helena, Mont.: Falcon Publishing, 1998.

—. *Utah.* Oakland, Cali.: Fodor's Travel Publications, 1995.

—. *Utah.* Oakland, Cali.: Compass American Guides, 1950.

About the Authors

Peter Massey grew up in the outback of Australia, where he acquired a life-long love of the backcountry. After retiring from a career in investment banking in 1986 at the age of thirty-five, he served as a director of a number of companies in the United States, the United Kingdom, and Australia. He moved to Colorado in 1993.

Jeanne Wilson was born and grew up in Maryland. After moving to New York City in 1980, she worked in advertising and public relations before moving to Colorado in 1993.

After traveling extensively in Australia, Europe, Asia, and Africa, the authors covered more than 80,000 miles touring the United States and the Australian outback between 1993 and 1997. Since then they have traveled more than 25,000 miles doing research for their two guidebook series: *Backcountry Adventures* and *4WD Trails.*

Photo Credits

Unless otherwise indicated in the following list of acknowledgments (which is organized by page number), all photographs were taken by Peter Massey and are copyrighted by Swagman Publishing Inc., or by Peter Massey.

30 Joe Tucciarone, Interstell; **32** (upper left) Utah State Historical Society; **55** Utah State Historical Society; **77-88** Bushducks—Maggie Pinder and Donald McGann; **92** Utah State Historical Society; **93-95** Bushducks—Maggie Pinder and Donald McGann; **99-102** Bushducks—Maggie Pinder and Donald McGann; **106** Utah State Historical Society; **121-148** Bushducks—Maggie Pinder and Donald McGann.

Front cover photography: Peter Massey